I heard the sound of cattle in the distance, baying for food. I opened my eyes trying to see where I was but it was dark, pitch black. Feeling with my hand along a cold damp wall, it felt like a traditional stone wall, trying to see any light at all, nothing, just black. I touched something cold and hard but exceptionally smooth unlike the surface I had been touching. As I moved closer there was a strong smell, I knew the smell but could not remember what it was; it was so strong in my nostrils. I kept moving, an inch at a time, but this smell was so overpowering, I shuddered slightly as I moved my head and felt something smooth touch me, but that smell was so strong, what was that smell? It felt reassuring as my face moved across this smooth surface, from my forehead along my cheek past my ear, it was so nice and felt so peaceful. A small pinhole of light appeared in the distance, beginning as a tiny dot it slowly grew bigger, it was so amazing to see the light as it was so black, the light grew bigger and bigger and started to illuminate my surroundings. In my peripheral vision, I recognised an alleyway made of traditional stone, suddenly realising where I was, the farm, I involuntary smiled and thought, sanctuary, thinking I was coming back to my senses.

I tried to move my head but it was so wonderful to have this smooth surface on my cheek, the area was in full view now as the light was coming closer I didn't want to move, but I slowly moved my head backwards, the light moved faster now lighting the area up more quickly. I gasped in shock on seeing what my cheek was against, it was the face of a woman covered with black shining tar, I gasped, TAR that was the smell that raged in my nostrils. I tried to move but this thing had a hold of me and I had no strength to fight it off. I tried with all my might to move as the light came at me faster now, an involuntary tremble went through my body as a loud BANG, BANG, rang in my ears. I tried to jump back but this thing was holding on so tightly, I was shaking, the light had split into two now and I realised it was a vehicle making the thundering noise of the BANGS. I tried to move away from this face that I had embraced but could not. The vehicle was upon me now I moved to the side to escape the crush of the vehicle wheels. People appeared at my side holding pints of what looked like lager and all roaring with laughter. I saw the figure on the vehicle now firing his mounted weapon the noise was deafening but these people beside me just stood and laughed.

I screamed but nothing came out, my eyes were so painful with the pressure the vehicle was there in front of me, I tried to crouch down waiting for the impending crush of the vehicle. In an instant I was inside something, a van, I recognised the seats at the front they were all buckled, and shards of glass tinkled around me, brightly shining like diamonds. My body moved to one side as I rolled, I grasped again as the two figures in front of me turned and laughed, there was blood everywhere then darkness again. I saw something glint in front of me it was moving towards me spinning in the darkness coming straight toward me, it was shining so brightly in the pitch-black background.

Realising it was a hammer, I moved my hand forward to catch this spinning hammer. I had to move so I started to rise.

I sat up in my warm bed and gasped for breath, a sheen of sweat covered my whole body. I panted realising it was a bad dream. As I looked into the dimly lit room, with the small amount of light coming through the curtains, I controlled my breathing and thought what have I done to deserve dreams like this.

Callum and Joe

Thank you for all your help through the years it isvery much appreciated.

Cheers lads.

The word love is only a small four-letter word until someone gives it meaning and I give meaning to my wife every day.

life worth living, every moment we are together and even more when we are apart, the love of my life and my soul mate, all my love to you my princess xx.

Table of Contents

Chapter 1

I remember lying in my warm bed but for some reason, I felt cold and shivery, my eyes felt gritty and my heart felt heavy. I moved into the fetal position clasping my hands together behind my ear. I knew that something important had happened but in a sleepy daze I could not remember what, I thought if I kept my eyes closed, I could stay safe and would not have to remember. My mind drifted back to a beach when we were on holiday, the sun warming my back as I played with my brother among the sand dunes. I smiled and thought, that was a while ago, I was fifteen years old now by three days. I slowly opened my eyes; it was dark as I was under the covers, I heard the door opening and a gruff male voice saying, "Hey min, it's time you got up".

I flung back the covers and saw my uncle Sandy standing at the door, he had a cigarette in his hand, he was not an uncle really, but we grew up with them and they were always called Uncle Sandy and Auntie Betty, they were good friends of my parents. Uncle Sandy asked if I was okay, I remember him having a very sad look on his face. I asked for a smoke he reached into his pocket and threw the packet towards me. As I rose with my arms outstretched to catch the packet all the horrors of yesterday came flooding back to me like a stream train, my Dad died.

All the emotions came flooding back now and I started shaking. Uncle Sandy put a hand on my shoulder and said, "Let it all go have a good cry you will feel better". I kept thinking, 'if I had not asked for a cigarette and if I had stayed under the covers everything would be ok, everything would be back to normalmy Dad would be downstairs. As I looked at Uncle Sandy a tear rolled down his cheek and I screamed, 'NO'. He sat on the side of my bed and said through a broken voice, "Hey min, you are a big loon now and your Mum needs you more now than ever before. Make your Dad proud", he stood and wiped a tear from his face as he walked towards the door he turned and said your Dad was my best pal and I am yours, if you need anything just ask I am here to help you ok. He stood there for a moment and watched as I tried to stop sliver bubbling from my lips with my sleeve. I remember shouting through a lump sore throat, "I want my Dad". He walked over to me grabbed me out of my bed and hugged me tightly and said, "He will always be in yourheart and your head my loon".

As he left the room I slumped back onto my bed, I remember trying to scream but nothing came out.

My throat had a huge lump in it and my eyes were swollen from crying. I rolled back into my pillow and hugged it for what seemed ages, then the door opened my brother came in and asked "You ok?" He sat at the side of my bed I told him to go away as I did not want him to see me crying but he just patted my back, it felt so reassuring. My big brother, by two years, was my hero. I looked up to him always. I turned around and he had a tear running down his face I told him I didn't want to go down the stairs he nodded and told me it was okay we will just wait until you are ready. "Wash your face you will feel better" he said, at this, he stood and walked out. I rolled around in my bed panicking wondering why I could not picture my Dad in my head. I rose, stood and looked out of the window it was dreary and overcast, I remember thinking that is how my life felt at this moment.

My Dad had suffered with kidney failure for a long time, he had improved but he was on the dialysis machine three times a week waiting for a transplant. Sadly, he suffered a massive heart attack. Doctors told my Mum they had worked on him for ages, but his body was so weak he sadly lost the fight for his life. My Dad was 44 years old.

When we went to view my Dad, not visit but view, what an awful turn of phrase, we all walked up to his coffin, I was only fifteen and had never experienced anything like this in my life before. It is bad enough losing a loved one, but this was my 'Dad' lying there. He looked so peaceful, no furrowing on his brow and a calm serene look on his face. I remember my Mum crying, me, I just wanted to hold him. I touched his hand, it felt cold I shuddered and whipped my hand away. I said, "Rest in peace Dad", I do not know why, but it just came out. My aunt held my hand as I started to cry and shake uncontrollably. She led me outside where I gulped in lung fills of fresh air. My family and I all headed back to my grandmother's house, grandmother's house where everything was safe and warm and nothing bad ever happened. But it just had.

The next day I woke, my brother was having a cigarette out the loft window in our Grandmothers attic, they had been converted to a couple of bedrooms and we loved it up there, it was like 'our' space. I rolled over and said, "Gives a drag". He shushed me and passed me the cigarette; my Grandmother was very anti-smoking. We both knew this was going to be a very long and hard day, but he said, "It will be okay little bruv I am here with you", his words were very reassuring as I knew he must be feeling as bad as I was. We lay on our beds in silence both contemplating the day ahead, about an hour or so later we heard movement downstairs so up we got and headed down. I saw my Mum sitting in the kitchen with red tear-filled eyes; you could tell she had not slept. My grandmother was busy setting out dishes for breakfast, no one was hungry. I hugged my Mum, felt the lump in my throat, tears started running down my cheeks. My Mum turned to face me and said, "You have to be strong and do this last thing for your Dad". I ran outside to get away, I needed to get fresh air. All our family was there, and everyone kept asking if I was okay, I know they mean well but what was okay when your Dad has just died?

My brother and I began to put on the suits we had worn just two weeks before to one of our uncles' weddings. It felt strange, two weeks ago we dressed in these 'grown up' suits to go to a wedding, all my family was there. Happy days. Little did I know this would be the last 'family' outing we would ever have.

I had a moment of panic before leaving my grandparents' house, I did not want to go, my grandfather placed a hand on my shoulder and squeezed it, whispering in my ear "It will be ok". I loved my Dad I told him, he replied, "I know son we all did".

The funeral was held in one of the biggest fishing villages on the Moray coast, and they said in the local paper it was one of the biggest turnouts for a funeral the town had ever seen, just goes to show how well-liked he was. I do not remember much of that day; the only thing that sticks in my head is the lowering of the coffin down and me staring at the brass plate with my Dad's name on it. It was so surreal; this could not be happening to me. I started to shake, I felt a hand on my shoulder pulling me back and pushing me through the crowd of well-wishers.

I learned later that my Mum had asked two of my Dad's friends to make sure I got away from the graveside as quickly as possible. I can remember returning to my grandmother's and people were sitting about having cups of tea and drams. I heard laughter but could not understand how people could laugh on a day like this. I realise now that it was a celebration of my Dad's life, a way to let go of the emotions. In hindsight it was reassuring to have so many people there celebrating my Dad's life; he was a good man, well-loved, and well-liked. Someone handed me a dram, I realised then why they were drinking whisky - it sure took the edge off the pain.

The next day I got up early crept down the stairs and out to the garage, I got out the old bike that had lain in my grandmother's garage for years, it must have been made in the 1950s but my grandfather had kept it in good running order. As I headed away from the house, I knew where I was going, straight to the cemetery. As I approached the grave, I noted the fresh cut edges of the turf with the fifty-plus wreathes on top of it, as the sun shone down directly down on the scene. I sat down and started to cry uncontrollably when I felt a strange warm sensation – it was like someone was hugging me - it felt very reassuring as I swallowed the huge lump in my throat. Just as quickly as it happened the warmth went, and I felt cold again. I tried to speak to my Dad, but nothing came out, all I could do was cry.

Sometime later when I finally stopped crying, I raised my head, there was an old man standing at the end of the path, I never noticed him when I came in. He took the pipe from his mouth and said, "Your father was a good man I knew him well, remember son always put in a day's graft for a day's pay and be a good man. Never let anything stand in your way and most of all never give up. That's what your Dad would want from you". He nodded and smiled, waved an old hand at me and headed away. I looked back at the grave feeling reassured by the old man's words. When I raised my head again to thank him, he was gone. I remember looking for him amongst the gravestones, but he was nowhere in sight, I thought he couldn't half shift for an old man. I can remember his face and what he wore; I found it a bit strange.

When I returned to my grandmother's house, I was putting the bike back in the garage when my grandfather came out. He never spoke very much these days due to him having a series of strokes leaving him weak and unwell. He nodded knowingly at me and held open his arms. I hugged him so tightly feeling like a little boy again. He said, "You always liked a bosie (a cuddle) when you were a wee loon, you're ok now". I nodded and he guided me into the house for some hot soup, my grandmother asked if I had been at the cemetery, when I nodded, she said "I thought so". My Mum was sitting at the table, she smiled at me her eyes were so red. I wanted to mention the old man at the grave but for some reason I did not, I don't know why.

After the funeral was all past I was sent up to the farm. The farm – the one place I felt really at home. I spent much of my childhood at the farm with my Dad. It was up here he taught me and my brother all aspects of farming. He also taught us how to shoot, map read and many of the other skills he had learned during his time in the Army, including boxing. I loved the farm. We learned how to live off the land, how to trap animals humanely and shoot.

The shooting was always my favourite, roe deer, red deer, foxes and game birds. My brother was good with a rifle, but my Dad never really said much about my ability. I tried hard, always hitting the target, my grouping was tight, but he never really acknowledged my ability. He always pushed my brother and paid me little heed, I hated that, and I was always trying to better myself. As we got older, I would go off to practice by myself, all my Dad would say was say "Mmmm that's ok", it pissed me off.

The turning point came one night when my Dad and I went stalking. We got into position, I was all excited. Dad told me to calm down and control my breathing. We crawled on our stomachs to the tree line where we spotted a deer in an open field. Two other deer, which we had not seen, bolted. I jumped up and cracked off a round, I watched the deer fall instantly. I smiled feeling pleased with myself, but my Dad slapped me lightly on the head and said "We are stalking for Christ sake what were you thinking".

This shocked me as I had hit one, surely, he should be pleased, but he just frowned and shook his head. We walked in silence, me feeling more than a little bit disappointed at his reaction, over the field to where the deer was lying. I had aimed at the back of its head and was inch-perfect. It was then my Dad looked at me and said, "Where did you aim". I told him I had aimed at the back of its head because it was running away from me. He smiled, shook his head and said "You have some talent with that" as he pointed to the rifle in my hands. I beamed a huge smile, my Dad had said 'I was good', at long last I felt worthy of his praise. He handed me a knife and said, "Prep it then". I had watched him do it many times, but this was my first. My Dad continued to talk as I prepped the deer, "I have taught you the humane way of killing a deer the heart or neck shot only a clean kill for a noble beast", then I saw him smile and he put his hand on my shoulder and said, "That was some shot". As we walked back, me carrying the deer, I didn't notice the weight of it, I was smiling so much that I had pleased my Dad with my shooting.

After that, every time I went with my Dad shooting, the distance got longer and more difficult, he taught me all about wind direction and how to compensate when taking on a distant target. The target not a roe deer but a neap (turnip) balanced on a post or a stump of a tree. I never missed; I could not afford to miss. It made my Dad smile and shake his head in recognition of a good shot and I loved it.

Just before my 15 birthday, I was out with the rifle, a .22 with scope; I saw a deer moving from one field to another and enter a small open wooded area. I diverted to the left and ran up the side of the field, I knew that the wind was in my favour and the deer would not smell me. I got into a position on a large flat boulder at my guess I was aiming at a 9 degree down angle from where I thought the deer would appear and about 180 yards out from the wooded area. I stayed still, going through in my head everything my Dad had taught me.

Cradle the rifle, relax, let the natural elements of the shot take its place. I waited for what seemed ages, then I saw the roe deer emerging from the woods. It was not where I had expected it to come from it was much further away, but I had it in my sights. Again, my Dad's words echoed through my head 'always a clean kill never let a beast suffer' it would be the longest shot I would have tried on a deer. I started to control my breathing, put the first pressure on the trigger, then finally on the out-breath I squeezed the trigger. I recoiled with the rifle but came back on target, I saw the deer fall to the ground then getting up and staggering down the embankment out of sight. I jumped up and headed down toward it thinking 'please let it be a clean shot and not let the beast suffer'. I kept thinking of the distance as I approached. I looked over the embankment there was blood but no sign of the deer. I approached slowly and there it was steaming in a small ditch area. I had aimed at the heart and that is where it had been hit. Clean kill for an honourable beast, my Dad would be very proud of me. I smiled to myself, then got to work cleaning the beast. I struggled to get it up the small embankment, as I got my breath back I looked back at the distance, must be at least 280 yards and thought that's ok, bet I could get one further though. I could not wait to tell my Dad.

Chapter 2

A year and a half had passed since my Dad had died and sometimes I would still break down when I thought of him. My family moved to a new town to start a new life; it was hard to live in our old house now my Dad had gone. My brother had gone off to college, so it was just me, my Mum and sister.

I left school at the earliest opportunity and spent most of my time at the farm. It was different now, I was 'working' at the farm and I made some amount of money for someone my age. All I had in my head was working and making money. I think it was the only way I could get on with life, I still missed my Dad so much and getting tore into work from dusk till dawn was my way of dealing with it. I kept up my boxing training too, but it was never enough, I could not settle. I wanted more but I did not know what.

One day I had to go into town with a tractor that we had traded in for a new one. I parked overnight and stayed at my Mum's. I could see my Mum fussing over my sister, then she handed me a plate of food. It felt odd to me, this was not my home and I could not explain it. My family were here but something was missing. After dinner, I went through to the sun lounge my Mum said, "we are away to the cinema", I asked what we were going to see and she replied, "Oh, you're not coming it is a 'girlie' film". It was then I realised what was wrong, my Mum had made a new life for herself and my sister and I did not figure in their plans. I sat down looking out the window, a tear rolled down my cheek. My Mum noticed this and asked if I was okay, I shook my head, she sat down and said, "We all miss him". "I don't fit in here anymore do I?" I asked.

at the farm I worked every hour I could just to stop from thinking about him, I had no life other than work. My family had each other I just didn't fit in.

Where did I belong?

After they left for the cinema, I went to the pub, I always looked older for my age and never had any problems being served. After a few pints, I went to thetoilet when I came out two blokes bumped into me and I said "Hey fuck sake watch it eh", as I walked towards the bar one of them put a hand on my shoulder and said, "Hey you, ye bastard", without thinking I grabbed his hand, spun round raising my hand so that his fingers were fully extended in the wrong direction, he screamed and

I smiled and let him go, his pal threw a punch I stepped forward in his direction and I blocked it, crouched down slightly and gave him a couple of rapid punches into his side. Just for good measure, I headbutted him in the nose, he went down in a crumpled heap. Next thing I knew I was being thrown out of the pub by the barman and a few others. I smiled as I stood there, I lit a cigarette and thought, 'thanks Dad all that training came in handy'. I was just about to set off back to my Mum's when a man came out of the pub. I remember him being tall and very straight-backed. He said, "Nice moves young man not seen anything like that since I was in the army" he shrugged his shoulders and said "Maybe that's where you belong eh" he nodded and turned and walked off. I stood and watched him until he turned the corner. That was it 'the army' that was where I belong. I could not sleep all that night thinking about the stories my Dad had told me about his time in the army. Could this be it, what I was looking for, my future?

The next morning, I delivered the old tractor, they were still servicing the new one, so I decided on a walk into town, there was only one thing in my mind, the army careers office. I arrived at the office, it was only 8am, so I started looking at the pictures in the window of all the activities you could do. Big words over the door announced - JOIN THE ARMY AND SEE THE WORLD - I thought to myself, 'I am having some of that'. I was totally lost in thought when a voice behind me said, "Fancy that do ye". I turned and saw a man dressed in army uniform, I replied "Wouldn't be waiting here if I didn't", he frowned said, "A little less lip son and I will make you a coffee". I was surprised at his voice very tough and to the point, I apologised and stood to one side he opened the door and said, "That's better". We had a cup of coffee and a chat then he asked if I wanted to do the test. Test? What test? I didn't think I needed to swot to join the army, but I agreed. Why not.

Once I got going, I found it easy, he scored the test, congratulated me and said I could have the choice of infantry or infantry. I thought for a bit and said, "Oh well, infantry for me then". He said, "Because of your age, you have a choice, what will it be? 21 weeks basic training or 1 year at Aberdeen junior leaders". He explained the 21 weeks was a lot harder, but you got to your regiment quicker. What can I say - 21 weeks for me! Because I was under 18 my Mum had to sign the papers. That was a thought, I had never even mentioned to her about joining the army what would she say? As I began to leave the office, papers in hand, the recruiting sergeant said to me, "Hey your Dad was a good man he would be proud of you, I knew him very well". He winked and said if I could get them signed, I may be in the January intake. I left that office with a huge smile, not only was I doing something I wanted to do, but I would make my Dad proud. Now just to get my Mum to sign the papers!!

"No! No! No! I am not signing that; you don't want to go to the army just work at the farm!" my Mum shouted over supper that night. I walked out and down to the local pub. As I walked in the barman said "Out! You're barred", I thought, "I am not wanted anywhere". I walked around town for a couple of hours and headed back to my Mum's house. My sister met me at the door and told me Mum was upset because I wanted to join the army. I went through to the lounge where my Mum was sitting holding a photo of my Dad, clearly, she had been crying. I felt bad for upsetting her like this, but it was something I had to do. I leaned over and cuddled her as she wept. In my determination, I told my Mum if she did not sign the papers I would go anyway. I would not be coming home, and I would join the army at 18 – without her signature. "Please let me go with your blessing" I asked.

We sat and talked for a long time until she finally looked into my eyes and said, "If this is what you really want, I will give you my blessing" and she signed the papers.

I phoned the farm in the morning and told them that I would not be back with the tractor until the afternoon, as Mum wanted me to do some chores around the house, I lied. I headed up to the army careers office with my papers. WhenI handed over the papers, I was told they would be in touch, everything will be sent to me and any problems to get back to them. He told me to keep up the boxing training and start running with weight, "What kind of weight" I asked, he said "Anything, just so you can build up your fitness".

When I returned to the farm my Mum had already called them to ask if they knew about my plans to join the army. No, was their reply. She told them I would be away in January. Well, the proverbial shit hit the fan; they went mad. They had assumed I would just stay and work the farm, not thinking I could possibly want anything more out of life. How wrong they were. Army here I come.

Chapter 3

I started training with a couple of old sacks, fashioned with rope, strapped to my back filled with barley, my old uncle said it would mould into the shape of my back. He had come to terms with my plans, secretly I think he was proud of me but he would never say so. I ran up hills with this weight on my back, I started wearing it all the time even when feeding the cattle, just so I got used to it.

Every other day I would add more barley to my bag. My shoulders were red and slightly burned with the rubbing of the ropes, but I pushed through it, I was joining the army. My old uncle said, "Better not fuck yourself up too soon, a bit at a time my lad", this just made me work even harder.

A few weeks later came a call from my Sister telling me there was a letter for me 'from the government'. My army papers had arrived. I jumped onto my motorbike and headed down to my Mum's. When I arrived, I was surprised to find my whole family there. Mum, both grandparents my brother and sister. I excitedly opened the envelope. This was it, a rail pass, my army number, and some documents to sign and return. I was already on the payroll and my first payment would be paid by postal order. This was it I had joined the army. It stated I was to learn my army number and report to Glencorse Barracks, Penicuik, Edinburgh on the 4th of January. We all had a few drinks to celebrate. My Mum put on a brave face, smiling and laughing, but I knew she was not as happy as she made out. I kept pinching myself, I was really going.

The next morning, I went to the bank to sort out my money. I had saved up quite a bit of farming and contracting and I wanted to know how best to manage my money. The manager advised me well, although I know he made a good bit of money from it too. I thought I was rich and would never be poor again.

Stupid me!

When I returned, I found my brother standing in the kitchen with a grin on his face, he recited my army number by heart, I couldn't believe it I had only looked at it. I laughed and headed to my bedroom. I sat and looked at the pink papers they had sent me and read them all over again. I began to learn my army number, to help I wrote it down on pieces of paper and put one in my pockets, one in my wallet, I even sellotaped one to the bathroom mirror so that I could get it into my head. It took a while as my brother changed them for a laugh, he did not make things easy, but in the end, I managed to get it offto a tee.

That Christmas and New Year was fine but all I could think about was the army I even went down to the library and got some books on the army and battles. Christmas morning, I was out pounding the streets of the town with my bag of barley just to keep the training up. I was stopped about 300 hundred yards from my Mum's house by a passing police car, they got out and asked what was in the bag as I was running so fast, I think they thought I had stolen something. I explained that I was in training for the army, but they insisted on looking in the bag. One of them picked it up and exclaimed "Gees, that is some weight", it had been raining a lot lately and my bag had gotten wet, I hadn't noticed the wet barley had gotten heavier. They smiled and said enjoy your Christmas, son, I nodded and pushed off at speed again.

When they drove past, they peeped the horn and one policeman shouted outof the window, "Best of luck with the army mate", I thought it weird as I had never been called mate before, especially by a policeman.

Chapter 4

All too soon I was standing on the platform waiting for the train, it was cold and windy, I felt great I was in the army. My Mum got upset, as Mum's do, she wished me well and told me to take care of myself. As I stepped onto the train my sister had a tear in her eye even my brother, who was my hero, had a sad look on his face. I waved, moved off and found my seat, I felt great. My brother had put a can of lager into my sandwich bag without anyone seeing it. I found it later when I went into my bag for a sandwich, I smiled as I ate egg and onion sandwiches washed down with this can of lager. The girl on the tin was KAREN I remember thinking, 'cheers big bruv'.

I arrived in Edinburgh I saw an army corporal standing with a sign saying, 'Army Recruitment', I approached, he just said, "Name", I answered and called him sir. He smiled and said "Do I look like a wanker to you", I said "No", "Then you can call me corporal ok, get your gear on the bus and then go and have a pint, we have about an hour to wait until the next train gets here". I just walked onto the bus and sat down with the rest of the sorrowful faces, the corporal appeared at the door and told us all to go and get a pint, no need to offer twice, we all headed off to the pub full of expectation and excitement.

The corporal joined us but had a soft drink. He regaled us all with army stories, had us all laughing, I thought "If this is what it is like in the army bring it on".

When the other guys arrived, we got back on the bus, the corporal sat back and told us more stories. As we were about to enter the gates to the barracks, he walked down to the front put his Glengarry on and sat down in the front seat. When the bus stopped, he started shouting at us telling us all that we were pieces of shite. 'Fuck me' I thought he was such a fine bloke half an hour ago, what happened, did he have a brain lapse or something, he saw me muttering something and shouted "What the fuck did you just say boy", I shrugged my shoulders and he shouted again "Don't piss me off". I smiled and that really pissed him off. I was roughly pushed off the bus and made to stand in a line. Another corporal came up to us shouting about standing still, he was about an inch from my face and I looked down. He shouted "Look up," I thought, 'what the fuck have I done. The army likes to shout'.

The rest of the day was a blur. We were taught the

rules of the camp then had to introduce ourselves to our section training corporal. When it was my turn, I started to tell my story, he stood in front of me and slapped me on the face, "Speak correctly you highland bastard" he yelled at me. I was shocked at this, but I continued, when I finished, he had a look of pure anger on his face. He snarled at me and moved on to the next recruit. I seemed to be pissing everyone off 'what the hell had I done?'

The following day we were up at 5.45 hours, normal for me at the farm, but some guys struggled. I showered and dressed, our training corporal came into the room, my bed was just as he walked in the door, he threw my bed all over the floor and snarled. I thought 'I think I may have made a friend'. Over the next few days, we were shown how to make bed blocks, basic cleanliness, I couldn't believe some guys didn't even know how to shave properly.

When it was time to get our army kit from the stores, I was so excited, it was real now I was getting an 'army uniform'. The corporal was still being a pain, nothing was right, and constantly shouting. He introduced his, 'black persuading stick', a stick about 10 inches long, drilled out in the centre and filled with a steel bar to make it heavy, a flick in the balls and you were in agony. I hated this him, but I had wanted this army training so much. I remember one of the other guys saying 'that fucker has it in for you', I shrugged and said 'fuck him', just then pain shot through my back, he had been in the corridor listening, he whacked me on the left kidney. My first experience of the 'black persuader'. You can be sure that after that I kept my mouth shut and adopted a saying my Dad used to say when we were learning something new, 'look, listen and learn', and that's exactly what I did.

As our training continued, we were shown dry training, with fake rounds, how to fire or misfire, stoppage, change magazines, and unload in all different firing positions. We went through these drills so often that when it was time to get on the range and fire real rounds, we were all very proficient in all aspects of our weapons. The weapons we used were SLR (self-loading rifle) GPMG (general purpose machine gun) and the SMG (submachine gun) 9mm Browning pistol, these were the weapons of the British army at the time. I looked, listened and learned and I loved it. Everything except the marching, polish boots, bed inspection and the rest of it but I suppose that was all a part of the training and making you a young soldier. I did enjoy the log races and fieldwork, camouflage and concealment, digging shell scrapes, trenches, the BFT (basic fitness test), I got my teeth into it all.

When the boxing part of the training came up, this PTI (physical training instructor) asked if anyone had any boxing experience, of course, I put my handup. We were told, when you are pointed at to get up and 'go for it' so I did.

My opponent came at me with cartwheel arms and fists, I sidestepped and struck him on the side of the face he went down. The PTI said, "Nice footwork soldier, let's see you against someone that has boxed before". My next opponent was something different. I looked at him, as my Dad had taught me, his stance was good, arms up tight, head bopping from side to side. He came at me too eager though with an overstretched leg making this his weakest point. I stepped in close, ducked down, up weaved, by this time he was exposed so I jabbed with my left then came the right a humdinger, bang, he stood upright for 100th of a second then went down in a heap. Our PTI shouted "Ok, that's enough", I saw him wink at my training officer. I was told to sit down as two corporals helped my opponent up.

Chapter 5

It was now becoming a regular occurrence that the corporal would come in, wreck my locker and my bed block, it happened so often I got used to it and the rest of the guys used to help me square things away after he left. I refused to let him break me, but that black fucking stick though was something else. I had that many whacks from that fucker, I hated everything about him and as he snarled at me, I thought he felt the same way, fuck only knows why.

One day I was summoned to the platoon commander's office and told that I would be boxing for my platoon, he asked if it was ok, I answered "Yes sir". He said, "Good man do the platoon proud then", I was thrilled. I saluted, turned and marched out. As I walked past the toilet area, guess who was waiting for me, my friend the corporal, he said, "Hey don't think I will let you get away with anything ok", I answered "Yes Corporal". Then he flicked me in the balls with this black stick, I went down in a rage of pain, the sergeant came out of his office and shouted, "What the fuck happened". "I think he slipped" was the reply from the corporal. As he helped me to my feet he said "You slipped didn't you", I nodded the officer came up and said, "Are you sure that's what happened soldier", what else could I say but "Yes sir". He patted me on the shoulder then said, "That's ok then can't have anything happen to you with the boxing coming up", staring at the corporal as he said it. I am sure even to this day they all knew what happened.

On the range we went through dry drills again, then it was time to get real ammo. Zeroing our rifles on the 30-metre range - it was a real competition to see who could hit the targets at a distance. It felt great as I was told to get down into the firing position, the range warden shouted that the targets would fall when hit. The targets were at 30 yards, 100 yards, 200 yards and 300 yards. A bellowing voice shouted, "With a magazine of 20 rounds, load, make ready, in your own time, fire". I thought I would go for 300 first and get shorter so I fired 4 rounds, all targets were hit and down they went. As I made my weapon safe, the sergeant came up by my side and said, "Ok show off do it again". My targets appeared again, I made ready and waited till I was told to fire. I was told this time 30 yards then 100 and so on. I fired off 4 rounds and all targets went down. We all made our weapons safe and walked up towards the butts to see our targets, the sergeant was walking behind me, almost in my footsteps, as we approached the target they swung up again so that we could identify the hits on the targets they were on prints of a charging German soldier. I had hit square in the middle. The Sergeant said, "Good shooting lad let's do it again". We walked back just as the next wave of recruits got themselves ready for their turn on the targets. I got down with them and did it all over again then, again and again, the training staff of my platoon were all standing around me as I fired. I made my rifle safe and stood up they were all smiling even my great friend the 'prick of a Corporal'. He was actually smiling at me!!

I was asked by the Officer, how I was in other firing positions, I told him I was fine. He nodded and the targets flipped around again, I got down on one knee and fired at the 4 targets, all went down. I made my weapon safe and stood up. In the standing position, I was asked to fire at the next target that flipped around. I did this, it was the 300-yard target, and down it went. I made my weapon safe again and as I turned the officer said, "Very impressive young manwhere did you learn to shoot like that," I said, "My Dad, Sir". He nodded to me and said, "He would be proud, let's go and see where on the target you hit".

As I walked away towards the target, I heard the

other training Corporals shouting 'we want all of you to be able to do that level of shooting ok'.

The mood had changed a bit with the corporal, he was not so harsh on me, but he was still a prick. I got my head down and focused on my training. I enjoyed it, it felt so natural to be out living on the ground in shell scrapes or basher (sleeping canopy) at night, eating rations and night raids etc. We were three-quarters of the way through our training by now and I had a long weekend home on leave, before I returned for the boxing competition.

I was up against some bloke I didn't know so it was a battle of unknown skills. I won in the 2nd round. He was a tough opponent but in the end, we shook hands and laughed as we were led away to the changing rooms. He told me he was in the same regiment as me but was four weeks ahead of me in training, he said he would keep an eye out for me when I got to the regiment so we can have a few pints I readily agreed, I was up for that. Later the Officer came in and congratulated me on my boxing win and said that after battle camp he would get a few cases of lager for us to celebrate.

Battlecamp was 2 weeks away at another training camp, where we were to be put through everything we had been taught in the last 17 weeks, from live firing to land mines and everything about fieldcraft. We were told it would be a tough two weeks, but me being me, I loved every minute of it. We were beginning to act like soldiers, our fitness was at a good standard and we all pulled together proper teamwork. When we started, 17 weeks ago, we were 53 raw recruits and now we were down to 23 young eager soldiers.

All of us passed the battle camp. On the way back in our two 4 tonners you could tell how happy we all were, laughing and singing, it was the comradery that we liked. We knew that on our return we had a 10-mile run with full kit and a target shoot to do, but we all knew we could do that no problem. From then on it was intensive marching and drilling routines to get us all ready for our passing out parade. Saturday night before the passing out parade as promised, the officer produced 4 cases of ice-cold lager and we all had a hoot. It was decided to have the drink in the shower and toilet area so as not to mess up our billets and we all sat on our sleeping bags on the floor, we had a right good laugh, mostly making fun of the training staff.

Chapter 6

Our passing out parade went very well, we were all excited and the march past was wonderful, a great feeling of achievement, with all our families there to see us. It was a proud moment for us all, we had made it, and boy were we proud soldiers.

We all marched up and saluted for our wages, I had saved over £1100 during the 21 weeks of training, we got it in cash. I remember handing it over to my Mum saying keep good care of that while I changed out of my ceremonial uniform. We were all soldiers now and we thought we were as hard as nails, but hey we had just been through 21 weeks of hardship and bullshit. Now 17 day leave then off to our regiments. I was off to one of the Scottish regiments as a rifleman, an old and well-respected regiment, in the words of Winston Churchill, "Probably the finest regiment in the world ". When I was walking with my whole family towards the car park, our officer came up and said, "Would it be possible to have a word young man?" I was now in civilian clothes, I replied, "Yes Sir".

He pulled me to one side, there was another officer and a sergeant there, the officer said, "You will not be joining your regiment when you return here in 17 days ok". I stood very still I felt a lump come up in my throat, in a 100th of a second I thought, 'what the fuck have I done', my life was shattered, I started to tremble slightly, then I saw him smile and he said "You are off to the British army shooting competition, young man, between the many army battalions".

What a relief, I thought I was being thrown out. "Soldier you will be shooting for your regiment, we sent off your exemplary shooting record to your commanding officer and he agreed you should go straight to the regiments shooting team", he said. He shook my hand and continued, "You should be very proud of yourself". He wished me well and the sergeant pattedme on the back and wished me all the best too. As I walked away, I could hardly believe it, my family were standing waiting for me. My brother said, "What's all that about", I shrugged and said, "Tell you later". My family had hired a minibus to take them all to the parade, as there were quite a few of them. When I jumped in I began to tell them what the officer had said, my Mum said "Oh that's fine" and everyone nodded it was then I realised that they were all civvies and did not understand what an honour it was to be asked to shoot for the regiment, especially as I was a newcomer. I looked out of the window and thought, 'fucking hell, pity my Dad wasn't here he would be so proud of me'. When I looked around my brother smiled and winked at me and said, "Always knew you were a good shot little bruv, Dad would be so proud", suddenly I choked back a lump in my throat I smiled and thought 'yes Dad you would have been proud'.

I stayed at home for a few days, went out on the booze with my brother most of the time, it was great to relax and have a laugh. I went into the army careers office to let him know of my progress. It was so different from the time I enlisted, the sergeant shook my hand and congratulated me on my success in getting into the shooting team. I thought, 'how the fuck did he know that', but he winked and said, "They informed me only this morning well done lad, well done indeed. you keep your nose clean and you will go far".

After my brother headed away back to his work, I went to the farm. It felt great to be back in a tractor and do a bit of farming, I still trained hard but drank plenty at night. I messed about with girls at the local village, my old uncle said, "Keep that thing in your trousers or some of them will have a belly full of arms and legs, use a condom for Christ's sake". I remember thinking, 'fuck off that's like washing your feet with your socks on, I was a young stallion in his prime, a soldier'. When I was down at the local bar, I thought I was Jack the lad, these girls were all in awe of a soldier and I loved it. My cousin, who was a bit of a womanizer, said, "Hey min, ride them all and work high reverse when you cum ok", he was a lot older than me and more experienced.

I found that the training I was still doing was a piece of piss now so I started running 10 miles every day and kept up the boxing on the bag, pull-ups and heaps of sit-ups, It felt great to be so fit but I wanted to push myself further every day. When the time came to get my shit sorted ready to go back to Edinburgh I could not wait. I said cheerio to everyone and headed off for the train. I felt good about going back and beginning the next chapter of army life.

Chapter 7

We all returned full of stories about girls, drinking and of course fighting. We headed to the NAAFI to get some pints in before it closed, it felt good to be back with my mates again. My 'real family' as I thought of these guys. Over the next few days, we were messing around waiting to get sorted, I had to report to the company commander, as the rest were sent off to their chosen regiments to join them at their barracks. "You will start your journey tomorrow down to England, get the travel clerk to issue you with your travel documents any questions", he said, I replied, "Where about in England Sir?"

His reply was, "Welcome to the Army son you'll figure it out." I saluted and marched out, as I walked down the corridor, I thought, 'what a prick he could have just said where it was I was heading'. I heard my name being called so I went into the office, where the voice came from, and there behind a desk was an attractive female soldier from the WRAC (Women's Royal Army Corp) with the rank of a lance corporal, she said, "I have your travel detail here", I smiled and asked where I was heading, she stood up and walked very elegantly to a map on the wall she pointed to an area down in England, "There you go soldier, that's where you are going. Your rail warrant will get you to the train station, after a few changes of trains, of course, there you will be picked up by the duty driver any other questions just ask, fancy a coffee while I get you sorted out with money", I said "Aye ok corporal", she smiled "Its Kim".

As I sipped on sweet milky coffee she looked at my army record so far, just a thin folder, she said I must be a good shot going straight to a British army shooting completion, I shrugged and said it's just shooting, I was a bit embarrassed. When she handed me my documents and money she smiled and said, "We are all going out for a drink after work if you fancy it, since your mates are away now, it's a going away party down in Penicuik, just a few drinks, save you sitting in an empty billet by yourself". I tried to sound calm and worldly as I replied, "Aye ok where will I meet you?" We arranged to meet in the NAAFI and head out from there.

I rushed into Edinburgh city centre to buy some new clothes for the night out, Kim was beautiful, and I wanted to impress. I remember when I arrived back at the barracks how strange it felt walking through the gate showing my identity card to the duty corporal. The last 21 weeks were full of bullshit Corporals always shouting at the recruits and now this man said, "Hey pal fancy a brew". I was shocked but said yes corporal, would you believe he replied "Its Matthew or Mattie, now mate come into the guard room, I heard you were coming with us for a pint or 20 tonight" he said with a big grin, I told him Kim suggested it as I would be sitting alone in my billet. He Laughed and said "Watch her she will eat you alive" he sniggered and pushed his cigarettes, I thought this was great I didn't know this guy but he was so friendly, if this was the forces I am up for this big time.

I packed up all my gear, for all there was of it, I had been told that I would get kitted out when I arrived down in England. I would be ready for the dawn move the next morning, I was being picked up by the duty driver at 06.45 hours to be dropped at the Edinburgh train station, with still no idea exactly where I was going.

I showered, got dressed in my new clothes and left for the NAAFI, feeling just a little excited. I walked in and Kim was at the bar with about six others she smiled and said, "It's my round what you having," she introduced me to the lower rank permanent staff of the barracks. It felt very comfortable and comradely, we had a few drinks then we all headed out to Penicuik to meet the rest of the party. What a great night, we were all very pissed and had a great laugh. I had never drunk tequila before but it was shot after shot, a good night by all accounts. Kim and I staggered up the road and I seemed to sober up a bit, we went into the barracks and walked towards the billets. Kim said, "That's far enough soldier boy these are female quarters," "Pity" I replied, she smiled and kissed me. "Some other time eh" she said. I watched her walk off and then headed in the other direction towards my empty billet, alone.

I sat on my bed, checked all my travel details for the journey ahead again then decided to have a shower. When I walked back to my room with just a towel wrapped around me, Kim was sitting on my bunk she smiled and said "I meant some other time by a few minutes hey if I am caught I will get busted," I winked and said, "well there is no one else here."

The duty driver was sitting waiting for me at the guard room the next morning. I threw my kit into the back and we headed off to Edinburgh. My head was banging from the tequila. When we arrived, I thanked the driver and got on the train. My seat was booked so I settled down with my Walkman and a tape of The Clash, 'London's Calling'. I smiled at the memory of last night, it was a good laugh and Kim was very energetic. When she left at 3am I was knackered but a happy knackered. Before she left, she gave me her contact details and said if I was passing this way again to give her a shout. I said "Yes corporal" she sniggered and disappeared out the door carrying her shoes. As the train slid gently through the countryside, I fell fast asleep with Jon Strummer singing in my ear.

When I finally arrived at my destination the duty driver picked me up. He was a fine bloke from Newcastle. As we drove towards the barracks, he made me laugh with some stories about some of the things the officers and sergeants get up to on nights out. He told me he has to drive them home, sometimes he said, "Tell you something son they will shag everything, some blokes wives, girlfriends, if it's got tits they will shag it". I laughed all the way. He should have been on the telly as a comedian, I'm sure he embellished a bit but the way he told it was funny. When he dropped me off, he said if I fancied a pint then he would meet me tonight in the NAAFI. Once I got my kit from the back of the vehicle I turned and saw an old-looking corporal. He wore the same cap badge as me. He said "So you're the new shooter eh?". He introduced himself as 'old Eddie'. I followed him into the rooms, there waiting for me were eight men all kitted out for the ranges. Eddie introduced them all and we shook hands. He said, "Your bunk is through there, get sorted, your new kit arrived yesterday so get squared away and we will meet you for a dusk shoot, give you time to settle in and see the boys in action". I just nodded.

That night I was an observer only. As I walked with Eddie I noticed that on his jacket he had a badge with crossed rifles and an 'S' above, which meant he was a sniper. I was in awe of him as he told me about the weapons I would be using. We stopped at a guy he introduced as Fergie, he had an L96 7.62 sniper rifle. I reached to touch it but he shouted "Fuck off you", I told him I only wanted to see one up close but he said "Not a fucking chance", Eddie said, "Come on leave him he's a bad-tempered little fucker but a bloody good shot though". I was admiring the weapon but Eddie said, "It's a long way off for you to be firing one of them. It's the SLR you have been entered for, you might get a chance of the 9mm Browning but we will see how you get on".

The next day on the range I zeroed my rifle but thought something didn't seem right. I went to the proper range and opened up on 200 yards target with my shooting team standing behind me. I had fired 10 rounds when a voice shouted: "What the fuck is he doing here?". Eddie told him to be quiet then he made me run down the range to see my target, on the run back I thought 'shit I hardly even hit the target'. I stood with the rest of them and they all started complaining about how bad I was. Eddie said in a gruff voice, "Lad you will have to improve big time if you are to stay here", I agreed and asked to try again, he nodded. As I got into position, I heard someone say "Fucking sprog". I remember breathing lightly and it was as if my Dad was by my side, I could hear his voice in my head going through the drills. I loaded the SLR, cradling the weapon, slowly taking aim and fired, again and again, I finished the magazine on the 200 yards target, made my weapon safe and stood up. Someone said, "Oh aye so you can shoot eh sprog" as he looked through the binoculars. I looked over at Eddie who winked and nodded, which reassured me. I asked if I could carry on and did the same from the standing position. One of the lads said, "Fuck me that's impressive, what a grouping". Even Fergie said, "Well sprog keep that up and you'll do ok". I smiled.

After a few hours or so I walked up to Eddie and said, "I'm sorry, I don't know what happened with the first target" he replied "It was nerves, we were standing close to you and you were trying too hard, I noticed how you held the rifle, it was almost unnatural for someone with your records from training. That's why I made you run down the range to get your head clear so we could really see what you could do". I looked around and everyone was packing up for the day Eddie said, "Its pint time, can you drink laddie? You will get plenty of practice on the range tomorrow, and for the next 3 weeks. Better we have a few bevies so you get to know the lads, we are a team, we train as a team, we shite as a team and drink as a team. The only time it's not a team effort is if there's a piece of skirt involved, well only if she's a willing participant". As I laughed he patted me on the back and said, "Tell you what, you keep up what you were doing today and I'll teach you everything you want to know then you too can have one of these", he pointed at the sniper badge on his jacket.

The next few weeks were brilliant, we started working as a team. Eddie worked with me a lot for the first few days then one morning he turned to me and said, "Right laddie you're on your own now, remember what I taught you, I need my practice as well you know". I settled into my practice, repeatedly, round after round. At lunch break, we cleaned our weapons only to start all over againin the afternoon and sometimes into the evening for night shoots. I thought it was brilliant most of the lads were great, except Fergie he was still a bit of a prick, but he started to nod to me after the first 2 weeks, I thought to myself, 'he must be warming to me'. I stopped him one day to ask his background and where he learned to shoot, he loudly responded, "Listen sprog we are not mates, ok?", Eddie butted in, "Fuck sake Fergie, he's only asking a fucking question give him a break". Fergie turned to me and told me he was from a farm and that his Dad had taught him to shoot. I told him that's was the same as me, and that my Dad passed away a year or so ago and that's why I joined the army, to get away. He went silent and stared at me for a few seconds then he lowered his voice and said "My Dad passed away as well", he touched me on the shoulder, winked then said "Listen sprog this afternoon fancy a shot of the L96?", one of the other lads shouted, "Fuck sake, Fergie getting soft in your old age", Fergie smiled and said, "Well lads he's proven that he can handle an SLR, let's see what he can do with a real weapon at distance". My face nearly burst with the huge smile on it, I looked at Eddie he shook his head, smirked and winked at me.

That afternoon I walked with Fergie to the longer range which was 600 to 900 metres. Fergie taught me the drills, how to strip the weapon down for cleaning and assemble it again. I did that four times in a row to get it perfect, once I was done assembly Fergie said "Right let's get you zeroed in". I walked behind him thinking he is ok but I'd better say nothing just now. My Dad's voice came into my head - look, listen and learn.

I zeroed the rifle on the 100 metre target, which on this range was specifically for zeroing rifles. I squeezed the trigger, there was a smooth recoil, it was excellent I adjusted the scope and fired another couple of rounds. We then settled down on the target at 600 metres. Fergie said, "I will be your spotter ok?" as he looked, through fancy looking binoculars, at the target ahead. After a long pause, he said, "Sprog listen to what I tell you ok, target 600 metres at an elevation of four degrees, fire one round only". I controlled myself and took aim, slowed my breathing and relaxing, then while exhaling I squeezed the trigger. The rifle leapt into life, I recoiled smoothly but stayed on target. Fergie mentioned a couple of adjustments, so I made these and at his signal fired again, he lowered the binoculars slightly and told me to fire one more round. After a short pause, he said, "Fire at will". I settled back on the target and fired again exactly on the spot where I had aimed before, after a few seconds, he shouted, "Unload, make safe". I did so smoothly and correctly. Without lowering his binoculars he said, "Ok sprog off you go back to your SLR and get the practice in, that's all for the day we will have a pint later". I slowly stood up and walked back towards the other range, my head was spinning I thought what had I done to be elevated to having the L96 experience then to be dropped down to earth again, I shrugged my shoulders and carried on walking. Later that afternoon Eddie asked how I got on with the long rifle, I said, "Aye good I think, got three rounds down on target, but Fergie said that was enough, so I walked back and carried on with the SLR". Eddie nodded and said, "Ok, brew time. A cigarette and clean weapons eh, then shower, shite and shave, in that order".

I smiled these older army lads had some sayings.

Over the next few days I worked hard and fired hundreds of rounds on the SLR range. I started getting some pistol work in as well, it was great! I thought I was Dirty Harry as I shouted at the targets, "Go ahead make my day punk" before opening fire. One afternoon Eddie heard me and told me angrily "It's not a game ok! You must be professional at all times". He laughed smiled and said, "You're probably a better shot than he was anyway". I smiled and realisedthat I had gone that little bit too far, so I stopped all the playing around and settled into good honest training. No more Dirty Harry, well, not out loud anyway.

The day before the competition I decided not to fire my weapon. When Eddieasked why I told him I thought I better prepare myself mentally, I have fired enough, he nodded and said, "Ok, it's your show".

It was a fantastic sunny day with not a breath of wind, I decided to walk past allthe other ranges in the vicinity and watch others firing. Halfway round I spotted two black range rovers coming towards me I thought it a bit strange as all army vehicles were British army green. I stopped at the side of the road as they drove past until they reached the pistol range. I continued my walk, making my way up towards the pistol range where I stood by the vehicles. I watched in awe at these six chaps on the range, it was not conventional range work they were doing, they were moving in strange ways firing straight from the holster and walking away from the targets, turning to fire crouching down then firing again.

I had never seen anything like this being done before on the range. I was about to approach and introduce myself when someone caught my arm and pulled me back, the six men stopped what they were doing and stared at me. I turned my head and saw it was Eddie who had pulled me back. He waved a hand at the men, shouted an apology and pulled me back onto the road. He walked me at speed away from the range, I tried to resist but Eddie had hidden strength it seemed like he was breathing heavily trying to get his breath back from running.

After a few hundred yards we stopped at another range, he sat down and started making a cigarette, he roared at me "What the fuck are you doing up here?", I apologised and told him I was just walking and asked who they were. I was told in no uncertain terms to forget them. We sat in silence, me feeling a little confused, when we heard the roar of vehicles thundering towards us as the two range rovers sped passed and out of sight. I turned to Eddie and said, "I have never seen anything like what they were doing on a range, they were jumping around and...". Eddie stopped me mid-sentence and said, "Forget what you just saw soldier, those lads are special forces". I turned in awe and said "SAS?" he nodded and said "Or SBS, so just forget what you saw eh laddie". We walked back in silence, all that I could think about was these lads and how they were messing around on the range.

The next day the competition went very well for us, as a team we won seven awards, myself included. I managed to win a first in my category for the SLR and I came third in the 9mm, so it was celebrations all round. After receiving our awards, we headed back to the barracks to get spruced up for a night of drinking. I was sitting outside waiting for a shower to become empty, having a smoke, feeling pleased with myself on my success at my first competition. I was lost in thought so never noticed the man walk up the side of the building towards me, he was dressed in civilian clothes, jeans and a black padded jacket. I stood up, as I didn't know who he was or what rank, better to be safe than sorry, he asked for alight for his cigarette in what I detected was a slight Aberdeenshire accent. I gave him a light as he puffed on his cigarette he turned and said "Nice shooting today", I thanked him for the compliment, it was at that moment I realised he was one of the lads on the pistol range that Eddie had pulled me away from the day before. He sat down on the step and gestured to me to sit, he asked where I came from as he had heard my accent while I was on the range during the competition and recognized it. I answered his questions and told him a bit of my background. He asked when I was going back to my battalion, I told him we were leaving in two days to travel back but that I had not been to the battalion yet due to coming straight from basic training at Glencorse. He just looked at me for a moment then went back to his cigarette.

After I had rambled on like an idiot for a while, telling him about my Dad, the farm and my reasons for joining the army, he turned to me and said "Stick in, that was really some fine shooting today for someone your age without a lotof experience", he crushed out his cigarette, stood up and walked away. I shouted after him "Nice to have met you", he never turned but replied "Aye you too". As he disappeared back round the side of the building a voice asked "Who was that?", I nearly jumped out of my skin as I turned and came face to face with Eddie, I did hear him coming. I told him I thought it was one of themen from the pistol range the other day. Eddie looked surprised and said, "What did he want?", "He just said nice shooting and asked about my background" I told Eddie, he only nodded but I could tell he was not happy with my answer.

After drinking hard that night I decided to get up early and go for a walk beforebreakfast to clear my head. I made my way towards the ranges; we had been shown a shortcut up a bridle path. When I reached the ranges, I decided to start jogging as my head was beginning to clear. I heard vehicles coming along the road behind me, so I moved into the side to let them pass. The vehicles slow down and I turned to glance at the vehicles realizing that it was the two Range Rovers again. They slowly passed as I carried on jogging then they sped off. They were stopped at the pistol range again, I thought that chap yesterday was friendly enough but I remembered that Eddie had told me to stay out of their way, so I moved off the main road up another track. I had jogged for about four miles in a wide circle, coming over the ridge I realised I was at the pistol range again. In front of me were the lads in civvies. I went to run past, but someone shouted at me to stop. I thought, fuck, I was not sure what to do so I stopped and stood still. In a well-spoken English accent, a man asked, "Getting some exercise son?", I turned and replied, "Yes sir, better to keep fit sir", they all laughed and I looked awkwardly around, what had I said that was so funny? Someone said, "Don't call him sir for fuck sake, he will think he's above his station". They all laughed, the man I had spoken to yesterday said

"Relax, here have a smoke".

He gestured a cigarette towards me, I looked at the rest of them and slowly walked over and took the smoke while another chap at my side offered me a light and I stood there puffing away. I didn't know what to say but they broke the silence and asked questions about shooting, my basic training, my background and they offered me a brew from an urn they had in one of the range rovers. As we stood drinking our brew I started to shiver as I was cooling down from my run one chap passed me a jacket. They were having a laugh slagging each other off and telling jokes, I thought these guys have got it sussed, a real comradery. About half an hour later the man that offered me a smoke, by all account his name was Doug, said "Listen off you go we have work to do". I said, "Nice to have met you all", we said out goodbyes and I started to jog away. I was stiff from standing around but I thought I would push through it and show them that I was ok, it was hard and I struggled for the first five minutes but by that time I was well on my way back to theaccommodation.

After showering, we as a group, went for breakfast. I told them I had run into these lads again at the range, someone said, "What the SAS lads?", he wanted to know what they said and so I told them that I had a brew with them, and they all said, "Fuck off sprog you're speaking shite". I told them it was true but none of them believed me. I ate my breakfast in silence and as I finished most of the lads had moved away to get themself a smoke or head back to the accommodation. It was only Eddie and myself at the table, he told me SAS ladskeep themselves to themselves normally, I told him that is what happened   as I put my dishes away. As we left the mess hall (dining room) in walked the SAS lads, they all nodded and winked at me but said nothing. When we walked outside Eddie said, "Seems like you've made a few friends eh" I only nodded and smiled to myself.

That afternoon Eddie asked if we fancied going for a pint, I declined with the excuse I didn't have a lot of money left, it was a lie but I had had enough drink for a while. I said I would mooch around here and meet up with them all later. They all headed out and I went for a walk around the area for a while, I met up with the Geordie duty driver who had me laughing in minutes, I asked him about the SAS lads and he said, "Aye they are here one day away the next I see them now and then but better to give them a wide berth unless they approach you", I nodded we went for a pint and met up with the rest of the group who by this time were well on their way with the drinking games so I joined in it ended up a good night by all account I was pissed out of my skull.

Chapter 8

When I arrived at the Battalion, it was strange, I was used to being on first name terms on the range now I had to say yes corporal no corporal so it was a shock being back in the regimented way again. I had to sleep in the guard room that night as the quarter master was not available to give out my bedding. Next morning the RSM and the duty officer were at the guard room, I stood very still and straight in my civilian clothes. RSM turned to me and shouted "Who are you", I said my number rank and name he nodded told me I would be up in front of the commanding Officer at 14.00 hours, he would inspect me at 13.45 hours. I was then told to go and get breakfast then start getting squared away with my kit. At that I turned and marched out of the guard room not knowing where to go. I heard a voice say, "Sir, he has not been out of the guard room, someone will have to show him where to go", the RSM shouted halt to me and I froze he told one of the guards to show me the camp and we were told to double away.

After a big hearty breakfast, I staggered with my mattress to my room in the training accommodations lines. I barged in the door and saw that my gear had been dumped in the room, I put my mattress and bedding down on a normal army issue bed. A voice behind me told me to get everything squared away, I spun round and a corporal was standing there, he told me I was here on my own as the rest had been through their battalion training, hopefully they would get me through mine in a couple of weeks. I said, "Yes corporal" he smiled and said, "Ok its Terry when there are no senior ranks about", I nodded he handed me his pack of cigarettes and we had a smoke. He explained what the battalion training was for and that everyone had to do it before they go to a rifle company. He said he would help me get ready for meeting the Commanding Officer at 14.00 hours. Terry was full of stories and I sat and listened to him for an hour or so, he chain smoked, I tried to keep up but I had to say no to the fourth cigarette almost in a row. His stories were funny, it was good to be here.

The RSM office was up at HQ. When Terry lead me up through the camp I saw other soldiers doing rifle training on a small 30 metre range, others marching, running they all seemed to nod in my direction.

I stood outside the RSM's office and waited until he shouted my name, I marched in and up to the front of his desk. He shouted "Get out boy and do that march and halt again", I repeated it, he said "Much better". He moved from the his side of the desk to inspect me and said in a harsh tone "Ok lad, you will do for the CO ", as he shut the door he explained what would happen in the CO's office, I nodded and said "Yes sir", he told me to stand at ease, so in a swift movementI did just that.

Sitting on the corner of his desk he said in a low voice "I would like to be the first to congratulate you on winning the SLR award and the great effort with the 9mm pistol, well done laddie", he shook my hand and said "Well done indeed". He stood up from the desk and ordered me 'at the double' out of his office. I was then marched in and halted in front of the CO. I shouted out my number, rank and name, as instructed by the RSM. He began by welcoming me to the battalion, then went on about the awards that I had won for the battalion. He congratulated me then I was marched out and given the rest of the day off to sort out my kit.

Back in the lines Terry said, "That's it for the weekend, training will start Monday morning", I sorted out my gear and decided to go to the NAAFI for some cigarettes and boot polish. As I approached someone called out, in a loud resentful voice, "Here you!" I turned and saw it was a lance corporal with the RP (Regimental

Police) on his shelve. He came right up to my face and shouted, "Who the fuck do you think you are walking around the camp like that", I told him I was marching, he asked my name, I told him. He frowned "Oh aye, so you're the sprog eh?". Someone behind me shouted "Leave him alone you toss pot", the corporal smiled, moved sideways, and shook Eddies hand. I stood still, not sure what to do, he said "Ok sprog off you go". I wasn't enjoying being called 'sprog' but that was just something I would have to put up with for now. As I marched away, I heard Eddie saying "He's something with a rifle best I have seen in a long time he's a good lad, give him a break eh?".

Over the next two weeks my training went well, I covered everything easily, even my fitness was still at a high level, I could even outrun Terry and the other training corporals. "He's fit alright, I put him through the different levels of fitness, he was hardly out of breath, never seen anyone, just out of training, do press up and pull up like him".

At the end of the two weeks Terry invited me down to his house for a meal anda few drinks with him and his wife. When I arrived, I was met at the door by Terry and his wife, he had that never-ending cigarette in his hand as he handed me a beer. He introduced me to his wife and told me to go on in.

When I entered the living room there was Eddie, a big smile on his face, his wife and two others. We were introduced then the drinking began. I thought we were having a meal but as I looked down at the table there were crisps, dips and a few nibbles, it was then I realised that the main course of the meal was alcohol. His wife passed me as I came out of the bathroom she slapped my back side as we passed I just turned and awkwardly smiled, I wasn't sure what to do, she leaned in close and said, "If you ever fancy a fuck come visit me when he's not here". I was shocked and walked off back to the living room. I thought I better get out of here as soon as I could, but I carried on drinking for another few hours. When I next went to the bathroom I made sure that I was in and out very quickly.

During the next seven months in the battalion we were on training exercises for weeks at a time, which I loved. All the guys in my platoon were excellent, living life on the edge; train hard, drink hard, play hard and a great laugh. They were really switched on and I learned a lot from some of the old sweats. If I was not sure of something they would take time and show me, it was excellent experience for me and I felt that I was part of a big family, there were a few battles between myself and others, which is normal in an all-male environment each trying to get to the top of the tree. I usually managed to calm people down before it came to blows, but sometimes it just went a bit too far. It usually started by someone taking a swing at me, I would quickly take up the boxing stance, it usually ended in a double thump from me then it all cooled down. I never classed myself as a 'hard man', as I don't think there is such a thing, but I would never let anyone stand on my toes. I always asked for a handshake after to show there was no hard feelings, something my Dad had taught me from a young age. He said to always make up regardless of who wins a fight because you never know when they might have your back. I had managed to gain a bit of respect by now, I was no longer the sprog which was a bit of a blessing. I trained most of the time with my platoon but every so often I would be away with the shooting team on the ranges and of course I was entitled to access all weapons even the L96. I would put round after round down and enjoyed the banter with the guys.

One night we returned after a dusk shoot and was summoned into the OC 's office, he told me I was going on a sniper's course. I was delighted. He said,

"Keep your head down and stick in, ok, I have put my neck on the line over this". My reply was a definite 'yes sir'. He nodded and said, "Well-done lad you do the regiment proud on this course!" When I marched out, I almost burst out laughing with delight. When I turned into the corridor there was Eddie standing with a wide grin he said "Well-done mate, now I think it may be your round down the bar" I had no problem with that and thanked Eddie for all his help and encouragement. He replied, "Why? You did all the work mate I just honed it a bit".

Chapter 9

I packed up all my gear and left the platoon, heading for the sniper course in Warminster. I was so looking forward to this. My mates wished me all the best and they wanted to have a drink before I went away but because it was all last minute we did not have a chance, but I promised we would grab a pint when I returned.

I did well on the sniper course and passed no problem, I was so proud of having the crossed rifles with the "S" on my arm. I learned a lot and the instructors were brilliant putting me at ease right from the start. I looked, listened and learned. It was fantastic, we spent most of the time on the ranges. My spotter, whom I found difficult to trust at the start, made sure every round I fired hit the correct spot on my target. I soon relaxed into it and started to respect his advice and when it was my turn to be the spotter I made sure that I did a good job for my sniper too.

Our camouflage part of the course was a great laugh, some of the lads turning up from the barrack rooms looking like walking bushes. They had been ripping down branches and collecting grass and leaves all morning so that their ghillie suits (sniper suits) were covered in foliage. All I had on was my Ghillie suit, no branches. The instructor stopped in front of me and gave me a puzzled look. I explained I would wait until I got on the ground to see what the surrounding area was like before camouflaging up, you don't bring camouflage with you, you acquire it there on the ground so you fit in with the area you are operating in. The instructor was pleased and said, "You'll do for me".

My Dad had taught me camouflage and concealment, but he had never known that myself or my brother should join the army, but on reflection, itwas as if he predicted one of us would.

The instructor said, "The rest of you have done well, but he is right, your camouflage in the field might need changing every quarter of a mile so betterwait to see the environment first, but I know that you have put a lot of work into looking like this. When we arrive at the training ground area take all that shite off and re camouflage yourself, but well-done lads good effort especially when there is no camouflage in this area except the trees and bushes atHQ" he smiled.

Once I had returned to the battalion I got stuck into training again and although my fitness was at a high level, I kept pushing myself further and harder. A couple of months later we were away on a skiing course in Bavaria, which was excellent, the cross-country part wasn't enjoyable, but we had to be able to move over deep snow with speed carrying weight. Then came the normal ski experience, what a laugh, at the start I was never off my backside but one of the PTI'S I had trained with in the gym took me to one side and said he would help me. Once it all clicked I did very well. It was a great experience; we would ski during the day and drink at night. German beer took a bit of getting used to due to its strength but not being one to quit I persevered, we ended most nights just having a great laugh. I still did my sit ups and press ups every morning just to keep my upper body strength. When the two weeks were up, we were getting ready tohead back when the sergeant came in and shouted my name and pulled me outside. He said, "Son, one extreme to the other. You are joining a training team that's heading to Kenya so when we get back sort your shite out, I think you have a few day before you go but don't count on it". We both nodded and hewalked away. When I told my mates, they were a bit disappointed that I was off to blue horizons, but that is what Army life is all about.

When we arrived back at camp, the sergeant had

been wrong, I had only a day before I was heading to Brize Norton. I set about sorting my hot weather kit and getting it packed ready to move. I headed to the training room to be briefed by our company commander, there was myself and five others, we were to head out to Kenya and join a training team. One of the other men was a sergeant, I didn't know him but some of the men did, they all nodded in recognition of his capabilities. The company commander said "Just remember that we represent the Battalion so let's show them what we are capable of. You will be briefed properly when you have boots on the ground, ok chaps enjoy". I shrugged and smiled at the thought of Africa. My grandfather had been in Nigeria for ten years as harbour port authority and my mother had lived there for years when she was young, so I had been told a lot about Africa and seen the photos also the reels and reels of silent home movies my grandfather had taken all those years before. It excited me to be seeing the place itself.

The night before I was due to leave, I phoned my Mum, she had just come home from work and sounded tired, she did not say much but told me to come home safe. I thought she would have been more excited for me as she used to tell us of her fantastic memories of Africa but that was all she said. I said goodbye and went back to the lines to get changed and readied myself with some stretches for a ten-mile run, a good way to clear my head but I also was thinking about the long journey tomorrow. As I started my run out of the camp gates one of the guys on guard shouted, "Your keen, it going to piss down shortly" my reply was "Who gives a fuck and don't call me shortly". We both laughed as I headed away, but he was right just half a mile into the run it began to rain heavily, it really didn't bother me, I enjoyed all types of weather. My opinion was, whatever you were doing you just have to adapted to the weather condition, get your head in to gear and get on with it. Every mile I would stop and do 30 press-ups and 30 sit ups and then sprint off again just to keep it interesting. By the time I got back I was like a drowned rat and most of me covered in mud. I showered and headed out to a have pint with the lads. I always felt great after a good run and a hot shower. When I walked into the bar some of the blokes were already quite drunk. I had a pint, but I just could not relax into the evening, I was too excited about Africa. I went to leave when I heard someone I thought was a good friend shouting, "There's fuck face leaving for Africa must have crawled some to get on that team eh", I just shook my head and headed out into the rainy night. It bothered me, he was supposed to be my friend, but it was probably the drink talking.

Chapter 10

The journey from Brize Norton to Africa was uneventful, there was the dull roar of the C130 Hercules plane, it was not very comfortable as we were bundled in with a land rover, a trailer and pallet after pallet of equipment all marked HM forces. Not long after take-off I told the Load Master that I had never been up to the cockpit of a C130 and asked him if I could. He told it wouldn't be a problem so up we went. When he opened the door he said "Here's a young squaddie wanting to see the cockpit", As I walked passed him he whispered, "Watch they don't bite". I was introduced to the flight team and shown around the flight deck, it was very impressive. Both pilots were sitting there flying a massive plane puffing away on cigarettes and drinking coffee. The young female 'trainee navigator' called Tracey showed me where we were and the route we were taking. As I leaned in to see the map more clearly, I caught a faint scent of perfume, as I looked at her. I thought she was stunning but well out of my league. I thanked them all and as I turned to leave Tracey smiled and said "Any time soldier boy", I beamed red and joked, "I am no boy" she just smiled.

I started to get bored about halfway through the flight so decided to do some pull-ups on the Land Rover to pass some time. As I did my sixth set of twenty, I turned and there was Tracy standing holding a cup of coffee and smiling she said "Keeping in shape are we", I replied, "Aye the flight is a bit boring" She put her hand on to my biceps and squeezed saying "Wow soldier you have arms of steel". I thought with the noise of the engines no one could hear but there was a roar of laughter, I just smiled as she turned away heading back to the cockpit. I watched as she walked to the bottom of the stairs, she turned and winked, I could do nothing but smile as I went back to the pull ups, when she was out of sight Knuckles shouted "Oh you jammy bastard I'd be into that like a rat up a roan pipe". I stopped doing the pull ups and came from behind the land rover grinning from ear to ear I nodded, then Ginge shouted jokingly "Go on then fill your boots son, join the mile high club", at that the load master shouted "That's enough lads settle down that's someone's daughter have a little respect" then in a low voice he said "What a body eh, fucking hell if I was only that fuckers age" nodding at me.

As we landed the tailgate opened and we were hit by the heat. We collected all our kit and left the plane, the pilots said goodbye and Tracy said, smiling, "Keep doing your pull-ups soldier", I smiled and watched as they walked off to a waiting vehicle. We were transported to Laikipia Air Base in Kenya, there was a skeleton guard at the barracks as the rest were on a training exercise down south in the country. It was all quiet and after we got some food inside us we sorted out all our own gear and got our heads down, as I lay there thinking of the last few days, from the snow-packed Bavaria mountains to this barrack room in Africa, my mind was a blur, it was ok though I knew most of the team. Ginge, the sergeant, was a fine bloke and very switched on, he liked a laugh but when it was time for serious stuff he switched on big style. He had made a name for himself while on tour over the water in Northern Ireland. Some of the boys told stories about him before we left camp, I was looking forward to having a chat with him about Northern Ireland as we were due to go there in afew months for a six-month tour.

It was all first name terms and we were all trained in a different skill so we could operate as a formidable team. I was the sniper, Alex was my spotter come second sniper, Ginge was signals and patrol commander, we had Knuckles the explosive expert, a medic called Malcom and a recce lad who had trained in Africa for two years before, called Les, a mortar fire controller, thin and wiry but totally switched on guy. All good blokes, all very professional but liked a joke now and then. I was the youngest so as normal it was look, listen and learn.

The following day we acclimatized with a six-mile run and some circuit sets outside, we were all sweating buckets, I loved it. Once we were showered we headed to HQ where we were told that we would be in camp for a few days until they can get a heli to drop us off where the exercise was. Ginge asked for a briefing on ourtask and was told the briefing will be once the heli drops us off and only then, the officer said, "Chill out and get used to this fucking heat".

We left HQ and walked back towards the room we were allocated. Ginge said "Well nothing left to do but get some ammo and get some range work in", a slight roar went up, we were all up for that. We had a mixture of different weapons from sub machine guns to SLRs, and of course the L96. To make it more interesting we had a small completion, it was hard as the heat was so intense, Les said we would be a couple of days before our bodies adapted so drink plenty of water. Later in the afternoon we had a quick kick around with a football, by that time we were all exhausted, so it was rest up before dinner. Of course, it was then time for a pint or two as we had been invited to a bar by someone that Les knew from the guard room.

Dressed in our only jeans and t-shirts, we all set off. As we walked in, we realised it was a really posh place, nice leather chairs and wooden carvings on the walls, a club more than a bar. I looked around the room it was jammed packed, I was handed a beer and started walking around looking at the wooden carvings and paintings, what skill these people had with wood it was fantastic. As the night went on, we were sitting at a table having a laugh and then suddenly, the blokes all went silent, I looked at them and then turned around to be faced with Tracy, the load master and some engineers. She smiled and said, "Fancy seeing you here, mind if we joint you?". We all stood up to offer them a seat, she smiled slyly and said, "Give me a hand at the bar soldier". She was dressed as if she was going on safari and she looked stunning. As we walked to the bar, we instantly started smiling at one another, she explained that they were here for a few days before flying on to Canada then back to the Brize. I made a silly comment about how she got about, she just smiled, laughed and said, "Aren't you glad to see me then?". I just nodded and smiled, I was ecstatic. She smiled back at me and squeezed my arm again. As the night went on, we all started to get quite drunk, it was a great laugh listening to the load master and all his stories, what a character. As we headed out, I was grabbed by Tracey and walked towards a taxi she shouted to Ginge "I'll have him back by morning". There was a roar of laughter as we set off in a taxi, we stopped at another bar on our way to a hotel. It was a lot quieter and we found a small booth ordered drinks and giggled and kissed like a couple of long-lost lovers.

We headed to a hotel and spent the night together in a huge suite. The receptionist who booked us in smiled and offered us breakfast in the morning. We both declined as we would have to be away first thing.

I arrived back at camp the next morning to all the questions asking for details which I declined to give. Knuckles shouted, "Fuck she has some body", I just smiled, nodded and headed off to have a shower. Ten minutes later I was toweling myself dry when Ginge walked in he looked at me strangely and said "Watch what the fuck you're doing ok. Shagging a female officer, even if she is a trainee, is a no no in the forces". I acknowledged it implying he was jealous, he raised his voice "Listen mate, I am up for a promotion to Colour Sergeant when I get back and if anyone finds out about you and her it will be me that they will come down on, so be discreet eh. We are away to join the exercise in a couple of days, so enjoy yourself but never fuck it up for your mates". I nodded and apologised, he winked and said "You're a lucky bastard she's tidy as fuck but remember what I said, ok?". When he walked out, I thought about what he said, I realised he was right I better screw the nut.

That evening Tracey and I met up at the same hotel we had dinner and spent the night together. It was wonderful but at the back of my mind I knew that itwas wrong. When she came out of the bathroom, I must have looked troubled because she asked, "What's the matter? You look worried?". I told her what Ginge had said and she replied, "It's just a bit of fun for fuck sake what's his problem". I explained what he said about his promotion, she replied, "If anyone finds out it will be from your blokes not mine" so that was that. She sat at the end of the bed looking out the window I crawled up to her and sat beside her with my hand round her waist I leaned in and kissed her she turned I felt her breast and we rolled back on to the bed.

Next day I arrived back at the barracks, showered and headed for breakfast. I heard a helicopter in the distance, it was low and coming in fast, the rest of the blokes came out of the Mess Hall to see what all the commotion was about. There was a blast of dust as the Puma came in to land and we saw a stretcher being wheeled out of the medical centre towards the helicopter. I saw a soldier was walking wounded with his arm in a makeshift sling and another was in a really bad way, he was lifted out and on to the stretcher, we went forward to help but in a moment, they were all inside the medical centre, the helicopter shut down and the two pilots came away from their craft. We waited and Ginge asked if everything was ok, and what had happened. There was no reply.

They just walked right past us and towards the accommodation building without even turning their heads, it was as if we weren't even there. Whatthey had witnessed we could only imagine.

Chapter 11

We had managed to get our hands on some maps of the area where we were to be deployed, so we had a chance to study them, Les also had some slides to show us. When we were finished with the maps the lights went out, projector on, and Les talked about all the nasty shite that can fuck you up in Africa.

Lions, Crocs, Water Buffalo, Hyenas, Snakes and that is not including insects and other things, we all sat in silence and listened. Les really knew his stuff, it was all knowledge and I loved it. I could not wait to get boots in the dirt and get on with it. Sitting around was ok and a good laugh but there has always been something in me that wants to get going and get on with it. Les went on about the Black Mamba snake, a real serious piece of work, fastest and most venomous snake in Kenya. If that was not bad enough, he then said it was the most bad-tempered snake in the world so watch out for them. I looked at Knuckles and he mouthed for 'fuck sake'. Les then told us about the Puff Adder, which has the highest snake bite deaths in Kenya, a slide came up on the screen, I glanced round the room, there was complete silence. I hated snakes, I had been bitten by an Adder up on the hills above the farm when I was 15, the very thought sent a shiver down my spine.

I was lost in my own thoughts when the door burst open, the lights went on and a youngish looking officer walked in with a soldier behind him, I recognized him as the walking wounded soldier with his arm in a sling from the Helicopter, the officer was about to speak when the soldier said "I will take it from here thank you". As the officer looked at him, he tried to say something, but the soldier said "With all due respect Sir leave and close the door behind you" gesturing with his thumb towards the open door. A remark was made by the officer as he walked out but was ignored. Once the door closed, he walked to where Les was standing, he stopped, then spoke in a very deliberate voice. He looked at Ginge, asking if he was in charge. Ginge nodded. What happened next totally surprised me – he called my name. I looked at him and said, "Yes sir that's me". His face showed total disgust as he said "Outside". I looked at Ginge I thought he was about to say something but must have changed his mind. My mind was racing - was this Tracy's boyfriend, surely not, I was lost in a panic thinking shit what to do now. He looked at Ginge and said, "I'll be needing him for a few days, three at the most, it's all cleared at top level you can phone your Commanding Officer from the radio room ok". I was still sitting there, shocked, he looked at me and said, "I will not ask you again outside". I looked at Ginge and he nodded, he stood up and said "If its ok I will contact our battalion" the soldier just nodded.

Outside he walked past me, without stopping, and just said, "Follow me". I walked behind him in the sunshine. I squinted at the bright sun and he told me to look down, so it will not fuck up my vision. As I walked behind him my visionstarted improving and we went into another accommodation block. He stopped unlocked the door nodded for me to enter the room. When I entered, I saw a bed with a backpack, rifle, pistol magazines filled with rounds, two smoke grenades and four high explosive grenades, just lying there. Under normal army regulations that would be a definite no no. There were also radios and other equipment I had never seen before. He gestured me to sit while he leaned against the window ledge, the curtains were closed. He said "You will be working with me for a maximum of 3 days, we will leave from herein a heli in 2 hours, you will do exactly as I say. Do you understand?" "Aye" I said. He asked how old I was, and I told him. "Do you have any problem takingorders?" I just shook my head. He looked me in the eye, I felt as if it he could see into my very soul. As I looked away, he said "Are you as good as they say you are with a L96", I nodded and said, "I think so". The next question startled me a bit he asked, "Have you ever killed before?" My reply was only deer and rabbits. He said "Are you okay, your shaking?" I didn't realise I was. He just said we will have a brew in a few minutes put the kettle on then get outside.

When I went outside there were several guards standing there with fire hoses. "Come on then let's see if you can take orders soldier" is all that was said. He made me stand against a wall as they all hosed me down. I was then told to leopard crawl from the building to him and back again, all the time the hoses were on me. I did as he asked but by this time the dust had turned in to mud, as I crawled through the sandy mud, I thought to myself 'what the fuck is this all about'. With some relief I heard Ginge shout "What the fucks going on here, with all due respect, he is still under my command".

The soldier with the sling shouted at me to get up and the guards were told to hose me down. I was soaked through when he told them to stop and gestured to the guard to tidy away the fire hoses. I was told to walk around in a large square until the sun dried my combats. I started to walk off when Ginge said to the soldier, "I have not contacted the Battalion yet, what are you doing?", He replied, "I would advise you to make the phone call asap".

Ginge held up his hand and said, "But what the fuck are you doing to him?" The reply was, "We are going in the field and he smells of Adidas deodorant and aftershave. This way he will not be smelling of anything", in a firm voice he added, "No scent". Ginge looked surprised then nodded in acknowledgement because what they had done was to mask the smell of everything on me.

"Now get that phone call done" he commanded Ginge. The soldier looked at me and said, "Get walking", as he disappeared inside, I kept walking. He emerged a few minutes later holding two plastic mugs, walked up to me handed me a mug saying, "Get that inside of you", he walked over, sat in the shade and lit a cigarette. I was dry within ten minutes. I walked over to him he handed me a packet of cigarettes and said "Smoke?", I only nodded. I stood there puffing away and he said "Right mate I'm Mike and that's all you need to know just now, I will brief you when we get on the ground, get your kit together and get it to my room in ten minutes". I glanced down and noticed there was blood on his sling, I said, "You're bleeding", he looked down and said, "Ah fuck that", I pointed out that in the field animals will smell the blood.

He looked at me and smiled saying, "That's very good, you're right now get going". I turned away with a smile on my face thinking 'fuck you and thanks Les for our briefing on how to survive in Africa'.

I entered the room, got all my gear together, as I headed out Les appeared at the door and said, "Keep your head down and remember what I told you ok see you for a pint in a few days eh, if we are not away on exercise that is". He smirked and punched my arm. I asked Les if he knew who the soldier is, he just shook his head and said "No, but I have an idea what he is, the only soldiers to have that influence over an officer must be special forces. I saw them a lot when I was here on my two-year posting". I looked at him shocked as he said "Just remember what I told you, you better get going and do as he says". I turned and walked towards the soldier's accommodation, as I entered Ginge ran up behind me and said, "It's all cleared you are to support in an operation that they are running so you will do fine ok mate". As I looked at him, I said, "I am not sure what the fucks going on but if it is cleared from battalion, I am up for it". He just smiled and wished me all the best.

Mike turned my Bergan inside out, then tipped my webbing on to another bed in the corner. He laid out all the equipment I would need, including rations, the rest of my gear he kicked under the bed. He told me to get it packed and squared away. When I finished with my kit, he returned and handed me an M16 assault rifle with 8 magazines and rounds for the L96. He said, "This is your first weapon the L96 is your second". I nodded. He instructed me to strip and reassemble the M16. It is an American rifle, but we had a couple in the camp armoury, the shooting team got to play with it, so I knew what I was doing. Handing me two high explosive grenades and a smoke grenade Mike said, "That's fine, ok. Pack these into your webbing and kidney pouches" he also told me to pack a 24-hour ration pack and fill my water bottle and get it in to my webbing as well.

Once that was all squared away, I was told to get all my kit on. As I put on my webbing and Bergan, Mike told me to jump up and down, I just looked at him, he just said "Do it". So, I started jumping up and down, he stood and watched and said, "That's fine". It was then I realised what he was doing, if there had been something knocking against a mess tin or some other thing it would make a noise and he was making sure I was silent as I moved.

I looked at his arm, he had the wound redressed. He noticed me looking and said, "It's fractured and there is a laceration from the elbow halfway down the forearm, if I need help, I'll ask for it ok", I nodded. I was told to dump my kit by the door and go to the cook house and ask for two melons. I was told to be back in 10 minutes as the heli is leaving in 30. When I got to the cook house, I asked them for the melons and a couple of bottles of ice-cold water. As I turned to head back to the accommodation block, Knuckles appeared from nowhere and asked "What the fuck is going on?", I could only shrug my shoulders and say "I really don't know, but can you let Tracey know that I am away". He smirked and said, "With pleasure my dear boy I show her what a real man can do". I scowled at him and he said, smiling, "Get a grip for fuck sake". He patted me on the shoulder, and then headed away. As he walked away, he turned and said, "We came here as a team we should all be involved", I told him Alex could step up as sniper and Malcolm will be his spotter. Knuckles grinned and said, "That blind cunt couldn't see a tit at the edge of his nose". I replied, "Well you better not get too close to him then". We both burst out laughing and he said, "You'll pay for that youngster keep your head down pal" then he turned and walked away.

When I entered Mike's room he had all his gear ready and said "Ok make two runs to the heli, I'll wait here with the weapons", I ran out to the heli with thefirst load of kit and came back got the rest of our gear and headed away, Mike locked the door. As we boarded the heli I could see him struggle because of his arm I went to help him, but he shrugged me off saying "I will let you know when I need a hand".

We sat there in silence as the pilots did their checks then started up. As we slowly lifted from the ground, I saw my entire squad come out of the accommodation block, no one waved, they all just stood and watched as we headed away.

Mike was talking on his radio mouthpiece all the time. I just sat there and enjoyed the views of my first real look at Africa. We were heading south West from the barracks. Mike kicked my foot and mouthed "You ok", I nodded and showed him a thumbs up. We had been flying for about 20 minutes when I saw the ground coming up fast, I realised we were going to land. We hovered then landed. As Mike got out, he gestured to me to grab the sack with the melons, he headed away from the Heli, he returned a few moments later and gave a thumbs up to the pilots. We took off again flying at a very low level, the door was left open and I what was going on, as we hovered again and landed.   Mike gestured for me to get out and handed me my L96. We both moved a few steps from the heli, he pushed me into the kneeling position looking away from the heli, then the rotors sped up causing dust to go everywhere then the heli was gone. It was a weird experience, the noise of the engine, then, suddenly it was silent.

Mike stood up and said, "Right set up your rifle, you will see the melons at a distance of 800 metres". As I got down, I saw the heli, in my peripheral vision, disappear off to my left. I looked through the scope, there was a little head wind but nothing too serious, I closed my eyes and took a deep breath, I opened my eyes and relaxed into the shot as normal, I did all my checks controlled my breathing and on the out breath touched the trigger. The rifle recoiled but I stayed on target with the scope, the melon exploded. Mike shouted from behind me, "Do it again". I took aim on the second melon controlled myself relaxed and then pulled the trigger, again the melon exploded into pieces. Mike said that was enough, and he got on the radio and called the heli. In an instant the heli approached. I had hardly enough time to pack away the L96 when Mike put a hand on my back turned me so that we were looking in the other direction and gestured me down on one knee. Again, the wind from the rotors almost blew me over as the dust surrounded us, he patted me twice on the shoulder as if to say let's go. When we boarded the heli he handed me a set of radio earphones so I could listen in to what they were saying. The pilot said to Mike "All ok?". Mikes reply was "Oh fuck aye".

We were told by the pilot that endurance is 2 hours 13 minutes and to get our heads down and rest up a while, at that Mike put his head on a Bergan and was soon fast asleep. I was busy watching animals run and looking at the landscape, after a while I thought I better get my head down too although trying to sleep was hard but I soon drifted off, it felt like only a minute had passed when I heard the pilot over the head phones say, "Wakey, wakey 20 minutes to landing Guys".

Mike poured a couple of mugs of hot sweet tea from a large flask, we drank them down, and he handed me a bottle of water and told me to drink it. Over the headset Mike said to put my webbing on get a mag into to my weapon and make ready, safety on. I nodded and did as he instructed. "When we land, we have a 25-kilometre tab ok". As I looked out of the window it was still day light, but the light was fading fast, he went on saying "Once the heli has gone just keep up ok". I nodded and said, "Aye ok". I looked at his arm, which was now in a makeshift sling of green camo net. He shook his head and said again "If I need help, I will ask".

By the time we landed it was almost dark. Once the heli disappeared Mike looked around, he pointed to a small cluster of bushes and rocks at the side of us and said, "Remember that ok". I looked and could just make out the rocks as the night was closing in. He then said, "Look at the surrounding area but remember that cluster of rocks and bushes". I nodded.

We headed off back in the direction that we came in, I thought, 'what the fuck is he doing'. I wanted to say something but thought better of it. After tabbing (tactical advance to battle) for about 30 minutes Mike slowed down, pulled me by the arm, turned sharp left as if on a corner of a pavement and we headed in that direction for a couple of miles or so. We then turned left sharply again he said quietly, "We put deviations in our routes, we call them dog legs, so if we were seen being dropped off of the helicopter by anyone, they will think we are heading in another direction". I nodded assuring him I understood what it was all about.

We tabbed at a good pace and after a while we stopped at a rocky mound formation. Mike, using hand signals, gestured to me to get down and drink some water. Mike raised his night vision goggle and scanned 360 degrees. Once he was sure there was no one about he settled down into a seated position and got some water himself.

"Right, listen in, I will make this very brief", Mike said in a very clear and concise tone, "The reason for all this is, eight days ago we were tasked to set up an ambush in a village not far over the border in Tanzania to apprehend a P.I.R.A. (Provisional Irish Republican Army) man who has been on the run in Africa for a few years. He has claimed the lives of several people including soldiers, R.U.C, 14 intelligence group in Belfast and surrounding areas. He fled from Ireland after his last couple of kills and disappeared. Now, a few years later, he has raised his head again. He is advertising to terrorists' organisations throughout the world as a gun for hire. He is also a trainer in weapons and explosives. He runs with his ruthless band of very well-trained African killers. Under normal circumstances he would have been taken out by now, but our chaps from the government want a chat with the fucker. All the money he makes from training terrorists he sends to America, where it is used to supply weapons for the P.I.R.A. We have information that they have an inside man who has the capability to supply ground to air missiles, (GTAM), our government wants to cut off the head of the snake as it were. Stop the supply. At the very least we can fit trackers to all weaponry to enable us to keep them in sight.

Learn how they are handled through the channels and get to the hands of the P.I.R.A. Can you imagine the devastation they could do with those missiles, so we were tasked to man an OP to keep the evacuation route clear, for a four-man team to cross the border into Tanzania to 'persuade' him to come over for a chat. He was the most wanted man in Ireland at one time and he is still high up on the wanted list. Our people set things in motion and through contacts they came up with a bogus story, they were looking for an expert to train locals in fighting skills and weaponry, for a large sum of money of course. After a few months, through different channels, he agreed. He is known to be very clever and trusts no one, probably why he has survived in a country that would sell their granny for a bowl of sugar, let alone a wad of cash. Our team reccied the village and settled down to ambush for him".

Ewan and I were set to protect a way out for the team if it went noisy (kicked off into a firefight). We settled in but as 'bad' luck would have it, Ewan managed to get himself bitten by a puff adder. I wrapped his hand in a tight elasticated bandage, but he took a very bad reaction to the bite and I knew I had to get him medivacked out asap. We had to bug out of the OP, leaving Ewan's kit behind and only bring weapons and grenades. As the other lads were well dug in it would have compromised the entire operation if I were to call one of them back to help medivac him. I made the call to get Ewan medivacked to hospital and I was to return by myself. I struggled with him and I slipped on some rocks and that when this happened, gesturing to his arm in the sling, but I had to get him to the pickup point. Once I got him settled in the medical centre, I contacted our base but was informed the other lads from our regiment were too far away, in the rift valley, training. Intel came throughsaying that a team had just arrived at the barracks from the green army unit, (normal infantry battalion) "Your lot" he said, "I was to use you lot if needed, they thought three men but I fucked them off saying all I needed was the sniper, the operation will be all quiet hopefully, so your name came up I didn't have time to fuck about so you fitted the bill and the rest you know". I puffed out my cheeks and said, "An SAS operation in Africa and I'm involved", he punched me in the arm and said, "Get a grip and focus we are all soldiers and we all have a part to play ok so fucking focus". I nodded in realisation this was a real and serious situation I was in, I had better step up my game, after a moment he continued, "About one and half miles from here is the OP, we will dump our Bergan's here and do a recce in silence so just stay with me ok". I nodded and he continued, saying, "Webbing and rifles, leave the rest here, this is now RV 2 (rendezvous point), if anything goes wrong you have got your compass" he gave me a heading to go to if it all went to 'rat shit'. I looked at him "Rat shit?". He puffed out his cheeks and said, "Another term for we're fucked", I just nodded. I said "Where the heli dropped us will be RV1 yes" he nodded and said that compass bearing I gave you will take you to that cluster of rocks and bushes I pointed out to you when we landed , get under that bushes and stay there, the heli will return in 72 hours whether we are there or not, standard operation procedure, unless we radio in alternative bug out orextension to task or different location ok. He gave me a thumbs up and I nodded. He patted me on the arm and said, "Right lets soldier".

We reccied the area in a large circle moving slowly and silently. Day break was about 2 hours away when we returned to our Bergens then made our way into the OP (observation post). It was under a large cluster of bushes. Mike did a quick recce of the OP, to see if anyone had been near it or in it. He also checked for snakes and other nasties, but there were no signs so in we went to the bushes, got down and went on stag for first light. He whispered "We will sort out our shit once day light comes in ok. I will point out locations for your targets, to give you target distance and elevation. I will be your spotter if it goes noisy". When day light came, we checked the whole area for anything unusual. Mike told me to get my head down and we would do a two-hour stag. When the sun began to rise it looked wonderful as we were slightly elevated, we looked straight up a large open valley with good vision all round. Mike said, "Bergan's are at the back of the OP so if we have to bug out leave them and get going ok". I nodded in agreement. The sky was so blue on my third rotation of stag, funny the things you remember. I was totally taken away with the scenery. I had seen some animals but no people.

In the last half hour of one of my stags I decided to eat some AB biscuits and I drank a little water when I heard a noise. I placed a hand on Mikes sleeve, he was already awake, we lay there is silence breathing with slightly open mouths so there was no noise. I glanced to my left flank and saw two local boys dressed in red wrap around garments, both had sticks and tapped a tan coloured cow gently every time it stopped. They were headed towards us, I looked at Mike but he gestured that they were no threat to us and to keep silent. They stopped about eight yards from us, as we were slightly elevated, we were looking down on them. One of them came closer and stopped about two yards from our OP, he relieved himself splashing urine everywhere. After he finished, he walked back to the other boy. I slowly looked at Mike and he gestured with his pinkie finger at the size of his penis I almost laughed out loud. The boys were chatting away and started gathering branches. I watched in wonder at what they were doing, it was as if they were making a large makeshift barrier around them with a little opening. They worked till almost dusk, by that time they were well protected in a large circle of stones and bush branches about 4 foot high. I continued to watch as the night closed in, they started a small fire within their little bushed up area, one of them started to sing. We had noticed earlier that they hobbled the cow with a piece of rope.

They sang into the night once the stars were out one of them moved from the area and had a shite not far from us. Mike handed me the night vision goggles you could make out the boys glow, as he stood and walked back to the enclosure his shit was lit up in the goggles like a lantern laying on the ground. I laughed silently as I watched him pick up his stick and break up the ground round the outside of the bushes. I remember Les saying that snakes are not too keen in moving over broken ground, I thought these young boys were about twelve or thirteen years old but very switched on in this environment. I could not see many lads their age doing this back home.

We took our turns on stag during the night. There were messages coming through and Mike used 'batco', a paper full of inscriptions he could use to decode a message from the other team. It was all done under a light not much bigger than a pin head. I watched him decode messages, he was excellent at it, but he never mentioned any of the things he had decoded. I whispered, "All ok?". He nodded, and gestured with his head to look outwards because I was on stag.

Next morning, we were both awake for the sun rising, we watched the two boys come out from the bush circle. They both stretched and ran around in circles to get their circulation going. One untied the cow's leg and lead the animal out of the bushed area. I watched in awe as one of the boys started to dismantle the bushed area by throwing the branches back and spread it all out, the other bent down and started milking the cow into a small bowl. When he had finished milking he laid the bowl to one side , he then took a knife and pierced a sharp prick in the neck of the cow, the cow never even flinched, there was a slight spray of blood which he caught it in the bowl that had the milk in it, once it was full he laid it down and picked up a hand full of dusty earth and rubbed it into the cows neck to stop the flow of blood. He then picked up the bowl, said something to his companion, and he drank the milky bloody liquid and passed it to the other boy. I looked at Mike and he just shrugged his shoulders. It took about ten minutes and the boys were away, the area they had been in was back as they had found it and the fires black mark brushed away. No one would have known anyone had been there.

When my stag was over, I fell asleep quickly in the

heat. It felt about an hour later when Mike shook me. I opened my eyes and though 'what the fuck', I looked down and he had decoded another message while he was on stag. He said "They have him, they are making their way out now, but it will be morning before they come up that valley. I would say they have to put in a big dog leg and a few detours to put his band of militant wankers off in another direction, let's set some claymores just in case". I looked at him and asked if there were any problems he just shrugged and said it was just a precaution. the hour that followed I cleaned both of my weapons while Mike was on stag.

That night when I went on stag the sky was so clear. Mike had been out and set some claymores. I went over and over my spot targets and distances in the back of my mind. We stood to at 03.00 hours, sorted out our gear and made ourselves ready. Mike was still decoding messages. About an hour before sun rise Mike said, "Ok, listen in, I've had another message, the team are four clicks (kilometres) from here coming up the valley on our right-hand side ok".

I kept watch up the valley for what seemed like ages when I saw a movement. I quickly glanced through my scope. I touched Mike on the sleeve he looked at me and I used hand signals to inform him

I have seen movement. Mike asked if I was sure, I nodded showing three fingers. He went on to the radio giving the call sign and passed the message. It all sounded gobbledy gook to me, but they came back immediately 'all copied'. I thought it was strange as he had used batco for the last two days then suddenly he had broken radio silence? I looked at him and he just said, "We have company, keep an eye on where you saw movement, this shit just got real soldier".

It was all silent as I checked the wind direction not even a light breeze. There was a moment, I thought the whole world was at peace as everything was so calm, what a wonderful feeling, the warmth of the sun through my combats and the birds singing, a very surreal moment. Then I heard it, away in the distance, I felt an involuntary tremble running through my body and my eyes widened. It was gun fire from an automatic weapon. Mike said "Relax and only fire when I tell you. I said "RELAX? Aye right". He just nodded and smirked.

Next thing I knew I was seeing men in the distance, dressed in combats. Mike said, "That's our guys ok". They were making their way toward us, I heard vehicles in the background then thump, thump, thump, it could only be 50 caliber rounds.

Mike said "We will secure their way out ok; they will cross from your right to left about 850 yards out, there are some large boulders and mounds of grass and earth they can use as cover. I have a little boom party of claymores for anyone that follows my team. They will come toward us about 100 yards on our left ok". By this time, he was shouting, not giving a fuck about silent routine, he gestured with a thumbs up, "Follow my lead" he shouted with a massive grin. I thought, 'this cunt is not human all this happening and he still manages to smile', me I was shitting myself. I shook when I heard more automatic weapons fire that's when I saw the vehicles with their mounted 50 caliber weapons. Mike had his own weapon resting on a sandbag as his arm was still in a sling. We saw his team return fire as they made their way out. Mike was looking through a laser range finder then shouted, "Vehicle, 790 yard put a round through its engine block".

I took aim I realised I was shaking but then relaxed and fired. The bonnet of the vehicle flew up as it rolled to a stop. Mike shouted, "More distance for the next vehicle". I fired again I hit my target I had stopped the vehicle but not its weapon from firing. Mike shouted an order I could not make out, but I had gone through the drills with him so many times over the last few days instinct kicked in. I moved slightly to my right, there was a man standing on a ridge loading an RPG 7 rocket launcher. Mike shouted, "Target 710 yards, no wind, fire when ready". I had him in my sights then it felt like everything went into slow motion, everything felt still as I touched the trigger. It felt like ages before anything happened. It was then I saw the spray of blood flying high above the target's head and his RPG falling to the ground, he was falling backwards out of sight, but it still felt like slow motion. Mike was shouting another target; I was in a daze for about one-hundredth of a second. I reacted to his commands and moved the rifle barrel towards the target firing the 50 caliber. Mike shouted out the distance then clear to fire; I touched the trigger. Instantly the man jolted backwards over the side of his vehicle. Mike shouted another order and I turned to the other vehicle. I had the man in my sights when I saw him fall, he had been taken out by one of Mikes team. There was a huge, loud, bang and dust everywhere, Mike shouted "That's someone tripped the claymores". I couldn't see anything for dust. Mike shouted, "They're leaving". I saw the men running back through the dusty haze. I just watched as Mikes team ran past us about 100 yards to our left, then the noise from the automatic weapons stopped and it was all silent again. A weird calm sort of quiet.

We had talked about this moment, so I knew what to do when the time came to bug out. We waited for what seem ages then Mike shouted, "Let's go". I had not been out of the OP for a couple of days, so I was stiff, but I still ran for all I was worth carrying our kit as I went. We ran past Mikes team then we got down and covered their retreat. We carried on this routine for some time, we then got into formation and basically patrolled to our RV 2. We laid down all round defence, while some were on stag we got water inside us.

One of the guys got his medical kit out and I saw him treat the P.I.R.A chap who had been hit on the shoulder by his own men. Someone said, with a snigger, "Well they are well trained paddy I'll give you that. At least they shot the bad guy". The medic told us it was only a flesh wound he had. A cloth bag was placed over his head, his hands were still tied, you could tell he was a muscular no-nonsense type of person. I sat there in a daze thinking 'what the fuck just happened', my mind raced over what had just happened it was all a blur. In that moment, sitting on the ground in the middle of nowhere somewhere in Africa, I knew my life would never be the same again.

Mike whispered, "You ok?". I just nodded. I felt sick, my stomach was all over the place, another member of the team came up and said, "It's delayed shock, you'll be ok" then he grinned and continued saying "25 kilometre tab, shave, shite, shower and a big plate of egg and chips will sort you out". He winked at me, I tried to smile but I only managed a nod.

That day we patrolled to the Heli pick up point, we had two guys covering our retreat, watching for anyone following. When the heli was due they appeared and said there was no sign of anyone behind us. We waited till almost dusk before we heard the chomp, chomp, of the helicopter in the distance. Next thing I knew I was jammed into a helicopter between two guys. When we landed back at the barracks, I thought I would have a shower and just chill out. When the helicopter shut down, I went to get out and was told to stay by the helicopter. So, I waited although I did not know why, next thing I knew Mike and his team returned with all their kit packed up and threw it into the back of a four tonner. They walked over to me and Mike said, "You are coming with us ok". I said I would have to get my kit. This guy with a well-spoken voice said "No leave it, we will take care of that. Just get on the 4-tonner" I nodded.

Before I knew it, we were boarding a C130. I panicked thinking what if Tracey sees me like this, having not washed for three days, what would she think.

Panic over when I realised that it was a different aircrew. I sat down and one of the team members came over and said, "You ok we will get a brew once we are in flight". All the other team members started shouting at a chap that emerged from the cockpit as he struggled down the steps but all I could hear were words like fanny, tosser, a wee snake fucked you up wanker. They were totally ripping the piss out of this guy. He just waved at everyone with a big smile on his face then I realised it was Ewan the team member I had replaced. As the flight took off, I was still not told where I was heading, I had a couple of brews and forced down a cheese and ham sandwich but I still felt sick in the pit of my stomach. I could not hear much of what people were saying but one by one they all fell asleep eventually and so did I.

The plane landed and the rear door opened, the sun blasted in and I heard someone say "Welcome to Great Britain in the sunshine". I watched four people in civilian clothes come into the plane and removed the P.I.R.A man. They nodded at some of the team members as they made their way off the plane. Mike came up and said, "Its Gibraltar". Later when I jumped into the lorry my mind was still buzzing with all the events in Africa. I was shown into the accommodation block, I dumped my kit and started cleaning my weapons as instructed to do by one of the team members, then we put our weapons into the armoury and handed over the remaining rounds.

Returning to my room I had the longest shower ever, after not showering for a few days, the water on my skin felt amazing. I was standing under the water, my mind still a blur, when someone came in and said, "Debriefing in 20 mins, second door from yours on the right, ok?" I shouted, "What am I supposed to wear?" "It's on your bed mate" he said as he left the room. There on my bed was a thin green coverall. I got dressed and walked bare foot out of my room and headed for the debriefing room. When I entered the team were all there sitting on the window sills and tables, I sat on a chair and looked around. Maps of Africa covered three of the walls, on the other there was a whiteboard with call signs and routes. It was clear to see that the task we had just completed had been planned from this very room.

Mike introduced me to the team, and they all nodded. A man walked in wearing full dress uniform, it took me a moment to recognise he had the rank of full Colonel. I sprang to my feet and stood at attention, he didn't even look at me, he said, "Relax gentleman". I stood, still at attention, Mike said, "Oh sit down mate".

We proceeded to debrief the whole task from start to finish, everyone speaking when it was their turn as the task unfolded. I sat in silence Mike gestured to me when I was mentioned in the events of the task, the coronel just stood and listened. When they had finished, he said, "Good, good job, well done lads" then looked and nodded in appreciation at everyone except me. I looked round and realised the team were all staring at me, the Colonel was staring too. After a long glare he said, "I am sure you will be fully aware of what has happened in the last few days is not to be mentioned" he paused then went on, "It didn't happen, ok son. Never mentioned unless it's inside these four walls or if you are invited to Hereford, do you understand?". I said, "yes sir of course sir". He just kept staring at me and said "Wait till you are fifty, it's something you can tell your grandchildren ok, by all accounts you did a sterling job young man, if anyone asks you were on a training exercise ok. Any questions?". I said, "Yes, one sir". Mike leaned closer and said, "Well were all a team what is it?" I hesitated and Mike said, "Spit it out man". I said, "Well you had me fire on the vehicle engine blocks first, I thought it should have been the man firing the 50 calibre?" Mike said "I knew my team had good cover so that was not a problem, my problem was could you perform in battle or were you going to freeze up and not being able to continue, or worse, get up and run. It happens, everyone reacts to battle in different ways". The other men all nodded, and he continued, "But you, you carried out your part with no problem. If I had told you to hit the man with the 50 calibre first and you missed, then the situation would have been very different. I had to be sure you could still hit the targets, when I saw the man with the RPG7, I had no choice, I had to get you involved in taking out the target". I just nodded; the rest of the team were nodding too. I looked at the coronel he said, "Ok now", I nodded and replied, "Yes sir". He said, "I have contacted your battalion so you will fly back to the UK with the team in a few days well that takes care of that YES" , I replied "Yes Sir". The Colonel nodded to the other team members, "Get him down the town and get him some civvies eh lads", they said, "Thanks boss". I thought it weird they called him 'boss' and not 'sir'. As he walked towards the door he said, "The Star bar has £200 in credit have a pint on me". Never turning his head, he left the room. I slumped back into my chair, releasing a breath I had not realised I was holding, and said "Fuck me". They all roared and laughed. Someone said, "Right let's get you shit faced and silly". I was up for that.

They all scrounged around and got me a t-shirt, pair of shorts and flip flops. When we headed out, I was in high spirts. It felt good to be among these guysthey were all so friendly, there was no bullshit, even the one that talked like an officer was up for a laugh. Mike asked, "Can you drink?" Oh, could I drink!

The drinking changed everything, we laughed and listened to some of the guys stories. We drank and drank all-night into the early hours of the morning. I woke up in the doorway of my room. I had been drooling saliva from my mouth, there was a pool of it on the floor. As I staggered into my room, I saw three members of the team lying sleeping, there were beer cans and empty whisky bottles all around the room. That was some night. My head was pounding, and I was so hungry. I went and had a shower and intended to go out to getsomething to eat. When I came back into my room all the cans had all been cleared, ashtrays emptied, my room was spotless. I put on my T- shirt and shorts and realised I had only one flip flop. I went through to the other rooms, there were guys toweling themselves after having a quick shower. Someone shouted, "Its bacon butty time". A loud cheer went up, I think they were all feeling as bad as me. During breakfast Mike asked if I was okay and said, "You can't half drink". Then with a grin on his face, said, "We will see what you are like today, if you don't want a drink just say no". After having had two egg banjos and a bacon roll, I leaned forward smiled and said, "I am gagging for a pint", the rest of the team roared 'you'll do for us matey'.

Mike said, "It's just our way of letting off steam but first we are going to run the rock, you up for it?". I told him I only have one flip flop. "No worries we'll kit you out". I looked at his arm still in a sling he said, "Don't worry I can still jog, and I can drink from the other hand". We both laughed.

Run the rock is a term the forces use when running down, round and up, the rock of Gibraltar or Gib as it is called. It was hard to start with and I was sweating buckets but after my second sweat I settled into it. I was managing to keep up, these guys were incredibly fit. When we had finished, I was like a sponge dripping sweat everywhere, it might have been the heat of the day, but I suspect it was the drink coming out. We did press-ups, sit up and pull ups, Mike did a couple of one arm pull ups and one arm press ups. When we returned, I was in the shower when there was more kit thrown on to my bed. We then went to an office to sign for some money and we were off again, and before I knew it, I had a pint in my hand, and we were chatting away to some female tourists.

We drank all day and most of the night, I think I ended up drinking myself sober and thought it was about time I went back to the accommodation. I staggered into my room and collapsed onto my bed and slept till morning. I was woken by someone shouting, "Ho! Fuck face, fancying going scuba diving?". I showered had breakfast and met up with three of the team, they had all the kit ready. As I had never scuba dived before they gave me a quick run through, it was in shallow water anyway, or so I was told. We did a thirty-five-minute dive in forty foot of water. I did all my drills I had been taught in the fifteen-minute briefing I got before going into the water one of the guys was a diving instructor, so I was to stick with him. It was amazing, something I had never experienced before. When we surfaced and walked back up to the rocks, they all said I did ok for the first time. They said, "You know what goes well with diving?", I said "No? What goes well with diving? ",

"Drinking". I smiled at the thought of an ice cool lager, 'here we go again'.

Chapter 12

The following day at around 16.00 hours we were to fly back to the UK, I didn't have much kit. I signed for my weapons and made my way to the four-ton lorry.Once I had I dumped my kit I looked round and the whole team approached saying they had been tasked to another job and were staying there for now, they all shook my hand and wished me all the best. I climbed on to the lorry asthey all walked away, I was sad to see them go, what a great team they were. I had not noticed Mike had jumped into the front of the lorry. We reached the plane and I jumped down and began gathering my kit when round from the front of the lorry Mike walked and said, "Right mate listen in, if you see any of the team members again don't just walkup and start chatting. We may be on an operation, so let us approach you ok mate". I nodded he shook my hand and said, "You did brilliant all the best mate". He turned and jumped back into the lorry, as I watched it go, I heard the loadie shout, "Come on then mate". I walked on to the plane and sat in my seat and was really disgruntled, I wanted to go with the team, the load master said, "You ok son?" I nodded, he said, "Three hours twenty-five minutes to UK". I settled down and stared at the boxes of kit marked HM FORCES, my mind drifted to Africa and I shook my head trying to get my thinking straight.

Having returned to the battalion barracks gates, I signed in and was escorted up to the battalion headquarters by the duty guard. Once there I was told by the RSM that I was up in front of the commanding officers ASAP. I marched in halted at the instruction of the RSM, then the door was closed. The CO was sitting at his desk, he put down his pen and clasped his hand together, he said, "You were tasked to aid in an exercise with another regiment", I said, "Yes sir". "What did that entail? Can you give me some details and learnings from your experience?". I replied, "With all due respect Sir but I cannot answer that question". He leaned forward and said, "Well keep it that way ok", I just said "Yes Sir". He then said, "I don't know the details but it comes from the top that you did very well, you are a credit to the battalion, If I hear that you have being telling stories I will lock you up do you understand?". I said, "Yes Sir but the other lads-". I was cut short by the CO, "The other soldiers that you arrived in Kenya with have been briefed, I would grant you a week's leave but as you know we are training for Northern Ireland and you have missed the start of the training, so I would like to get you up to speed I would also like to offer you a promotion, making you a Lance Corporal but only when we return from our tour in Northern Ireland, it is too short notice for you to take over a brick. Keep up the good work young man you are turning into an exceptional soldier", the RSM agreed, "Here, here". The CO sat back on his seat and gestured to the RSM to have me stand at ease. He asked, "What motivates you? By all accounts your training record so far is impeccable". I said, "I just want to make my Dad proud sir". He smiled at me and said, "He should be, he should be". The RSM said, "His father is deceased Sir", the CO said, "Ah the voice in your ear and the shadow at your shoulder eh lad". "Something like that sir". "Well I can say this, he would be a very proud father if he were standing here today, well done again, carry on the good work". I said, "Yes sir thank you". I knew my Dad would have been proud

Chapter 13

Our training for Northern Ireland was excellent and we went in companies to a place called Tin City, it was a purpose built town made of tin and blocks that we could learn to patrol through and how to react if we had contact from gun fire. My brick (four-man team) was made up of a Brick Commander, Signaller, Sniper and Tail End Charlie, we would be a team for the next six months. We trained hard and got extremely good at reacting to gun fire or coming across a riot (that was put on by other soldiers from other regiments dressed in civvies). My brick was picked to go to Sennelager, a training area in Germany, to be search trained. If we did a house search, we would know where to look and what to look for. P.I.R.A were the best terrorists in the world and were very inventive in hiding weapons and moving them from location to location, so we were trained to find weapons and ammunition. The best bit was being able to identify bomb making equipment. To do that we were shown how to make IEDs (improvised explosive device), that you can make a bomb out of your basic kitchen was unbelievable. Our brick had a great time learning all about this and blowing things up, a course I will never forget.

Having returned to the battalion we had a long weekend before the advanced party were to leave for Belfast. Our brick was to go to a barracks just off the Fall's road. Having landed in Belfast we were sped away on souped up pigs (armoured troop carriers) as they were called, we arrived at the barracks and Inoticed the netting cast over the whole camp, to stop mortars landing as most of the camp was made up of portacabins. We got settled in and were allocateda bed space. We were due for a briefing in one hour so after getting squared away we made our way towards the briefing. The regiment we were taking over from were ready to go home, but we were the advanced group so we would filter our regiment in and theirs out over the next two weeks.

We were not supposed to go out on patrol for a day or so, but that night we heard gun fire in the distance. Two rounds were fired, we were asked if we wanted to start our tour now. I shouted out "Fuck aye" next thing I knew we were dressed in our combats and a flak jacket with an armour piece of plate on the back and front to protect your heart. We rushed out the gates of the barracks spread out and formed a patrol brick. We patrolled down on to the Falls road and were tasked to patrol down another road, we heard screaming and started to run when a guy from one of the other regiments shouted, "Over here". When we turned the corner into an alley way there was a man screaming in pain. You could see the blood coming from his knees, he had been knee capped. I shook my head in disbelief. We cordoned off the area and someone gave the poor man morphine, then he was sped away in a pig to the hospital. I was crouching at a corner on stag and thought, 'fucking hell that's one of their own', I shook my head saying to myself 'better get a grip here, stay focused'.

Halfway through my tour, during which I had attended four massive riots, bus burnings and some of the other bricks had been shot at but so far, no causalities. I had witnessed a lot of terrible things, but this day was different. It was a Sunday morning when we were patrolling from the Falls Road to Kelly's Corner. It was still slightly dark, but the sun was rising. It looked like it was the start of a fantastic sunny day when we came up to Kelly's Corner our Brick Commander stopped us, in true brick fashion we stopped and kneeled down with weapons scanning all around as normal. It was then we heard him call it in. I could just make out someone at the lamp post, but there was a car in my way so I could not see properly, the brick commander let his weapon fall down by his side but never let it go, it was so out of procedure for him, your weapon was always at port arms. I ran up to see if there was anything I could do then I saw it. I stood still, an IRA snipers dream, then after a few seconds I came to my senses and all our training went into automatic mode.

There was a roar of vehicles as they were coming towards us, it was the Quick Reaction Force, in Land Rovers then the QRF2 in armoured Pigs. I stood there and could not believe what I was looking at, a naked female had been tied to a lamp post and hot tar had been poured over her head, a sign hanging round her neck with the word 'SLAPPER' on it. The smell of burned flesh and tar was terrible. You could tell she was dead, but we had to make sure, I leaned forward and touched her neck, it was solid, the tar had hardened. An officer came from one of the vehicles with the RUC and we all just stood there staring. A short while later the Doctor arrived and pronounced her dead, the whole area was cordoned off, then we were taken to the side to give brief statements.

That whole morning was a blur, we were piled into a pig and taken back to barracks once it was all sorted and the female had been taken away. In the debriefing room, we went through what had happened. I was sitting there, and I could still smell the burned flesh and tar, I wanted a shower so bad. We were told to rest up and we would not be back on duty for at least two days. "It is to be bed space, egg banjos and whatever music you have on your Walkman's" the officer said with a grin. I suppose he was trying to lighten the mood but after witnessing what had happened to that woman all I wanted was a shower. When we went to leave the room, I said to the officer "I don't want time off Sir, I want to keep doing our task", the rest of the brick said the same. He nodded and went to the telephone, a few moments later he returned and told us the CO has said we could carry on as normal. We all knew it was callous of us to continue as if nothing had happened but if we had just sat on our beds our minds would be on what we had seen. At least if we were out on patrol, QRF, or sanger duty (camp lookouts), we would have something to do and take our minds off it.

By all accounts, the female lived locally and had been seeing a British soldier, who was based at the airport camp, they had met at church on a Sunday about ten months ago. They would meet up most weekends in East Belfast for a meal or dancing, their relationship had not moved to spending the night together, she had been a nice clean-living catholic girl. Her only fault was not so much that she that she fell in love with a Catholic man, but that he was a British soldier. Someone had seen them together, reported them and the Provos had taken it in their hands to sort her out. It was terrible. If that is what they did to one of their own imagine what they would do to one of us. That thought sent a chill down most of our lad's backs.

We were sent up to a police station called 'New Barnsley'. We were to be there for a few days, there were bunks and sleeping bags in the accommodation. When we arrived, we noticed two cars, a Cortina and an Escort, parked within the police station, which was unusual. We were then told that we would not be able to enter the accommodation as special forces were using our facilities to wash and clean up so we all just mulled around for a while within the camp.

I was sitting on the bonnet of a Land Rover having a cigarette when the door to the accommodation opened and out came two men dressed in civvies, they went to the vehicles and put canvas bags into the boot, as they turned I noticed it was one of the guys from the African team. I went to shout out, but Mike's words came at me like a steam train 'don't approach us', I shrugged my shoulders and didn't bother. After a short while I lit up another smoke and was halfway through it when one of our officers came out and said "Listen in lads these guys in here need a hand loading gear", he pointed to me and said you and you pointing to another guy, Billy, who was beside me. I jumped down from the land rover and walked into the accommodation, Billy was hard on my heels. When we entered a chap said to Billy, "Put these bags into the escort and that boxes into the Cortina, then wait outside".

He turned to me and nodded for me to go through. When I walked into the room, I noticed there was a couple of the lads from the African team and they were smiling at me. We shook hands, it was great to see these lads again. We all sat down and had a smoke, someone handed me a brew and they asked how things were. I shrugged, "Ok I suppose". "It will soon be time for us to be heading away from here and get back home for some hard-earned rest and recuperation", he said, "We used the excuse we needed a hand lifting the boxes to see how things were with you".

I kept looking round thinking the officer was going to appear at any moment. One of the guys said, "Its ok he won't come in here", so I settled down and I was introduced to the other guys in the room. It was great to be in their company again, they had me laughing within a few minutes. I asked how Mikes arm was and they said all ok now, but they had not seen him in a couple of months. After about twenty minutes someone said, "Well we are off, nice to have seen you again". I walked back outside carrying an empty cardboard box and put it into the Escort and headed back to the Land Rover. A few minutes later the guys appeared, the gates opened, and they were gone.

We went inside and relaxed, some of the guys asked what they said, I replied "Nothing". I told them I had waited at the door and was handed a box to put into the car. I thought it best to say nothing. When I heard my name being shouted, I went to another room and an officer and a sergeant were sitting at the desk. The officer asked what was all that about, I said "Don't know Sir". "They asked for you specifically and when you went into the room, I heard laughing, I repeat what was all that about?". I repeated that I did not know. At this reply the sergeant stood and shouted, "Answer the officer!". I stood very still and said, "Sir with all due respect I cannot answer that question, but can you contact the Commanding Officer or the RSM", the Sergeant shouted "Is this some kind of fucking joke?". "No" I said, "It's no joke". They both just looked at one another. When the officer picked up the phone and dialed a number and he asked a few questions, his facial expression changed to one of shock. When he put down the phone, he gestured with his head to the Sergeant to sit down. As he leaned forward, he said," I haven't to question you and the CO said to pass on a message to you", "What was the message Sir?" I asked. His reply was "Well-done keep it up", the officer was not happy as he dismissed me, I turned on my heel and walked out I smiled to myself.

During our tour we had bombs going off, a failed mortar attack on our camp and shots fired into the camp. It was miserable but after five months and one week itwas time to go and get the next arrivals from the airport, it felt great. A week after the new lads arrived it was my turn to go home. I remember the plane lifting from Belfast airport and feeling, for the first time in five months and two weeks, I could relax.

We arrived back at the barracks, got our gear out of storage, a wooden box filled with all your kit that you had accumulated over the past few years, and headed for a shower. Dressed in civvies I headed out for a decent haircut and then on to meet the guys for some heavy drinking. It felt great just to let off steam, telling stories, laughing and generally having a good time. Later, when the alcohol had flown too much and the fights broke out, I just sat there smiling. I carried on drinking my pint then it all got a bit wild. Someone had called the RMP (Royal Military Police). It was then someone slammed a chair on to my back, so I joined in the fighting. It was just a way for us all to let off steam. When the RMP arrived, flashing lights and sirens, the bar cleared. Out the back door we ran, through gardens and over walls, what a laugh, I could hardly run for laughing. I managed to get over a fence and jump on to a bus that had just stopped to let people off, I sat at the back, others jumped on the bus too. We all started laughing as the bus moved away. Once we got back to camp, I got my head down. I woke early next morning, showered and readied myself for going home. I wanted to see my Mum, Brother and Sister but in all honesty, I just wanted to get up to the farm.

Chapter 14

I was standing in a field at the top of the brae looking towards the local village in the distance, it was wonderful and I was breathing in the fresh air. In a flash there was something in front of me blocking my view I tried to move to one side so that I could still see the view to the village. Then it became clear, I was experiencing a flash back. I closed my eyes. I saw the guy with the RPG in Africa, then the other guy falling over the side of the vehicle that I had taken out. I tried to open my eyes but suddenly the female appeared with the tar all over her, she was standing in front of me. I raised my hands and I started shouting. I opened my eyes and one of my mates was standing holding my arms he said, "You ok mate?". I was sweating I nodded, "Aye I'm ok". He nodded and said, "Bad dream pal, you need more of this", placing a tin of lager on to the table. I was on the train, people were looking at me, I left the can where it was and gazed out of the window my mind was full of my dream. I heard my name being shouted and a voice saying" You ok or do you want a cuddle?", I smiled and shouted "If you have tits I'll take the cuddle", there was a roar of laughter, but the smile quickly fell from my face as I looked down, my hands were shaking.

I visited my Mum and stayed a couple of nights; my brother came down and we went out and had a few pints. On the second night the barmaid was asking me about life in the army, I was enjoying telling her some of my stories, she seemed quite interested. I was chatting away when suddenly, a bloke shouted, "What the fuck is going on eh? Chatting up my bird?". I stopped the conversation and looked over at him. He was standing at the door with two of his mates, the barmaid said "For Christ sake, we were only talking John". At this my brother stepped in and said, "Hey John, it's ok nothing in it". John said, "Hey butt out eh, he's big enough to know not to try and chat up other people's women", then the barmaid shouted "I was talking as I do every day! what I am supposed to do? Stand here and say nothing?", he shouted back at her and told her to "Shut the fuck up!". It was all getting a bit out of hand. I turned and said "Look pal I want no trouble, just have a pint and chill it's my round", my brother agreed," Aye let's all have a pint eh?" But no, John wanted to take things further, I shook my head and told him I didn't want any trouble and I would leave if it made him feel better, at that he swung at me. I side stepped and said "Ok mate that's one punch thrown, let's not have another", but his two friends were wanting in on the action as well. One came up as if to headbutt me, big mistake, I caught his head returning the headbutt. Grabbing Johns Jacket I moved my arm over his left shoulder grabbed his right shoulder and tripped him up with my foot, he landed hard, the other friend kicked me in the side but I didn't feel it, it was like I had blinkers on. I took him out with a couple of rapid punches, I knew his nose was having a bad day as I felt the bones break under my fist. I turned around, John was up and had broken a glass on the bar, he lunged forward but I side stepped it and pulled his whole arm up and punched him in the side of his face. he was out cold, the glass fell and what remained of it smashed on the floor. I turned and the other bloke shouted, "No more", "Oh no Fuck Face, you started it". I grabbed him and punched and punched, I didn't want to stop. Through the mist I heard my brother shouting, "For fuck sake! Stop!". I started to come to my senses, the bar was in a mess. I had taken out not just John and his pals but three other people that had tried to stop the fighting. I hadn't noticed them in the scuffle, I felt sick to my stomach at the scene of carnage I had created. The barmaid said to my brother "Get him out the back door, I will say I don't know who you are".

Next thing I knew I was standing in the alley, a good bit from the bar, with my brother. He handed me a cigarette while he paced up and down the alley. I asked, "You ok?". He replied "ME? Am I ok? For fuck sake that poor fuckers in there are in a real bad way! What the fuck is in your head, you're fucking nuts! I don't know what's happened to you, but that was not my little brother in there, more like a fucking unstoppable animal". I told him I was sorry. "I'm sorry!" he said "I have to come down here most weekend to see that Mum is ok and do things round the house for her, what the fuck I am I going to do now I can't go back there for a pint!". I said "Change bars then, that moron asked for it. I gave him the option not to start anything, but he was a stupid prick".

He flicked his cigarette towards me and said, "Just remember that we all have to live here when you are away playing soldiers, come on I will get you cleaned up". When I looked down, I could see by the streetlights my hands and sleeves were covered in blood. As we walked, he said "You better stay low for a while before you go back to the battalion", I told him I was heading for the farm tomorrow. He sighed deeply, probably relief, "Ok" he said "I will drop you off". We carries on walking when I stopped at a wall and leaned against it trying to breathe he asked if I was ok. I slumped down the wall and was in the sitting position. I said, "I should have just walked away I'm sorry". It started to rain but I just sat there, I felt him pull me up and walk me back to the house. He sat me on a chair and got a basin of hot water, telling me to clean myself up.

In the morning Mum was up cooking breakfast, the smell of grilling bacon was enough to get anyone up. I showered then headed downstairs, there at the table was my family, Mum smiled, and little Sister gave me a hug and big Brother just nodded as I sat down. My Mum asked what had happened to my hands but my brother quickly butted in and said "Little bruv can't handle his drink, he fell on the way home, I, on the other hand managed home no problems", with a large smirk on his face. We all burst out laughing as my Mum put a hand on my shoulder and said "You both should stop drinking but if you are to have a few don't try and keep up with him ok my loon", I nodded like I was five years old again. If only she knew the half of it!

My Brother dropped me a couple of miles from the farm, at my request. I wanted to enjoy this walk into the place I had dreamed about for such a long time. As I walked up through the woods into the clearing, the farm came into view perched on the side of the hill. I smiled and almost ran across the fields. I trudged through the mud at the gate and then I was in the close entrance, it felt like I was home at last. I walked into the house, it was exactly the same as when I was last here, nothing had changed, the smell from the Aga, the dogs barking as they came to greet me and there sitting in his favorite chair was my Uncle. He lowered his pipe and blew smoke up into the air then said, "You took your time getting here laddie". I just smiled and went upstairs to get changed.

When I came down there was a dram waiting for me on the kitchen table, my Uncle had his glass in hand saying, "Welcome home lad". As we drank, I heard the tractor stop outside, in walked my Cousin, with a grin he said, "Just in time for a dram", he looked at me "You've changed".

Somewhat surprised I said, "No, not me". "Aye you have changed" he repeated. Then my uncle said, "Aye he's right, your eyes are colder". I told them I was just tired, but I saw the look on my uncle's face, he was frowning. We all sat down at the table and the bottle went round and round until it was finished. My Cousin said, "Come on then, we have some cows to sort out". He told me he had a few beasts to get inside that he wanted to check over. As I went to walk outside my Uncle grabbed my arm and said, "Here you, if you ever want to talk just gives a nod and tell him", gesturing to my Cousin "Nothing, he's only interested in shagging and drinking". I joked, "So am I". "Nah laddie" he said, "You have seen some shite I bet, I can see it in your eyes". I walked outside breathing in the smell of dung, silage and wet mud. I was so glad to be home.

It was great being back at the farm I got stuck in with tractor work and cattle. I started seeing a girl called Laura from a farm close by. She was a good-looking lassie, she was halfway through her training to be a nurse. We would have a laugh at the local pub then turn the old Jeep into a passion wagon on the way home. She helped me forget all the things that had happened in Northern Ireland.

One afternoon I walked into the kitchen and my Uncle told me to give my Mother a call, she had already called twice. Thinking there was something wrong I called her straight away. Nothing was wrong thankfully but I had a phone call from a girl called Kim, I had to think for a bit then I remembered, Kim from Glencorse barracks. The message was she would be up at the local RAF base for a week. She left a contact number with my Mum and asked her to get me to call her. My Mum, being a Mum, asked all the question under the sun, I wasn't giving her any details, I only said that I would call Kim when I got a chance.

I telephoned that night around 17.00 hours, Kim answered the phone and she was excited to hear from me. I told her I was really busy at the farm, but I could meet up with her the following afternoon. She was looking forward to it and would arrange for a pass to be left at the guard room. I asked what she was doing in a RAF camp and how she knew I was at home on leave. She told me she had been promoted and had a couple of courses to attend, they just happened to be up here. She knew we had just finished a tour over the water in Northern Ireland, so she put two and two together. I said I was looking forward to it and hung up the phone. I stared at the phone and thought of Laura, thinking I will make up an excuse. I looked up as two faces stared at me, my Uncle said," Woman problems?". I just nodded my cousin shouted, "You lucky bastard! Is there a spare one for me?". I smiled and thought 'yeah very funny' as I raised my glass of whisky to my lips.

I arrived at the RAF camp all suited and booted. I had told Laura, the night before at the bar, that I had to go away for a night. I knew by her voice she was not happy, but I told her I was staying with my

Mum, so that seemed to placate her, I hated lying but I was a young, single, virile, man.

I picked up my pass from the guard room after showing my ID card and waited until I was escorted to an office block. I walked in and there she was with a big smile. I had forgotten how attractive she was, she said, "Coffee?" I nodded, after handing me the cup she whispered, "I will be finished in about twenty minutes, enjoy your coffee", then winked, I felt a stir in my groin area at the wink, I could only think to myself how good a night it was going to be.

We had a meal and a few drinks at the local hotel, we had a great time. She was different to the other girls I had been seeing, she was forces so she knew all the terminology and the score. We booked a room, the girl at the reception gave us a little smile as we headed up the stairs to the room. We both had a fantastic night the energy used that night was tremendous. Next morning, she was up at 06.00 hours and said she would see me at Noon. I lay back on the bed but suddenly remembered I was supposed to take Laura to Inverness that night. I lay there for a while, staring at the ceiling then drifted off to sleep. I remember turning my head to one side and next to me was the woman covered in tar, she was trying to touch me with her tarred hand. I tried to get away but I couldn't move. I heard a bang then another bang, I looked around and there in front of me was a man with a 50 calibre machine gun laughing and shooting at me. I shot upright and realised that I was in the hotel room and the banging was a knock on the door, I heard a voice say, "Room service is after 11 o'clock. I stammered "Yes I'll be out in fifteen minutes". "No problem Sir" the voice replied.

I was shaking, my whole body was covered in droplets of sweat, I stood up and the bed was soaked. I opened the window and gulped in fresh air, after a moment I collected myself. Once I had calmed down I went or a shower and got ready. I went downstairs into the bar and ordered a coffee, the barman asked if everything was alright as I looked, 'white as a ghost'. 'Ghost', I thought, what an appropriate word, ghosts from my past were always there in the back of my mind. I told him I was fine, just a heavy night. When he handed me my coffee, I picked it up my hand was shaking, and I spilled it all over the bar. I apologised and he told me it was ok; he turned and poured a dram from the optics. He handed it to me he said, "Its ok, it's on the house mate". I picked it up and took a gulp, as I felt the warm liquid burn my throat I stopped shaking. The barman looked at me and said,

"Guessing you have seen some shit mate". I just shook my head. He introduced himself as Brian and said he could tell a squaddie a mile away. "I was one para myself, been out five years just work here part time I am up at the camp lecturing, that's part time also" he said. I passed him the glass for another whisky he pushed it back towards me and said, "Life's problems will never get any better by looking at the bottom of a dram glass, yes it dulls the images and will get you through the day but you don't want to start that. You look as if you train hard so keep training, focus your mind on other things and try and see the funny side of everything, whatever it is ok mate. You can always pick out something humorous in every situation". I stood up from the bar stool and shook his hand. I thanked him and as I left, he said, "Anytime mate, I'm here most days till 13.00 hours". I headed out into the fresh air I smiled and thought 'aye that's it get your head round it as my Dad would say'.

With a spring in my step I headed towards the taxi rank, I jumped into the taxi smiling and the driver asked what the joke was. I told him it was nothing. When I arrived at my Mums I showered and while I was getting dressed Mum shouted that's a girl on the phone for you". I ran down the stairs grabbed the phone and said, "Hi Kim, I will be about half an hour ok? I'll meet you at the gate", the voice said, "Who's Kim?". I realised it was Laura, I replied "I was just going to phone you, I am being picked up by one of the guys wives, she's going to drop us off at Aberdeen station, I have to go to Edinburgh for a few days. I'm sorry but its forces stuff, I'll be back by the start of the week". She went silent and I asked "What's wrong?", "I can't help it", she said "I miss you so much, can we go to inverness then for a day or so, we could get a hotel overnight so we can be together". My guilty reply was "Aye that sounds great, we will get that sorted when I get back ok, hey missing you already". She laughed and hung up.

When I turned my Mum shook her head, she said, "That's a dangerous game you're playing", I just winked and hugged her saying', "Its ok Mum". I asked her to book a taxi while I finished dressing, and could she phone the farm and tell them I am away to Edinburgh. Her reply was "I will not lie for you, you can phone yourself".

Kim was waiting at the gate when the taxi arrived, she jumped in and we headed back towards town. I asked, "You free for the weekend?". "Yes, why?". I whispered in her ear, "Fancy a dirty weekend in Edinburgh?". she said, "yes please! But I don't have a change of clothes or anything with me", I smirked, "Exactly it's a dirty weekend", she punched me on the arm saying, "Judging by last night that's not what you mean at all". As the taxi sped its way to the train station I smiled saying," hey if we don't have it, we can always buy it". We both giggled like kids.

Edinburgh was excellent. We booked into a hotel, went shopping, walked the streets of our capital in awe of the sights, ate nice food and went to bed early but stayed up till dawn. It was a great time. On Sunday night, when we were heading back on the train, Kim said, "When am I going to see this farm you are always on about". A sudden panic ran through me as I thought about Laura. "Oh, aye that sounds great", I said "When are you off again?". Her reply panicked me even more ". "I still have a couple of days left then I'm away down to Wellington barracks, in London. I told you I will be stationed there for the next year or so". I must have paled at her reply because she asked if I was alright. I said, "Aye sounds great". She leaned towards me and said, "If you don't want to, its ok with me just tell me". I said, "No it's not that, it will be fine". What a liar I was. I felt bad but it was just a bit of fun right? She said, "I had a lovely weekend you know". I winked and said, "Dirty enough for you?". She blushed then turned to look out of the window.

Chapter 15

My Uncle told me to watch what I was doing. If I was taking Kim up to the farm to be careful because Laura's family were friends. That night I phoned Laura and asked if she was free on Thursday, she said no as she had nursing training. I told her it was ok but at the weekend we will go to Inverness. I hated myself for doing this but it was all a bit of fun, wasn't it? I phoned Kim and said "How about Thursday? I will pick you up at the gate and take you up the farm", her reply was "Take me up the farm? Oh yes, that must be a new name for it" she giggled and continued "yes I would love to visit this place you call home".

I laughed at her comment and told her I would see her then. I put the phone down, waited about thirty seconds and then called Laura. I said, "Hey, what about going out tonight?", she replied, "Oh yes! Looking forward to that already! Have you missed me?". I told her I would pick her up at 7, strangely not feeling the least bit guilty. I hung up the phone. My Uncle was sitting in the kitchen and heard everything. He took the pipe from his mouth and said, "For fuck sake min, you are some cunt you! Fucking lassies everywhere!". I shrugged it off, "It's all a bit of fun eh". He said, "You're just a fucking whore". I laughed and said mockingly, "You jealous?". His reply was, "Aye laddie, its ok just now but it will all catch up with you yet and bite you in the arse". I ignored his warning.

I had a good night at the local pub with Laura but I almost called her Kim about thirty times. I had to watch what I said. On the way home I told her I was exhausted but she said that was a pity as she wasn't with a sly smile.

A few days later I picked Kim up from the camp and headed towards the farm. We had fun as I showed her places of interest on the way. She punched my arm and said, "They are all bars and pubs!". I laughed "I know!". We stopped on route at the garage and bought some things that I been asked to take back. When I rounded the corner, I saw the farm on the hill in the distance. Kim leaned over to me and said, "You really do love this place don't you?". She laughed and told me that as we turned the corner an smile warmed my face when the farm came into view.

I introduced her to my Uncle and Cousin. They were all very friendly, trying to talk a bit upper class which really didn't suit them. She sat in the chair as they messed around making coffee and putting out biscuits. Later Kim and I left the house and walked around the boundaries of the farm. I showed her places that I remembered as a child and pointed out things of interest like a fox's den, where the badgers lived and of course where I shot my first roe deer with my Dad. We walked through a wooded area, stopped and kissed. We fumbled around a bit but decided we would refrain from ripping each other clothes off. In the distance I saw my uncle standing at the top of the brae beside the house, then I heard a high pitched whistle. I knew something was up, we opened up the pace. When we arrived my Uncle said with a wink, "You better get home to your Mothers, she needs you". I thought something was up and Kim asked, "Whatever could be wrong?". I shrugged my shoulders and we jumped into the car. As we headed off, I could see a red Micra in the distance. I realised it was Laura's car heading towards the farm. I reversed the car and headed down the brae in the opposite direction. Kim asked what was wrong. I lied telling her that it was quicker this way.

When we got to the garage I stopped and told her I would phone to see what up with my Mum. Kim waited in the car while I phoned the farm it, rang and rang. When it was finally answered by my Cousin he said "Laura had phoned before saying that her pal, who works at the garage, said you were there with some lassie and she was heading over to see what was going on. I told her it was you Sister and the old man said you had to go and see your Mum. The old fellow is fucking livid with you, oh shit here he goes". My Uncle came on the phone, "Now laddie, you better sort out this shit for fuck sake! Laura is just away, she didn't see you but you are bringing us into your world of shit. It stops now! I could tell by your eyes that you have been through a hard time, but you are shitting on your own doorstep here and we will be left with all the crap. Do you understand?". I tried to reply but he had hung upon me. I stood in the phone box for a few seconds and realised that this time home I had really messed up. First at my Mum's house and now here. When I got back into the car Kim asked what was up, "Aye it's all ok. Hey, we will head back to camp now eh?". She looked disappointed as she said, "I thought we were spending the night together?". I said, "We will soon. I promise". She knew something was up but didn't push the issue. Our journey back to the camp was almost silent. I stopped just outside and said, "I'm sorry, just a lot of shit going on".   She said, "Come on, let me buy you dinner".

Chapter 16

I was patrolling along a road that seemed to be never ending. I was alone. I spotted a vehicle that was heading towards me. It had a mounted weapon that was firing at me. I tried to move and raise my rifle but it seemed like I was in slow motion. It took a lifetime to get the rifle up into a firing position. I tried to pull the trigger but nothing happened. The vehicle sped up, still heading right at me. I managed to move out its path but very slowly. I recognized it as one of the vehicles that was in Africa. I tried to run down a side road but there was the girl, covered in tar standing beckoning me towards her. I tried to run in another direction, but the vehicle was so close to me I had nowhere to go. I just managed to keep my feet from being run over as it screamed past me. I heard a voice shouting in the distance. I could feel a warm sensation on my cheek. I opened my eyes and Kim was shouting, "Are you ok? For fuck sake". I sat up and realised I was in a hotel room. She was sitting up, trying to control my arms which were waving about like mad. The sweat was dripping off me as I jumped out of bed and rushed to the window where I gulped in fresh air. Kim came over and gently touched my shoulder, I almost jumped out of the window. As I slowly came to my senses, she said, "Its ok. Here, drink some water". I pulled my boxers on and sat in one of the chairs, she pulled on a shirt and sat down in the chair opposite. It was silent, then I realised she was waiting for me to speak.

What was I going to tell her? I said, "I have seen a bit of shit since I saw you in Glencorse". She stayed silent. I asked her what the time was and she told me it was only ten o'clock, "Get dressed I need a drink". She said, "No you don't". I said, "Yes, I fucking do". I pulled on my clothes and headed downstairs to the bar. I ordered a pint and it didn't touch the sides on the way down. I ordered another with a large whisky chaser. The barmaid said, "Hey honey, haven't seen you here before". I told her I was just staying there for the night. She replied, "I can stay open till the wee hours if you are a resident", with a sly giggle. I nodded saying, "Well, just keep the whisky coming". She poured another and said, "This is on the house handsome" as she touched my hand. I heard," Hands off bitch or I'll tie your tits in two!". The barmaid looked up shocked as Kim, with a look of pure anger on her face, cameup to the bar. The barmaid said, "He can please himself". Kim leaned forward grabbed her by the wrist and twisted, the whole upper part of

159

her body ended up on the bar. She let out an almighty squeal. "Fuck sake Kim let her go, she was just being friendly" I said. Kim glowered at her and said, "I'll have a white wine thank you pet". You could have cut the atmosphere with a knife.

Next morning Kim sat in the corner of the room. She said, "You can talk to people about your nightmares you know". I tried to dismiss it by saying, "Aye no problem. I always try and see the funny side of things". "Hey you can always come to London and talk to me, you know that don't you?". I nodded. When we got dressed to leave it was a sad moment. She kissed me and said, "See you some time soldier". I grabbed her hand and spun her around to kiss her. She gave me a tight squeeze. As she left she said, "Remember and call me, you have all my contact details. Just leave a message with my Mum if you don't get a reply from my work number". That was it, in an instant she was gone. I felt so alone. I enjoyed her company and I already started to miss her. I thought about running down the stairs to catch up with her but then thought better of it. It was better this way.

I went back to the farm to collect my gear. I spoke to my Uncle. He had calmed down and said he understood. He also said "You say cheerio to Laura eh? Don't keep the lassie hanging on for you. You let her down softly". I said I would. My cousin came in and said, with a grin, "Well, well, shagger. How's it going?". I said, "It's not funny, I've been a bit of a prick really". His reply was, "Aye you have that but hey, that's life eh. By the way Laura is tidy, but that Kim is well above your fighting weight. She's model material and what a body! Is she a good ride?". I told him to simmer down and that was enough of that kind of talk. My Uncle said, "She's a bonnie lassie I give you that, very down to earth". I knew this already, but it didn't make me feel any better. I had really been out of order, treating the two of them like that, they both deserved better.

I stood from the table and said my goodbyes. My Uncle patted me on the shoulder and said, "You come back safe and sound, I'll be thinking of you and when you get a chance gives a call eh?". I felt a sad to be leaving. I loved being at the farm, but it was time to get going. 'A night with Mum and Sister, then early morning train', I thought as I drove away. Laura was not so understanding though. When I went to say goodbye to her, I tried to let her down gently, but she was having none of it. I told her I better go and she said, "Aye! Away to your fancy lass you fucking bastard!". I was taken aback, how did she know? "I know your Sister and Betty knows her too". I looked at her confused, who was Betty? I asked and she shouted, "Betty from the garage you fucking tosser!". There was a bang as she kicked the door of my car. I tried to say something but thought better of it, so I drove off with a footprint shaped dent in my car door. During my drive back to town I realised that I had messed up big style this time. Fighting, messing girls around and dragging my family into the bargain. I decided that I would be on the straight and narrow after that.

When I got up the next morning my Mum had already left. She was working the early shift and as it was a bit early for my Sister to be up so I headed off down to the train station myself. I still felt terrible with all that had gone on during my leave. When I boarded the train, I tried to clear my head and think what was in store for me in the future rather than dwell on my mistakes. I sat and stared out the window, watching the scenery fly past. I opened my bag to get out my Walkman and there was a silver package. I smiled to myself. I knew what it was, egg and onion sandwiches, 'Thanks Mum, love you too'.

Chapter 17

Soon after I returned to the Barracks, I was promoted to Lance corporal and told it was effective immediately. I had to get all my army kit and sew on the corporal stripe. Me a 'Lance Corporal' my Dad would be so proud. I was very proud of myself, but when I got my corporals mess bills and corporals mess dues, I thought, 'fuck this is where all my money is going, I better calm down with the drinking'. Fun over, I got back into to fitness big style. I boxed most evenings and ran at least eight miles a day. I also started judo every other evening. All this extra fitness was taking its toll on me, but I wanted to learn more and more, I loved it. I still drank at weekend, messed about with lassies, but through the week I was so focused I wanted knowledge in everything army

Over the next month we readied ourselves to go to Belize for jungle training we would be away for the next four months. I did dread it slightly just the thought of it, but when we arrived I took to this like a duck to water, I loved it, even with the snakes and creepy crawlies. I thought it was heaven to start with but I soon realised that the jungle was the hardest environment I had been in and it tested you every minute, it was so hard going, but we were all in it together so as normal I adopted the saying look, listen and learn. We trained hard, learned how to make an A frame for sleeping in the jungle whilst we were deployed in the jungle, how to stand to for last light and first light. We had to make sure we could get back from our stand too position to our A frame without being able to see, when the light goes you cannot even see your hand in front of your face, it was pitch black. There was some carry on to start with, soldiers in the wrong A frame, even with the wool or para cord that we put out from their stand to position to their A frame, it was hysterical. When I think back it was supposed to be a silent routine or as quite as possible. Night-time was the best time, you got out of your wet gear and into dry gear. At night, the jungle came alive, with all the sounds from above, below and around, I used to lie in my A frame and listen for what seemed ages till I drifted off to sleep. One thing I hated above all was putting back on my wet gear in the morning, it was not something I never got used to, but again you had to put up and shut up everyone was in the same situation. We learned new skills like; patrol, map reading through the jungle, what we could eat and what not, we did river crossings, ambushes, blowing trees for heli evacuation it was really hard going with the heat but it was all new and knowledge to me and I loved it. I asked the instructors question all the time, I think that by halfway through the tour everyone was fed up listen to me constantly asking about this and that. Someone said, "For fucks sake stop asking stupid questions". The instructors were great, they loved to share their knowledge and experience.

An Instructor called Ritchie said, "In this environment there is no such thing as a 'stupid' question it may save your life". When our tour was coming to an end everyone was so excited about getting home. I was a 'second in command' of a section of men, the lads were great, but they all wanted to get home. I, on the other hand, wanted to stay. I was speaking to Ritchie and he said, "You have a good knowledge out here you're a quick learner and a good aptitude, you are maybe meant for better things mate". I didn't know what he meant so I pushed my cigarette's and shrugged my shoulders, but it niggled me just what he had meant.

On our return I was looking forward to getting home and up to the farm for a bit of rest and recuperation. We all had really good sun tans, so I looked forward to getting home to show it off and go out pulling lassies and drinking,typical.

The next morning, as I came out of the shower, one of the camp guards was standing in front of my door. I said, "Hey Bert, what's up?". "Message from the TARA (short for RSM) you are summoned to the Commanding officer's office as soon as possible". I thought 'oh fuck what now', I knew I was pissed last night but I remember getting back to camp and I did not think there was any issues.

I asked Bert to put the kettle on and we can have a brew, that will give me a bit of time. "If the TARA says anything tell him I was not in my room, so you waited ok", I told Bert. He nodded and filled the kettle. What a pain in the arse as my kit was all packed away ready for my leave. I quickly ironed my kit and made my way up to the battalion headquarters.

When I entered I chatted to one of the female pay clerks, she was a really fine lassie sorted out any money problems you might have, she said with a giggle "What a tan you have can I see your white bits". I just smiled and winked, I did not have time to reply when I heard the RSM shout my name followed by 'front and centre'. The RSM was dressed in his civvies which was a bit weird but the whole battalion was going on leave, so I thought nothing of it. I stood still while he inspected me and then he said, "Who told you to get into uniform?" I replied, "No one sir I thought it was best". He smiled, "Well done good effort but its civvies today, right lad get in there". I marched in and halted, the commanding officer was at his desk in civvies, he lifted his head looked at me and frowned at the RSM. RSM said, "He thought it best to come in uniform Sir, he thinks it's a bit more respectful, good effort I say Sir", the CO nodded in agreement then he continued. "Well young man did you enjoy Belize?" I told him I had loved it. He nodded, leaned forward on his elbows and said, "Good well done, I have something to put forward to you". I was curious as I said, "Yes sir". He continued "I realise that you have just returned from four months intensive training in Belize and you are looking forward to your leave but how about putting your leave on hold for a few weeks? We are to put a team together for a little adventure in Cameroon Africa we need someone with your skills, what do you say soldier". I was gutted I was looking forward to my leave, but I said, "Yes sir". He nodded, "Yes we thought you would say that your leave starts when you get back with an extra extension of one week ok". I quickly counted in my head the days of my initial leave, that was seventeen, now plus seven that's twenty-four days, yeeehaaa. I almost beamed a smile. He continued, "It will be in time for the harvest I think". I replied, "Yes sir that is correct they need all hands at the farm at that time of year". He just nodded and said, "Well-done carry on the good work the RSM will fill you in on the details ok anything to add?" I replied with a false smile "Well Sir at least I will keep my tan up". He smiled and said, "That's the attitude we need". As I marched out the RSM marched me into his office and told me to sit down and relax, I sat as instructed. Behind me I heard the clink of glass I dared not turn around then he appeared at my side handed me a glass of whisky and said, "Here, get that down you". He even smiled.

He sat down at his desk, there was paperwork everywhere, he said, "It's a twelve-man team, there is a bit of unrest down there in Africa but nothing serious, we will class this as training ok. You will secure the beach and surrounding area for an extraction. There are some people coming back to theUK from the British embassy, as there is a bit of a coup going on in Cameroon, so no flights. Another regiment have removed the personnel and are all placed in a safe house, miles from the capital. It is all a bit over the top I think, but we have been instructed to stand to and aid where we can. The team is made up of our guys. Most of the team I think you will know already, they are at

Brise Norton now and they have requested you as there covering sniper. The Duty Driver will pick you up in ten minutes, he has signed, and you will countersign for your weapons and you'll get issued with all the kit you need at Brise Norton". I said, "It's all so quick Sir". He nodded and said "Your room will be locked and left as it is until you return, I will personally see to that. Do you have any money on you?" "No sir it's all in my room" I said. To my surprise he opened his wallet and handed me £100. "You shouldn't need money but just in case. I'll get that when you return ok?". He glanced out the window and said, "That's the driver, now finish that", gesturing to the glass in my hand. I scooped back the whisky. As he took the glass from me, he handed me a piece of chocolate. He must have seen the expression on my face, and laughed, "Its ok, it will mask the smell of whisky on your breath. I don't want you babbling that you had a dram with the TARA". I almost laughed. He leaned forward and said, "Well done, now get going and remember my £100 has a fucking big return spring". I stood, shook his hand and thanked him. As I headed out of his office he said, "See you when you get back son". I thought it weird as the RSM calling me 'son'. I jumped into the wagon, nodded to the duty driver, he put it in gear, and we headed off. Bring on the next adventure.

Chapter 18

The next couple of hours were all a bit of a blur, everything happened so fast. I was on a plane with all my new kit. I already knew most of the lads. It turns out it was Ginge, the Sergeant from Kenya, that had requested me. We all boarded the plane and I sat looking around. I realised Ginge had pulled all the guys from Kenya, Knuckles, Les, Malcolm also six others and of course, Alex, my spotter. He sat down next to me and said, "Well, are you up for this then?" I told him of course I was. He knew me well enough to know I really meant it.

We could hardly hear over the noise of the engine, but we had a bit of fun. Knuckles shouted, "Let's see if you fuck this navigator", gesturing with his head. I looked over and there was an older guy with a handlebar moustache standing there, I laughed and shouted back, "Not my type!". Knuckles shouted back, "That's a shame, he's so nice too". We all laughed until Ginge told us to stop. The poor older guy was not sure what we were laughing at, but I am sure he knew he was the butt of the joke. With a scowl and a deep frown, he headed up to the flight deck. After taking off we all tried to get as comfortable as we could, it was going to be a long flight.

I had been asleep as Ginge tapped me on the shoulder and instructed me to follow him. We went to a makeshift table where a map was laid out. Ginge started by saying, "Right lads listen in, I will give you a very brief outline of the whole situation then I will go through each step-in detail. Does everyone understand?". We all nodded, even though it was noisy he tried his best to be heard, he continued, "We are flying to Nigeria and landing at Port Harcourt airport. We will be picked up by helicopter, flown to an American Naval ship about sixty miles off Cameroon for refueling, we will not have a great deal oftime when we land so get your kit ready now and make sure all your gear is sorted. From there we will fly inland, under the cover of darkness, to the Sanaga River mouth, South of the city of Douala in Cameroon. There we will secure and patrol the Southside of the river, leaving RVs and sentries at certain points, until we reach an area called Pongo-Songo, which is about 22 to 25 kilometres inland from our drop off point. From this point we can see straight up the river. By that time there will only be four of us as the rest will be left at RVs protecting our withdrawal. Everyone fine so far?" Again, we all nodded. He continued, "We will wait in hiding, our people will be transported by boat to this point. Once they have passed through, and we are sure they don't have any company following, I will radio each group in the RV then we will patrol back in quick time, passing each RV. Ensuring there is no company coming at us from the South. We will rendezvous on the edge of the foliage cover near the beach and secure it with an all-round defence, until the helicopters arrive". Knuckles said, "If its sixty miles at RV1 from the American ship that's a thirty-minute journey". Ginge nodded saying, "It depends on the cloud base, the Americans have agreed to help with the refueling, but they will stay on the horizon. Once we are in position, we will radio them and two helicopters will lift off and head for us. If we are compromised, after the radio contact, the people from the Embassy will have priority. Hopefully there is no drama. Once we are on board the helicopters, they will bring us back to the American ship, refuel, and then onto Nigeria, board the plane and then home. Any questions?". No one spoke. "Lads we are not expecting it to become anything other than a training exercise ok, but if we are compromised then only fire if it's a real and immediate threat to life".

During the briefing, our officer stood still and listened, he knew that Ginge had a lot more experience than him. When Ginge finished he said, "Chaps, as the Sergeant has just said we will be classing this as a training exercise, let's be professional". We all nodded in understanding, "Right lads get your kit ready in thirty minutes then get your head down again, you may need to get some sleep".

Ginge and the officer went through with each individual, discussing their part in the exercise, eventually he got to me. "Right listen in. We will patrol through to Pongo-Songo, once we have our people we will leave you and Alex to cover us. It will be up to you to make sure there is no one following. He pointed to my sniper rifle and said, "Only use it if you deem it to be hostile company in pursuit ok? Once we get to the RV 3 from Pongo-Songo we will radio you, then you and Alex patrol out as tail end Charlie. When we do get going, we want to be out of the fucking place asap. Any questions?" I shook my head; it was all very clear to me what was expected of me. The officer said, "We will be relying on you, but with your skill we should have nothing to worry about eh, Lance Corporal". Ginge looked at the officer and said, "Sir, we all have a part to play ok?". the officer nodded.

I soon fell asleep after I had sorted my kit. We

were woken and told we had twenty minutes to land. We landed, walked off the plane into the dark heat of the night and straight on to a British Puma helicopter. The rotors were running as we piled in all our gear and took off. It was a tight squeeze, but we managed. Roughly an hour and half later we landed on the American ship but were told that we had to stay in the helicopter but the doors would be left open should any problems occur when refueling. I could see fuck all of the ship it was so dark. Less than ten minutes and we were off again. I looked at the luminous hands on my watch, it was a little after 01.55 hours. I thought to myself how well executed it all was. I estimated that we had about thirty minutes to the beach, then five minutes flying up the edge. This was done to distort the sound so that no one at a distance would be able to pinpoint where exactly we landed. We were to make a tactical landing and throw our gear off, it had all been well-practised in past training. The helicopter should be air born around one minute after we disembarked.

We were told three minutes until landing. The helicopter hovered before touching down. The doors were opened and in an instant we were off and the helicopter was away. It was less than a minute, it had to be. We lay in all round defence as we sorted our gear then made our way to the edge of cover. We waited a few hours, got water and some food inside of us, until day light started to come up. Leaving the first three guys in RV 1, we patrolled for about two hours covering a lot of ground. We could see that the foliage was becoming more and more dense. We stopped to leave 3 guys at LV2. Les was scout and I was behind him as we headed away. After half an hour he froze. I looked past him and to the right I saw it - a Black Mamba snake. Les looked for an alternative route and steered clear of it. We patrolled, moving nice and calmly through the jungle, we were making good time and Les picked his route well, I was glad he was with us. We patrolled all day. As nightfall came, we were about five kilometres from the river Pongo-Songo. We made base and called it RV 3. We sorted ourselves and stood too till dark as normal.

During the night we could hear the chimpanzees in the distance and all the noises of the jungle, scrapes, screeches and howls, amongst other things. After a restless night we stood too for day light, sorted out our kit and were ready to go. Knuckles and the Officer were to stay at RV3. As we were preparing to leave, I looked over and saw Knuckles roll his eyes in disgust as the officer passed him a message to send. I smiled, Knuckles was a really funny guy, a right character. I could not think of a better man to have protecting our withdrawal.

We patrolled in silence, moving very carefully. Les, me, Ginge then Alex as tail end Charlie. We could see the river in the distance every so often as the jungle opened up. Suddenly, Les stopped. He held his hand up and then lowered his arm. We knelt and waited for about five minutes, then we heard it, someone singing in the distance. We stayed still and silent as the singing got closer.

Three women appeared on a path about ten yards from us heading towards the river. We waited for them to pass and the singing to fade before we continued towards the river. From the cover of the jungle to the river's edge was very exposed, it was about one hundred yards and I looked upriver realising it was the same all the way. I said to Ginge, "Hope to fuck there is no one following them as they come out, it's so open". He nodded saying, "You and Alex find the best position you can to protect our way out, make sure it has a good view upriver. We will stay here". Alex and I moved away slowly and after about an hour we found an elevated piece of ground with great views straight up the river. When we looked around, we could make out the area where Ginge and Les were, at least if it did go badly, we could contact one another by hand signals. Alex made a thumbs up and Ginge returned it. It was a bit more reassuring for all knowing we were so close.

Alex and I settled down and waited. After about ten minutes Alex handed me a message he had just decoded from Batco. The message said, 'All in position'. It was from Les, the message was sent to everyone. Alex made himself comfortable and soon drifted off to sleep as I stayed on stag watching the river. When another message came through Alex opened his eyes, moving quickly to decode it. He handed me the message, it said that a patrol boat was scanning the area off the beach. The three guys at RV 1 had heard the motorboat in the distance. They stood too and waited. The boat had been going up and down the coast but now was headed North. Probably towards the port of Douala. I was about to whisper something to Alex when I heard a noise, we both froze, the noise was close. 'Was it an animal?' I thought, 'hope to fuck it's not a hippo'. After a few moments I heard a giggle. A few yards to our right three local woman came into view, I let out a slow breath. Alex turned to face Ginge and hand signalled that it was all ok. I watched the women approach the river, then, like out of a blue movie they all started to undress. I felt a bit of a pervert, but this was the job. Alex whispered, "Stag doesn't get better than this eh?"

I sniggered, but like a true professional soldier I watched up the river for anyone coming down. It just so happened that the three woman in the river were right in front of us as they washed and splashed around in a small pool at the river's edge. Alex whispered, "There can't be a lot of razors in Africa eh". I knew what he meant. I told him to get his head down as it was my stag. "Fuck you", was his reply, I just smiled. A while later the woman stood and dried themselves in the sun. They pulled on their loose garments and headed back towards us. We stayed still as they sang and walked a few feet past our position. Alex moved slightly and I heard the woman squeal. I thought 'for fuck sake' as I made a face at him. There was a rock thrown in our direction, then another and another. I thought to myself, 'if I get a rock off my head, I am going to boot fuck out of Alex'. After about ten minutes they stopped, they must have thought we were an animal of some sort. Alex decoded a message from Ginge asking if we had been compromised, Alex replied saying, "No. They probably thought we were an animal of some kind".

After about half an hour we received a message "Our people are on their way and should be here in about sixty minutes. Let us all get ready". Four men from Special Forces were bringing them out so we would be under their command from now on. We acknowledged. About thirty minutes later I looked through my scope and saw a boat in the distance. It was long and thin with what looked like a sun or rain canopy, moving slowly down river. I whispered to Alex, "That must be them, eh?". "No way", he said, "They will be in a fast boat going like fuck". I shook my head saying, "No way, that would attract to much attention". "A tenner says it's not them" he said. I nodded, then over the earpiece we heard, 'all call signs, 'we are twelve minutes from you, we do not have company following ', we heard Ginge acknowledging followed by, 'we have the area secure'. Alex shook his head saying another fucking tenner I just smiled.

The boat passed us on the left still going slowly, they came to a stop on an areaof beach behind us. I kept watch up the river as Alex gave me, a very quiet, running commentary on what was happening behind me, I continued to scan the area for any hostile company. According to Alex they ran the boat up onto the muddy sand and they all piled off, three woman and three men in civvies and four other armed men. The group all walked slowly up the beach, no running and no noise, then we heard the boat reverse away from the sand and out into the river. Alex said, "It must have been a local man's boat", as we heard the engine putt away, I realised the boat was heading down river. We both knew we would not be moving till we got a message from RV 3. It would take around an hour to get there, so we scanned the river it was all quiet, the sound from the river was so therapeutic. In the distance I saw a hippo and its young calf enter the water. It was so fabulous to see something like that this was such a beautiful country. Alex shook my arm and said, "That's them leaving RV3". I said, "Lets crawl out of here, once we are in cover, high tail it ok". We crawled to the vegetation then we started pushing it out using almost the same route that they used. I kept looking down for snakes but I started to get dizzy and nauseated I realised that with me looking down all the time my eyes were focusing too much on the ground, as my pupils were always trying to focus on certain object near and far, I lifted my head and looked ahead I felt better within minutes. I stopped about halfway between our start point and RV3 and told Alex to get some water inside him, we shared the water bottle, then headed off again. When we arrived at RV 3 Alex got on the radio and gave them a situation report or 'sit rep' as we knew it. As we headed away and made for RV2 I looked at my watch it was 10:05 am, I told Alex that we had better get a fucking move on and I opened up the pace, he was trying hard to keep up. When we arrived at RV2 we ate, rehydrated, and then rested up for five minutes. We were still standing.

Alex was as white as a ghost. I asked if he was ok, he replied with, "Aye, but feeling a bit sick." I told him we didn't have time to feel sick, we had to get out of here, and there was no way I could carry him. He laughed and said he would be fine. I told him to go scout ahead and we would go at his pace. He shook his head insisting that I get going; he would keep up. I told him if he felt any worse to let me know. He gestured with his head to get going so I pushed off, but I did slow my pace down a little. I had my compass in my hand most of the time as we pushed and pushed. I saw Alex on my heels, looking in terrible shape. He staggered a little so I grabbed his arm. He looked at me then his eyes rolled back and he went down like a sack of potatoes. I made him comfortable whie I waited for him to come round. He opened his eyes after about five minutes so I gave him some water. He was dazed when he looked up so I explained that he'd collapsed and asked if he was okay now. He said he was fine before promptly rolling over to vomit. "That's better!" he said as I poured water down the nape of his neck and got him to drink some more, a little at a time. When he sat up he said he really did feel better this time, but when he stood up he was still shaky on his feet. After drinking more water he said, "Aye, I'm feeling a lot better". I said, "Give me your weapon." In response he told me to fuck off. I laughed, he was definitely feeling better. "Let's get moving in case someone heard you throwing up". I pushed him up front and he started heading off. I sighed thinking 'thank fuck for that'. As we neared RV1 I whispered to him to take it easy. At this he turned to vomit all over my boots. I helped him to the ground, and gave him some more water. This time he said he felt better, but when he stood up and set off he was heading in the wrong direction. I pulled him gently back and told him to give me his kit. He shook his head at first but I insisted. He handed it over so I strapped it on to my Bergen and we headed off. It was so heavy but that was the last thing on my mind. I just wanted to get him to RV1. He carried his weapon and sipped water as we set off again. It was slow moving but at least we were making progress. We stopped frequently for a quick rest before continuing on. I was trying hard to patrol as normal with the weight of the two Bergen's and supporting Alex.

Finally, after a long, hot and very exhausting march, we approached RV1. I got Alex to lie down while I moved forward and gave the call sign. Les appeared and asked where Alex was. I nodded towards Alex lying on the ground. Knuckles came forward and lifted off the second Bergen. I thought I was going to float away when the weight was taken off my shoulders. Knuckles handed me a water bottle, and as I drank I watched Les help move towards the defense position. I staggered in behind them where I was greeted by Ginge with a, "Fuck me, what happened to you?" I told him Alex took sick, so we had a hellish journey out, but I remained vigilant and ensured that no one had followed us. Ginge nodded before approaching a guy I did not recognize. As they spoke, the other guy glanced at me, before walking towards me. He said, "I will send out a patrol just to make sure there were no followers, you rest up".

"No I want to patrol with them, I know the area".

"As long as you are sure you're up to the task".

As our eight-man patrol left I turned and saw Malcolm tending Alex who had been sick again.

We had webbing only when we patrolled back. We patrolled south, then east, then north, heading up to the river's edge. Our patrol commander was one of the guys from the Special Forces team. As we approached the river we could hear a couple of motorboat engines in the distance, so we lay in defense. The Patrol Commander moved back from his position at the rivers view and told us they were armed men in combat uniform, twelve in total.

"They seem to be having a smoke just now; hopefully they will fuck off soon. Just remember they may not be well trained but weapons are just as dangerous in a fuck-wit's hands as they are in a well-trained fighting patrol, so if they do decide to patrol towards us we will be ready". He pointed to where we were to go in a classic ambush position. "If they move towards us, let them through, we don't want to compromise the operation unless we have to. I will contact our team and RV1 if there are any problems". We moved slowly into position and lay there for what seemed like ages. Then I heard movement to my left-hand side. Thankfully we were well out of sight. We watched the patrol pass by on a nearby path. I could smell cigarette smoke and thought 'these guys are amateurs to be smoking on patrol' but I remembered the warning from the Patrol Commander. I counted ten in the patrol, so two of them must have been left behind to guard the boats. I deduced they were coming back this way as we never heard the boat motors start. After a while our Patrol Commander was on the radio updating RV1. From my position I could make out the river's edge through the undergrowth. Looking to my left it appeared to be a regular sandy beach. Then the sounds of automatic fire began in the distance. I realised there was no way they could have reached RV1 by this time as it was about eight kilometres from here. Down the line passed a whispered message from the Patrol Commander saying that they must have a range here or are just letting off some rounds, we would bug out in five minutes. As we moved from the position we patrolled away from the path, heading west towards the beach. I thought we would probably patrol up near the beach and head south, but I was wrong, the Patrol Commander headed along the river until we were about one kilometre away from the boats. We got into positions so that we could see upriver.

The Patrol Commander whispered, "We will wait here till they are away in their boats or when we have to leave for extraction". I nodded as I heard more automatic gunfire in the distance.

We stayed for a couple of hours until we were told that we should bug out if we were to get back before it became dark and the Heli pickup. We moved South West towards the beach, we were about half a kilometre. We were still in the undergrowth as we headed South. Every so often I got a glance of the beach in the distance. I remember thinking what a lovely place for a holiday, then everything went mad. We heard automatic fire. It was incoming rounds, I was just about to move to the right when I felt something hit my face and a crack, then a noise like someone punching a piece of meat. I went down. My whole face felt numb.

When I got up, I opened my eyes and looked around. My mouth felt strange. I felt with my tongue and there was a space where my front teeth used to be. My mind was racing with thoughts of what had happened. The next thing I knew we were on the move again, so I patrolled on, ignoring the pain in my mouth. We stopped about two kilometres later. There had been no more gun fire. Knuckles came over to me saying, "Fuck me!" in a hushed tone and motioned for the Medic. I looked at him and tried to speak but a weird noise came out of my mouth. He told me to sit down just as the Medic appeared. The Medic looked at my face and said, "Oh, you'll be fine. I've seen worse, you've lost your front teeth an your lip has been split. It's not bleeding too much. Are you ok to move?". I nodded and felt a flap of skin move as I tried to speak. The Patrol Commander came up to see if everything was okay. I couldn't do much but nod. "It must have been a ricochet round that hit you. You'll be fine, just tell the lassies it's a war wound and they will fuck you rotten". He smiled and patted me on the shoulder, "Let's get moving". I got to my feet and we continued to patrol heading for RV1.

When I arrived at RV1 Ginge took one look at me and said, "What the fuck happened to your face?" I couldn't answer, the numbness was wearing off and the pain was raging in my face. Malcolm grabbed me and sat me down looking at the other Medic he said, "You do have morphine, don't you?". The other Medic shrugged and checked his bag. told me he would take my pain away; I closed my eyes and I felt a small stab in my thigh. I looked up and saw a woman standing over me she said, "Is he going to be ok?". Malcolm nodded saying "He will need stitches". I heard knuckles saying, "Aye, and fucking teeth". I could hear the Patrol Commander giving details about the soldiers landing and letting off rounds in every direction saying, "It must have been a ricochet, bad luck really". The other voice asked if we were compromised, "No, he never made a sound. Just took the pain, got up and got on with it". Someone else leaned in and told me the choppers would be here in fifteen minutes. They said they would radio ahead to see if I could get patched up on the American ship. Knuckles butted in, "What do you mean if? If he doesn't get help on the ship it's a long fucking journey to the UK and he a mess!". The guy glared at knuckles, "I know but it's up to the yanks".

The Patrol Commander, who I now knew was Ricky, bent down and offered me a drink from a makeshift straw made from some piece of a plant inserted in a water bottle. He said, "Drink very slowly but try and rinse you mouth out". I tried but it was hard to suck up the water. I managed using the right side of my mouth. The woman stood over me and said, "We will get you sorted, I can assure you of that. What's your name soldier?" I was about to answer when Ricky said, "With all due respect, questions will be answered later. Let's get fluid inside him unless you want me to put in an IV drip". She stood straight and moved back to where she sat before. I looked at Knuckles as he leaned close to my ear and said, "See, you still got it with the lassies. If he hadn't said that she would have tried to shag you". I tried to laugh but nothing moved as my face was starting to swell.

When the choppers arrived they bundled me into one of them along with everyone else. Once we returned I was laid on a stretcher and wheeled away a room with bright light. I heard a voice say, "Relax son, we'll have you back as good as new in no time at all". The last thing I remember was my fatigues being cut off and a sharp prick in the back of my hand then darkness.

Chapter 19

When I awoke my eyes felt swollen but I could see a little. I lifted my arm to touch my face when a voice said, "Hey soldier, you're ok just lie still", I had no idea who it was but I tried to get up but was pushed back down. I grabbed the hand and squeezed. I heard a squeal of pain and it was then I could just make out Ginge and Malcolm. Malcolm told me it was okay so I released my grip on the hand. He said they had 'patched me up', what did they mean by that? My mind was racing, what had happened? How badly was I injured? A deep voice boomed out, "It's better than a patch up! I made a damn good job!". Just then a face appeared in front of me, "Once the swelling goes down your face will be as good as new. Not much scarring, I stitched mostly inside and a running stitch on the outside but unfortunately I had to remove what was left of your front teeth. I'm sure you will have a perfect smile once you visit the dentist". He turned to Ginge, "Let him rest". Malcolm leaned in and I faintly heard him say, "We are leaving in the morning so get some rest". I don't know if he said anything else because I had drifted off into a morphine induced sleep.

The next morning, I had the pleasure of a liquid

breakfast fed through a straw. Later, dressed in a hospital gown, I was wheeled into the shower. I just sat there and let the water splash over me, it was painful at first but what a heavenly feeling. I slowly stood up from the wheelchair and pushed it out of the shower so I could wash myself. I felt slightly dizzy at first but it went soon enough. After a thirty minute shower I towelled myself dry and got dressed in the clothes that were laid out for me. Back in the ward I shook hands with the surgeon and thanked him for all this help.

Malcolm showed me to where the rest were waiting to board the helicopter. There were loads of men dressed in light tan uniforms, one of them asked me how I was feeling. My immediate thought was 'shite', but I told him I was fine . I thanked him very much for all the help and assistance he had given me. He turned to everyone standing there and said, "The United States Navy is glad to be of service to you, you all have a pleasant flight". He waved, smiled then headed away.

When we landed in Nigeria we headed straight onto the plane. The Loadie looked at me, I could see he was about to say something but knuckles stepped up to him shaking his head as if to say, 'don't bother'. I sat there thinking about my face. I started touching the scars but Malcolm, who was sitting next to me, told me to leave it and if I was in pain he had pain killers. I thanked him but declined the offer. I woke just before we landed at Brize Norton, my head was pounding and my face felt like it was on fire. As we were led off the plane I couldn't help but feel glad to be home. I breathed in the fresh air as I walked towards a four tonner when a woman and a man appeared and thanked me. I just nodded as they headed to a waiting car. As I climbed into the truck Knuckles laughed and said, "See? What did I tell you, she wants to shag you. Still got it with the lassies mate", Everyone got a laugh out of it, it really helped to lighten the mood.

I got checked over when I arrived back at the barracks and was told it will heal perfectly except for a little scarring between my lip and nose. The doctor commented on the quality of the surgeons work. The ricochet had caused a gash from my lip right up inside of my nostril. Both front teeth were missing and a third one chipped in half. He said, with normal British Army doctor sense of humour, "You will smile like a bulldog chewing a wasp for the first week or so but we will get you your teeth when you get back from leave". It might seem vain but there was no way I was going home looking like that. When my check up was finished I marched into the battalion headquarters to report for duty but the RSM said, "Get yourself home and up to the farm out of the way. Keep your head down, that's an order". As I headed out of battalion headquarters the Commanding Officer walked in with a few other officers. They all shook my hand as the CO said, "Before you go, I want a word young man".

We headed into the CO's office and the door was shut. "I know it's your leave but once the swelling has gone down you will have to report to London. Some people at a high level have said that you deserve the best so as far as I'm aware you will get new teeth courtesy of her Majesty's Government. A lot better than bog standard false teeth, so I will make sure that you have a return flight from Aberdeen to London. Once the swelling has gone down of course. I have spoken to your Company Commander and assured him that a month's leave would be beneficial to all concerned, I think that's acceptable don't you?" I agreed and thanked him.

I made my way home on the train, sitting reading a book and glancing out of the window from time to time. Every passenger than came on or left the trainstared at my swollen face. In all honesty it did look quite grim.

When I arrived in Aberdeen station my brother was waiting for me. He was through collecting some items for his employer and Mum said he would give me a ride home rather than take the train. He looked shocked when he saw me, "What the fuck happened?". I shook my head dismissing his question, telling him we could talk about it later. There were two policemen standing outside a portacabin in the car park. As we approached my brothers car, they walked over to us enquiring why was my face so swollen, asking if I had been fighting and where was I heading. I showed them my army ID and said we were heading for home, explaining while pointing at my face that it had happened many miles from the UK. They apologised and opened the car door for me. We thanked them and got on our way.

My Mum and my Sister made quite a scene about my face. I explained to them that everything was fine and the swelling would go down in time. I said I was going to hide out at the farm until I could get my teeth fixed, I didn't want anyone else seeing me like this. My mum protested saying I should stay with her so she could look after me but I really just wanted to hide away. I slowly, and carefully, ate the meal she had prepared for me. I saw a tear rolling down her face. I told her everything was okay but she said, "I know, but it was so close it could have been your head!". Trying to lighten the mood my Brother quickly jumped in, "No Mum, nothing will penetrate that thick skull of his!". We all burst out laughing. I leaned towards my Mum and told her not to concentrate on what if, but concentrate on what has happened and that I would be fine.

After a few weeks the swelling had gone down and my face was back to normal, minus my teeth. I had to go to the local hospital to get the stiches removed after ten days. The swelling returned for a few days after they had pulled them out but it wasn't as excessive as before.

My Uncle and Cousin were excellent. They made sure that the drinks cupboard was well stocked as we busied ourselves with the harvest. My Mum and Sister visited often, making meals and fussing around. It was appreciated as it meant that we could stay out in the field longer harvesting knowing that a hot meal was being prepared for us back at the house. I spoke easier now but with no front teeth it was still a bit awkward to eat but it is something I just had to put up with.

Chapter 20

When the time came for me to go to London, my uncle and cousin drove me to the airport. We said our goodbyes as there was a mart sale they were going to afterwards. I had a pint at the bar to wait until I was able to board my flight. I noticed a lot of men coming in and dumping bags in a pile. I had just ordered another pint when the guys started pushing and shouting for more pints. I moved to the end of the bar away from them. The poor barmaid rushed about getting drinks for the crowd. Once they had all been served and it quietened down, she asked if I wanted another. "Oh yes please!" I nodded towards the group of men, "They must be thirsty eh?". She told me they were off the oil rigs and had not had a drink in a couple of weeks, so they come in and get a few down their necks before heading off. As she handed me my pint she said, "That's on the house for saying please, I don't get that a lot in here". I smiled and thanked her; I was about to say something more when I heard some bloke shouting to get more drinks. I finished my pint and headed towards my gate for boarding. I sat in my seat on the flight and began flicking through the on-flight magazine when I heard loud voices and swearing. It was some of the men from the bar, they were on my flight. They sat in front of me and demanded the drinks trolley. The stewardess informed them that they would have to wait until they were airborne.

As the flight progressed, the men in front got worse and worse, becoming louder and more animated. I sat there trying not to listen but the language was getting to me, there were children on the flight and their behavior was unacceptable. They had been asked to be quite a several times by the air crew and to calm it down, but they ignored them and carried on. I leaned forward and whispered to the one in front of me, "Listen mate, they have asked you nicely to stop shouting and swearing. Now I'm asking you to keep it down". He turned in his seat and I just stared at him. He must have seen the mess of my face and decided not to push it. "Ok pal, it's just a bit of fun". I smiled and sat back. Later the stewardess came up and said, "Thank you". I showed her my ID card and told her it wasn't a problem, she smiled and patted my shoulder mouthing 'thanks so much' again. As we were disembarking the aircraft the stewardess smiled and thanked me again. I told her I hadn't done anything, just asked them to be quite. I gave her a slight smile and headed off the plane. I chuckled to myself thinking about the look on her face if I had smiled properly, with a gaping hole where my teeth should be.

I was met at the airport by a duty driver. I showed him my ID and we walked to a car he had waiting. He asked if I smoked, when I said I did he said "Thank fuck. We can have a smoke here, but you're not allowed to smoke in the car". He asked if I knew where I was going, I replied "A dentist". He laughed, "A dentist eh? No expense spared where you are going my man. What happened anyway?". Straight away I was on the defensive and adopted the need-to-know strategy. I shook my head and got into the car. After a good while he told me we had arrived, I looked up and saw the street sign, 'Harley Street'. When he stopped, he told me the clinic would contact him when I was finished and I was to be put up in a hotel for a few days. I thanked him as I left the car. When I was walking up the steps, I remember thinking that the place looked amazing. When I entered, I was immediately made to feel very welcome and was offered coffee or a cold drink. I met with the dentist and after a lot of questions, he finally said, "Well, I think a bridge will be perfect". He explained what it entailed and how long it would take and that they would work around the clock to get my smile back.

He started his work and a couple of hours later I walked out into the fresh air and the car was waiting for me. I jumped in the car and we headed towards the hotel. My driver said, "I will pick you up at 09.30 hours ok?". I looked at him surprised, "Hey, I have my orders". I thanked him and headed into the hotel.

After showing my ID card at reception I was handed a key and told everything was paid for including the minibar and would if I wanted to make a dinner reservation for that night. I smiled, the desk clerk stared at me with a look of shock, I had forgotten the mess my face must have I been. I just said "What do you think mate?". He awkwardly smiled and informed of the excellent room service menu. I headed up to my room. As I only had a small bag I decided to carry it myself, much to the disgust of the porter. I opened the door to my room; it was a huge suite. I thought to myself I should lose my teeth more often. My head was starting to bang with the work the dentist carried out, so in true British soldier fashion, I opened the minibar and looked in awe at the number of miniatures saying, "Right, where do I start".

The next morning I headed down for breakfast. When I walked into the dining room the porter at the door said, "Room number Sir?", I showed my key as he looked me up and down with a look of mild disgust on his face. I don't think he approved of jeans, t-shirt and a leather jacket, but after I beamed a big grin he turned on his heel and said, "Enjoy your breakfast Sir", I sniggered thinking this smile of mine works.

I was picked up and taken back to the dentist again. Just before I got out of the car the driver, who I'd got to know as Tom said, "Is it ok if I meet you in civvies after?". I looked at him confused, he explained he had been told to show me the sights. I joked, "Don't you have a Sister that can do that?". He just laughed and told me, "There's nothing I can't get you in London, but I have been instructed to show you museums, theatres and whatever you want to do. It's all paid by the HM Government". He showed me his Access credit card and said with a smile, "I know lots of ladies that take this card also". I laughed telling him I would manage the lassies myself.

After a few hours in the dentist chair and having a set of makeshift dentures in place, the thought of seeing the sights of London really appealed to me. As I walked out Tom was standing waiting, no car in sight. I asked where the car was, and he said it is easier to get around London by tube. "Fancy a pint first mate?" he asked. What a stupid question to ask me.

We were on our third pint and laughing like mad at Toms stories when I said to him, "I know a lassie that's based in Wellington barracks". He laughed and told me he knew a lot of lassies in Wellington Barracks. "No, honestly. I have her phone numbers at home, I forgot them in the last-minute rush". "What's her name then?", he said. I told him. He stood up and handed me some cash "You get them in mate". I was about to protest saying it was my round when he cut me short saying, "Not down here you don't, it's all on expenses mate". He went to the pay phone and I went to the bar. As I headed back to the table Tom returned and said, "Your lassie is at work, but I have asked one of the lads to pass on a message. If she is not available to call here in the next hour or so, but if she's available, then to meet us at the lamb and flag in Covent Garden later. I have reserved a table, they don't normally take reservations, but I am good customer. I mentioned to bring a friend, fours company but threes a crowd" he smiled "Hey come on, orders are orders. Drink up mate well have a good time". I told him I needed some new clothes he just smiled, waved the credit card saying, "No problem, let's go". I told him I could buy my own, but he wouldn't hear of it.

While travelling on the tube, I was amazed at how easy it was to get from one location of our capital to another with no great difficulty. Tom explained how it all worked, the different lines and the connection. I was amazed. We went to the Natural History Museum, it was amazing. I was in awe of this place. we walked around for a few hours then headed to get my new clothes. Later Tom left me at the hotel and said he would meet me at the bar around the corner at 19:30 hours.

I had a couple of miniatures from the bar and an hour's sleep then got ready for the night ahead. I met Tom at the bar around the corner and we had a pint before heading to the tube station. We reached Bond Street and walked a few minutes to the pub. As we walked in the barman shouted, "Hey Tommy, your guests are already here". My heart gave a little flutter as I walked around the bar and saw the two women sitting at the table. Even though she had her back to me I recognized Kim straight away. I put my hand on her shoulder and said hi, she smiled and asked, "What happened to you?". I said, "I'll tell you later ok".

Tom introduced himself to Kim and the other woman, who was a good-looking girl named Alma.

Tom asked if we wanted more drinks and asked Alma to help him at the bar. I sat next to Kim and she asked again what happened. I glanced around and said, "Its ok, but I was on an operation and a ricochet round hit my mouth".

She went to speak again but hesitated. She took a deep breath and said, "Thank you for the invite. I wanted to see you again to tell you I have met someone else". I smiled and told her I was happy for her, I genuinely was. "He is a Guardsman and things feel so right between us". I told her it was okay and she didn't have to explain it to me. She inclined her head, smiled and said, "Thanks. We had a lot of fun didn't we? But that's all it was, fun. You are so focused on everything army there really wasn't enough room for me was there?". I smiled but secretly I had to agree, Hey let's have a few drinks and a laugh. Then when it's time to go I will wish you all the best for the future. He's a lucky man. As long as you are happy, so am I". "I think I need a large white wine", she said. I winked at her as I stood, I am sure she could tell how gutted I was, my heart sank as I forced a smile. "I'll go see where the others are and chase them up on our drinks". I touched her shoulder and she grabbed my hand, asking me how the nightmares were. I said, "Aye, fine. Never had once since", she held my hand and looked into my eyes, "you're lying I can tell". I said nothing, I was not about to tell her that I wake most nights with nightmares drenched in sweat.

We had a couple of drinks and a lot of laughs. Tom and Alma were really hitting it off. When we left the bar, Tom said he and Alma were going to a few other places he knew and asked if we wanted to come. We both declined. I looked at Kim and said, "I am really happy, for you if you ever need anything..." but in mid-sentence she place a finger over my lips as I saw her eyes tear up. She shook her head then leaned in and kissed my cheek. She then hugged me whispering, "I will always love you in one way or another". She let go and walked away. I told her to look after herself but she never turned around, she just headed towards a taxi. Alma came up and said for me to go with them. I sighed and tried to swallow the lump that was forming in my throat. As I watched the taxi drive away Alma said again to go with them. I told her, "No, thank you. Two's company but three's a crowd". I winked at Alma she gave me a hug and whispered, "You know Kim always talked about you all the time. Even when she met Steven, he is a nice guy you know. She told me everything about you. I think there will always be a special place in her heart for you". She leaned in kissed me on the cheek then Tom and her headed away arm in arm. I watched until they turned the corner then lit a smoke and wondered what I was going to do. I was devastated. The lump in my throat was huge ,I tried to swallow it away but I could still see Kim's face. I finished my cigarette, looked around and decided, "Fuck me. I'm in London, lets party", so I headed back inside the pub.

The following morning my head was banging. The dentist asked, "Had a nice night did you? I would like you to use mouthwash first please or I will be as pissed as you were last night judging by your breath". I apologized but he insisted it wasn't a problem. I sat inthe dentist chair as he worked and all I could think about was Kim. Before I knew it the dentist was finished for the day, he explained that I needed just one final session then we would be done. While I waiting for my pick up from Tom I sat in reception and all I could think about was Kim. I must have been staring at the ceiling for a while when a female voice asked if I would like a coffee and handed me a tissue. I realised that I had tears running down my cheek. She asked if I was okay, I told her it was just my teeth hurting from the procedure. "I'm sure they are but most people don't call them Kim", she said sympathetically. I apologised "I was lost in thought there thinking out loud about a lassie".

Tom was waiting for me at the door. He apologised for leaving me last night but saying, "Alma is gorgeous, and I have a date with her on Saturday". I told him it was fine and we headed to the bar. Tom asked how Kim was. I explained what had happened and that she was seeing someone else but I was happy for her. Trying to get away from the subject I asked what our plan was for that day and Tom said "Anything you want".

After another day and night in London drinking, seeing the sights and partying till the wee hours I was back in the dentist chair, using mouth wash again, before he fitted the bridge. When we were all done I thanked him. As I shook his hand he asked, "Where will I send the bill?" I looked in shock but he grinned, "Its ok, it's my little joke. It's all taken care of". I let out a sigh of relief. I soon forgot about it as I was so happy with my new teeth.

As usual Tom was waiting for me. He told me, "Your flight back up to Aberdeen is at 18.00hours so we will have to head towards the airport around 14.00 hours. Get a few in the airport eh? What do you fancy doing now?" I suggested we go out and get some proper food, I had mostly been living on fast food since I had arrived in London. Tom suggested we try the Captain Kidd in Wapping, saying it had excellent food. He wasn't wrong. I was some real wholesome homemade pub grub.

When we arrived at the airport I thanked Tom for his hospitality and shook his hand. He gave me his contact details if I was ever in London again and needed tickets or anything to give him a call. I wished him well with Alma. He said, with a twinkle in his eye, "She is stunning isn't she?". I told him to treat her well, we said our final goodbyes and I headed off to Departures.

When I arrived back in Aberdeen I was collected by my Cousin and driven back to the farm. I had twelve days of my leave left and I was going to make the most of it.

Chapter 21

When I returned to the battalion, I started my training again. Pushing myself even further and harder than I had before. Boxing, judo, even murder ball when anyone was playing. I often thought of Kim hoping that she really was happy.

One morning, as I prepared to join the snipers at the range, I was summoned to the CO's office. I was told I was needed over the waters, there weren't many details but I had been asked for personally. I signed for my weapons and went to get myself ready. Ginge entered my room and helped himself to my cigarettes. He was now a Colour Sergeant. He said, "Briefing at 09.15 am, you're in charge on this one mate".

In the briefing room there was myself, Alex and two others. Brian who was an excellent bloke and of course my old mate Knuckles. He mouthed 'wanker' to me when I walked through the door. I replied, "Hey, everyone likes a wank!" He laughed so much he almost fell off the chair he was swinging on. He was such a great character. Before we went to Cameroon, he had asked me to be Best Man at his wedding. He told me he asked everyone one else in the Battalion and even the engineers in the nearby barracks as well as a tramp he met by the canal but they all refused so he thought he would ask me as a last resort. I accepted of course but said that as I was the last resort, I would do it for Queen and Country. I hoped at the time he would settle down as his partner Alice was a really nice girl. She was very quiet but trying to get a word in edgeways with Knuckles was impossible at the best of times so no wonder she was quiet.

Ginge, a Sergeant Major, and another officer I didn't know Entered. Ginge started by saying, "Ok you are going over the water. You will be tasked to take over an OP. Information has come through that the Provos have been having fake funerals and there are arms and munitions in the coffins. They are only buried a foot deep. Clever really eh? You are all on rations as of now, so no curries and kebabs. You will leave tomorrow at 21.00 hours, but you are going out into the field in three hours to get rid of any odours, aftershave and deodorant etc. So get your shit together. You will be briefed when you land in Ireland". He looked at me and said, "you are in charge till you are picked up and briefed over the water, any questions?" No one said anything.

That night we were out in the woods, about eleven

miles from the barracks, in our bashers, non-tactical, so we lit a fire, ate rations and talked. We were probably sent out there to make sure we had no communication with anyone. Knuckles produced a bottle of whisky. I shook my head and said I thought that was a bad idea, but he said, "Fuck off we are not airborne till 21.00 hours tomorrow we can gonk (sleep) most of the day". I told him we would have to get a grip, but he still poured some into his black mug and passed the bottle round. I looked at my watch it was only 18.30 hours. Alex looked at me and said he would drink if I did, but if I didn't he wouldn't. I told him I wasn't drinking because I needed to stay focused.

Brian said he did not want any either. Before Knuckles took a sip of his whisky, he changed his mind and poured it out instead, saying, "Ok, no problem. I will leave the bottle here, someone will find it". I said, "Thanks mate. Right, get the fire out. Last cigarettes at 10.00 hours tomorrow, we will have three hour stags all night and day to get ourselves into a routine, ok?". Everyone nodded.

We were picked up by helicopter and transported over the water where we were briefed and told that we would be deploying around 02.00 hours. We were to be dropped off by quick reaction force vehicles in Belfast at the bottom of the Falls Road, to make our way North through the fields and into the cemetery. "You are to make your way to here", the officer told us pointing to a large blown-up photograph of what looked like a family grave. It looked as if it was overgrown with bushes and there was an iron fencearound it.

"Your task is to look over these two graves", he said pointing to another large photograph, "and report everything, ok chaps?" He continued, "We have requested some assistance from the green army (normal infantry Battalion) as we don't have the resources to carry out long watches at this OP. Stay alert, we will have radio comms at all times. If these P.I.R.A guys smell a rat, they are likely to try and fuck you up so get in and get settled. We have QRF standing by if it goes noisy. OP guys there already have seen nothing of any interest so far" he told us. Alex asked how long we are there for and the Officer replied, "We will let you know, any other questions?".

We were dropped off and made our way through the fields in darkness. When we reached the cemetery wall we climbed over and waited. As briefed, we were met by one of the guys from the OP. I watched him moving in through the night vision scope. I whispered our password and he replied with his. Then he lead us to the family grave area where we relieved the watch already in the OP. Once we were settled, I check to make sure we all had enough cover. We had a corner each, so we had all round defence and good views through the thick bushes. We had sub machine guns, 9 mm browning pistols, radio comms with throat mics and two sets of night vision scopes. I whispered, "Right, two hour watches. Alex facing south with his night vision scope, me facing north, we are on stag first and we will continue with that".

We were on our third day. All we had seen were people coming and going as normal, paying their respect to their loved ones, but as instructed we reported everything. In the distance we could see two four-man army patrols moving through the graveyard, it gave us a bit of reassurance that we were not alone. We ate in the morning just after sunup, if we were on stag, then again just before sundown. I thought that most people coming to tend graves will do it in the middle of the day. There was a funeral procession, but it was a good bit away,so no one came anywhere near the graves we were watching.

That night Knuckles was on stag. At 00.35 hours I felt him slowly touch my arm to waken me but I was already awake as I had heard something too. I stared into the darkness, I thought my ears were playing tricks but then I heard it again. Every so often it was like someone walking on a gravel road then it would go silent. I turned slowly as I felt Knuckles handing me the night scope. Ilifted it very slowly to my eye and looked through. I saw four men walking towards us. They stopped, turned around stood still with their backs to us, they were about ten feet away. I knew my sub machine gun was ready and my pistol was now in my hand, I was breathing out of a slightly open mouth. I dared not move as I felt something sticking into me. I had been lying on it and it was making my hip ache, but I couldn't move. As we watched, another two men appeared. I could see one had a weapon, maybe they were all armed, but I couldn't tell for sure. The weapon I could make out had a curved magazine, it was an AK47 Kalashnikov, a real serious weapon. Just then I heard someone whisper in a deep gruff Belfast voice, "Have a look around lads, let's make sure we are alone. These British bastards are a sneaky lot. Once it's clear we will meet back here". I watched as one of them turned and walked towards us, he passed by my side. I lay completely still until he had passed. Seconds later I heard a zip being pulled down and heard liquid splashing against the small wall that surrounded us. I felt a warm sensation on my lower leg, I thought 'For fuck sake', but Brian would be getting the worst of it. I heard the zip being pulled back up then again, silence.

I kept the scope on the man who stood in front of me as he walked right up to our position. He was so close that I could see his trousers and shoes about two feet in front of me. I heard a rustling and then a lighter barrel being spun on the flint and smelled cigarette smoke. He walked away and stood back in front of the graves. I could still smell cigarette smoke but I could not see the glow so he must have been having a tactical smoke, drawing on his cigarette under his jacket and keeping the cigarette cupped in both hands so as to not be seen from a distance. I then heard footsteps by my head, a weapon being cocked and in a hundredth of a second, I thought 'we are fucked, oh shite is this it, oh fuck sake'. I was about to spin around and let off a couple of rapid rounds when I heard a whispered Belfast voice saying, "What the fuck are you doing Seamus?"

The other man standing beside me replied, "Sorry. I forgot to cock this fucker", "You better get that sorted out. What if the Brits were here? What then? You pull your socks up or you're off the team, do you understand?". He sheepishly replied "Sorry, it won't happen again".

We lay there for what seemed ages until the rest of the Irish men came back. The chap in the front of me, who seemed to be the one in charge, said, "Seamus here forgot to make his weapon ready. Mick, sort that fucker out when we get back, we can't have that now. A little more training I would say".There were sniggers as they started to dig up the grave. I knew I had to pass on a message but I couldn't take the chance of whispering so I used the switch on my radio and started using Morse code, hoping that I was not going to make a noise.

I should have, as a professional soldier, sent a Morse Code message saying we have contact, but due to nerves or panic I sent out

- .... . -.-- / .- -.. . / .... . .-. .

(They are here) I kept on repeating and repeating with intervals of thirty seconds till finally after a good five minutes I got what I was after

.- .-.. .-.. / -.-. --- .--. .. . -.. / .-- .- .. - / --- .. - -

(All copied wait out). They were almost finished

digging when I heard over and over in the earpiece

(Can you identify?). I quickly pressed the button with a reply,

-. ---

(No.). I was watching through the scope when I noticed the battery was on its way out, we had spare but there was no way to silently change it. I could just make them out lifting the coffin from the grave and opening it. I looked like an RPG7 they had pulled out. I thought 'where are the troops'? but there were no troops to be seen. They replaced the coffin and put the turf back. My scope was on its last legs as I willed the battery to last but sadly the battery didn't last. We lay there for ages after they disappeared into the dark night with the RPG 7. I slowly turned my hip off the piece of stone or root that I had been laying on. I clenched my teeth as the blood followed back to the area, what a relief.   By the time daybreak came we were all exhausted. I whispered for the men to get some shut eye as Alex and I would continue the watch.

That night I received a message through the earpiece. "Bug out at 23.30 hours waiting at Drop Off Point". I looked at my watch saw it was 22.32 hours. I thought for a moment about how long it would take us from our point to the DOP, then looked through the bushes and realised it was a very dark night, the moon overcast. I thought we should move now so I passed along the message to be ready to leave in five minutes.

Five minutes later we were ready. I went out first; I was as stiff as fuck and could hardly move but I got through the overgrown bushes. I went over the iron fence and lay down to wait until we all got out. About ten minutes later we crawled off until we were well away from the area and then patrolled to the wall. I whispered back to the guys, "Right, over the wall we will patrol halfway through the field and wait for pick up". We climbed the wall and got into all round defence. I looked at my watch five minutes to go till 23.30 hours. We saw the vehicles coming towards the drop off point; two Land Rover's and two armoured pigs. We waited for them to slow down and stop. Then we made our way in the dark towards them. it was all very clever; they deployed men from both pigs who ran into the field shouting, "Stop! Halt! British Army!". Then after a brief password whispered between us, we ran back with them as if we were a part of the team that ran into the field. To provide cover to the pick up and cause confusion to any onlookers we shouted, "It's too fucking dark we can't see where he went!"

I sat in the pig with Knuckles and some other guys. Alex and Brian were in another. We headed for a camp called 'White Rock'. We unloaded our weapons when we disembarked and then made our way towards the debrief.

We were commended by the officer, he said, "Well-done lads that was a good spot". I said, "With all due respect Sir, what happened?". He told me the answer to that question was 'Need To Know', all we needed to know is that it was a positive and well preformed operation, "I want all note books and any other material you have handed over, well done again men". Once he had collected our notebooks he left. A Sergeant entered and said to us, "The cook house is always open, get some egg banjos inside you. You will be leaving in one hour". I asked, "Not even a shower?"

"No, you shower back in the UK. They want you out of here ASAP. Get some scoff lads" he said as he shrugged his shoulders and walked out.

Chapter 22

We were transported back to mainland UK and headed to the barracks; I thinkwe slept most of the way. Once back at the accommodation lines, the first thing I did was shower. What an amazing feeling! I stood there for ages with the clean warm water splashing on my skin. When I eventually went back to my room I lay on my bed and was out for the count in no time.

I was standing on a road holding my rifle as I watched a vehicle approach. I tried to move but I was frozen in place. I could hear a banging sound. I saw a man on a vehicle firing his machine gun towards me. The vehicle was almost on top of me! I was going to be hit by the oncoming vehicle. When I saw the man firing his gun at me, he had a menacing grin on his face. I was standing there waiting for the vehicle to run over me when I felt a hand on my sleeve pulling me to the side. I felt the vehicle rush past me. I turned to see who had pulled me away and realised it was the girl covered in tar. I tried to get away, but she pulled me back. I looked round and saw the vehicle coming back for me. I could hear the machine gun fire again. Then I heard someone shout for me. I shot up in bed to realise that someone was at the door shouting my name. I shouted back "Aye, what the fuck is it?". I was covered in sweat and out of breath. I opened the door and the RSM was standing there. I said, "Sorry Sir, I didn't know it was you". He asked if I was okay, I just nodded. He told me I would be debriefed at the CO's office in one hour. I thought it strange that the RSM would come down to the accommodation, and then I remembered that most of the battalion was on exercise for a few days.

I got ready and headed to Battalion Headquarters. I saw Knuckles and Brian standing with Alex. As I approached Knuckles asked if I was okay because I didn't look well. I told him I was fine. Just at that the RSM called my name I turned and marched into his office. He was standing at the window. He turned and asked, "Are you ok?"

I replied, "Yes Sir, fine. Still a bit knackered". At this he pointed to his head and asked, "But are you ok in here?". "Yes Sir, still a bit tired", he nodded, "If you have any problems tell me ok?". I'm sure he could tell I was lying.

I re-joined the others and we were marched into the CO's office. Standing beside the CO was the officer that briefed and debriefed us in Ireland. The CO said, "Well-done gentleman, that was a good effort over the water". He turned in his chair as the other officer started speaking, "Well done indeed", nodding his head, "It was an operation that was well executed, comms were excellent etc. On the whole the operation was excellent". He looked straight at me and said, "You did well with the Morse code, we knew they would be close, when we realised that it was Morse coming through, we thought we would keep Morse going in replies. As you know, when transmitting on certain radios, you can get an unwelcomed very high pitch squeak, so we were not going risk it". I thought for a moment, 'I had never experienced a high pitch sound before with a radio'. He continued, "I am sure I don't need to tell you that it's not to be mentioned ok chaps? Mums the word and all that, but it was a good effort all round. Any questions chaps?" We were all silent, the CO thanked him, and he left the room. We all stood still, the silence went on for a few minutes, the CO breathed deeply and said, "well that's that lads, as you heard you don't mention it out of this room ok?". He sat back in his chair "You are all on a weeks leave starting now". I said, "Thank you Sir but I am not long after....". He raised his hand and stopped me mid- sentence, raising his voice "You are ALL on leave for a week, no exceptions".

Later, as we all sat in my room, Knuckles said, "That was fucking strange eh? Allthat for fuck all". Alex replied, "You don't know if they were followed or what happened, so shut the fuck up, we got a week off out of it". Knuckles shouted, "Don't fucking speak to me like that you little cunt!". Tempers were flaring so I stepped between them "Come on lads calm down, we are all still fucked after that carry on, so calm down and let's get a brew on". They lookedat each other, laughed and shook hands, they both apologised but you could still cut the tension in the room with a knife.

After a few drinks at the local bar I was still knackered. I decided to head back and leave them to it. When I stepped outside the rain had just started, typical. After I was past the gate and heading for my room I heard running footsteps behind me, I turned it was one of the guys from the guard. "TARA wants to see you. He's in the guard room", I straightened myself back on the walk to the guard room.

"Had a few then have we?", he said. I told him, one or two. "Fine, follow me",he replied. He nodded to the Guard Commander who instantly picked up the phone.

We walked outside, I immediately fell into step

with him. We headed past battalion headquarters and made our way toward the gym. As we walked inside the huge empty gym hall he turned and said, "You ok?". I said, "Yes Sir". He shouted, "Are you sure?". I shouted back, "Yes Sir!". He asked if I had any questions, I told him I had none for him. He told me he knew I was over the water and that he had a pretty good idea why and what happened. He said, "But you can't figure it out? What it was all about eh?". I nodded and replied, "Yes Sir it all is a bit strange Sir". Just at that door burst open, the Commanding Officer walked in, I sprang to my feet and he shouted, "As you were". I sat back down as he walked up to me and simply asked, "Questions?". I looked at the RSM and back to the CO then said, "We did all that for fuck all Sir, we had them, but no one reacted and they got away Sir", I decided not to say too much. "In this army son, we are all tasked with things to do and no questions asked".

He continued to talk; he went step by step through the whole operation. I was surprised at the detail he knew. To finish he said, "You keep thinking what if they use that RPG on the soldiers that are there now aren't you?". I nodded saying, "Yes Sir we had them, but no one moved on it. We had time to arrest them all, fuck me we could have taken them out ourselves". He replied, "I'm sure you could have, but that was not the operation. It goes a bit deeper than that and the people that call the shots are aware of the situation. If they did not react then there was a good reason. You understand it is well above our level of 'need to know' ok?". I replied, 'Yes Sir' and he nodded as he turned to walk away, he said, "Well-done that was exceptional soldiering and good control on your part".

When he was gone the RSM looked at me and simply said, "Ok now?" I just nodded as he walked away. I was left there sitting, alone with my thoughts.

Chapter 23

When our week of leave was over, I got straight back into training and really went for it. I didn't go out at weekends; I trained all week carrying on through Saturday and Sunday starting again on Monday. Pushing and pushing.

I was sparring in the gym one afternoon, I don't know what happened really, I staggered as I stepped back into the ropes. My opponent landed a few good punches to my body and face. I realised that I was stuck in the corner, I tried to move but he was good, then it all went into slow motion, I stood straight, then I lowered and weaved, as I straightened again I managed a jab which caused him to back off. Once I had room I went for it, I just wanted to annihilate my opponent. Next thing I know I heard shouts and was being pulled away. Bud, a good friend of mine, was shouting "What the fuck are you doing mate?". I looked at him then turned around I saw my opponent on the floor out cold. I realised what had happened and asked for my gloves to be removed and went to help him. Bud was at my shoulder, saying, "Fuck mate, that's not sparring that's destruction". I told him to shut up as I helped my opponent up, the others had stopped training around us and were standing staring, I shouted at them to call a medic.

Later as I came out of the shower a Colour Sergeant was standing waiting, he asked if I was ok, I nodded and said, "How's..." but I was stopped mid- sentence. "He will be fine, badly bruised and may have a fractured eye socket, but ok". When we got back to my room he said, "That's not sparring mate". I said, "Well he didn't hold back while I was against the ropes did he?" he carried on saying "I heard that, but you will be in front of the RSM". I asked when and he told me "Now".

I got dressed and headed towards Battalion headquarters. I waited outside the RSM's office until he shouted me in. The RSM gave me a dressing down over the sparring incident. My opponent was going to be out of action for a few weeks while he recovered. "It's time you were posted I think". I protested, "No thank you Sir, I'm fine here". He said, "It's a promotion to full Corporal if you pass the course, then you will be at the training barracks in Aberdeen. it's a two year posting if you accept, it's a good move really". I thanked him but as I walked out, I knew there was something 'not for me' about it.

That night I went to the corporal's mess and had a

few pints with some of my friends. They were congratulating me on getting 'an easy number'. I laughed and told them I had to pass the course first. They reckoned it would be a breeze but something about it still didn't feel right to me.

I never slept that night thinking about being a training corporal. I would have every other weekend off, I could go to the farm, it was more money, I could teach young trainee soldiers my skills and it would be very good for my career. But every time I thought of a positive there were a plenty of negatives. No range work, no work with the sniper team, no battalion exercises, I loved being out in the field. I sat up in bed and decided to go for a run, it was about 3am. I got dressed and headed out. The weather was awful, cold, raining and windy but I loved it. I was reminded of a saying my Dad used every now and again, when things got tough or hard on the farm, 'Success is not final, Failure is not fatal. It is having the courage to continue that counts', but when you're a little boy standing in the middle of a field, frozen stiff trying to lift turnips with fingers you can't feel, it didn't mean anything. It was not until later in life that I realised it was one of Winston Churchill's quotes and it means a lot to me. I still live my life to this quote.

I pushed and pushed still doing press ups and sit ups every mile or so, I had run ten miles by the time I went back through the barrack gates. The run had given me time to work through the doubts in my head. Training Corporal was the right move. It had to be.

Once through the gates I saw a man jogging towards me in running kit, it was one of the officers, I didn't know him well, but I knew from others he was a good guy, a Lieutenant but due a Captain's promotion. He stopped and said, "Morning", I said, "Morning Sir". He asked where I had run so I told him the route, he nodded and said, "You must have been up early", I replied that I was as I couldn't sleep. "Are you training for something special?" I replied, "No just clearing my head, been offered a promotion Sir", He asked what was there to think about, I shook my head telling him that I wasn't sure if it was the right move for me. "It's for a Training Corporal at Aberdeen, I am more of a field man. Really not too big on marching and all the shit that goes with it". He replied, "I know what you mean", he nodded and headed off. I told him to have a nice run.

That afternoon we were practicing at the 30 metre range. Having cleaned our submachine guns, I marched them to the armoury to hand them in.

When I had dismissed them the officer, I had met that morning, came out of the Company Commander's office, he nodded at me and asked if he could have a word. I saluted and said, "Yes Sir", He said, "If you are training tomorrow morning, I will run with you if that's ok?. "I leave at 03.30 hours; I will meet you at the guard room". I smiled and said, "If you're late Sir you will just have to catch up". He laughed and replied, "The same to you Corporal".

The next morning the weather had not improved any. I was waiting at the guard room and was about to set off when I saw him in the distance running towards the guard room. I looked at my watch 03.30 hours. I headed away and told the guard on duty to tell him to catch up. He chuckled and said "Fuck off, tell him yourself!", I laughed. I had run about eighty yards when the officer caught up with me, "You weren't kidding were you about being on time", I replied, "If you're one minute late in battle it could make all the difference Sir". We kept up a good pace, every mile we stopped did sit ups, press ups then headed off again. After about eight miles we decided to forget the sit-ups and press-ups and just run, opening up into a much faster pace. We stopped once we had reached the guard room again. The Corporal asked if I did this every morning. I told him I did, it was a lie but he wasn't to know. "Ok see you tomorrow morning then" he said. I replied, "Yes Sir". "First name terms when we are training eh soldier"? he smiled and walked away.

One morning when we stopped to press-ups he asked, "What are you training for?" I told him I was just trying to push myself further, I would probably have a beer gut when I was at the Aberdeen barracks. He laughed saying, "So, you're going are you?" I came back up from a held press-up position and said, "That's all there is on offer at the moment, what are you training for then?"

His reply took me off guard, "I have been thinking about doing selection in January, at Hereford". We started running again but after about twenty yards I stopped. It suddenly dawned on me what he meant, SAS selection. He stopped too and asked what was up. I just stood there staring at my feet, my mind was a racing. "How do I go for selection?" I asked, he said, "you fancy that do you? Its fucking brutal". We walked back to the camp chatting about the selection course, he told me all about a friend of his that had tried it twice but didn't make it. I was lost in my own thoughts but then I realised it's only June, selection is in January, we had time to prepare. We agreed to meet in the gym at 18.00

hours, we were going to start circuit training, but as we both had other duties, we agreed to work out a training schedule so we could train most days. We shook hands in agreement.

Chapter 24

First thing I did that day was report to the RSM to inform him that I would not be taking the posting in Aberdeen and that I was training for selection. He advised me that if I turned it down it would go on my record that I refused a posting. "I am honoured that I was offered the posting but if I try for selection and it's not for me then I will have to start again and build up the respect of yourself and others to get promotion again". "Do you realise what you are going for? It's brutal and a whole new ball game to what you are used to", I nodded and he continued, "Right, after you have been training for a month report to my house on the Saturday night". He said pushing a piece of paper over the desk with a date written on it. I will give you a pass to get into the married quarters and take the officer with you ok". I thanked him asking "What's all this about sir?" He said, "If you are training every day you will burn yourself out, take the night off and come down for a few drinks. I have a friend that I think you would be interested to talk to", he nodded and said, "Carry on".

My training buddy and I trained hard, running ten miles most mornings, unless we had other duties. After the first two weeks we introduced weight into our bergens, I wanted to get my fitness up to a peak before starting to carry weight. It was better when we started to carry bergens and in full army kit, we had run all those miles at speed to build up our fitness now we were building stamina. That's what we needed, pure stamina. We trained through all kinds of weather. After we finished at night, we started circuit training. We had all our other duties as normal during the day, so we trained early morning and night. I ate constantly. I needed fuel all the time, but now I ate for what I got out of the food, not because it tasted good, so many eggs and so much porridge, it's what we needed to keep going.

One evening after boxing training I decided to phone my Mum, she complained that she had not heard from me for a long time, I apologised and explained that I was training hard just now. She kept asking if I was ok, I told her I was fine I just had a few blisters. "You need to harden the skin on your feet. Go down to the chemist and get surgical spirits, that will tighten up your skin". I knew she had an excellent medical mind but I asked how she knew that. "Your Dad always told me that when he was in Cyprus, blisters were a problem for him too, so he was told to use surgical spirits and it worked for him", I thanked her for the advice and said that

I would have to go. In true mother fashion, she asked when I was coming home as she would like to see me, also my brother was not doing so well he was struggling with money. The company he worked for was paying him now and then, but he could not manage it on his trainee wage, it was not his fault. He needed books for study and he had to live in an almost derelict house. "When you come home will you go up and see him please?". I promised I would, I felt really bad, but I had to go.

We met up at 03.30 hours next morning and we were off. We were heading up the hills, it was a harder going but we encouraged each other. When we finished the officer asked what I was doing for the rest of the Friday as it was a day off for the whole battalion. I told him I had to go into town to sort out some money things, but I would meet up with him in the gym around 16.00 hours. "Can we do it a bit earlier as there is a bit of a knees up in the mess later on this afternoon", he said. I nodded 13.00 hours it was. I didn't like breaking our routine, but I suppose he had things to do. I reminded him that it was only a week until we were invited to the RSM's house. He nodded.

Later that morning I went into town to the bank and asked to speak to the manager. He sat me down and I explained to him I needed a banker's draft cheque sent to my brother as soon as possible for £1000. He queried what it was for as it was a significant amount of money. I told him it was none of his business, just to get it done as quickly as possible. I stopped at the door on the way out and asked when he will receive the cheque, he said, "When I have time". I shook my head and said, "Fine, thanks for your time". As I passed the pay clerk asked, "You ok? You look annoyed", I told her about the bank draft and the managers attitude. "Leave it to me, I'll sort it out. He will have the cheque in his hand by Tuesday. Tell him it's as good as cash and he will be able to cash it that day". I thanked her and left the bank thinking that will help big Brother for a while.

Chapter 25

We trained hard all the next week getting faster and stronger, making good timings on our routes, we were always sweating buckets by the time we finished but I loved it. I felt my fitness was at a new level it really felt great.

The Saturday night came, we met at the gate all dressed in smart civvies it all felt very unusual. "I have asked the duty driver to drop us off", he said, my reply was "For fuck sake everyone and their aunty will know we were at the RSM for drinks". He told me he would have a word so no one would know, but I refused saying we should be dropped off a street away and walk the rest, he agreed.

The RSM met us at the door and shook our hands, in the hall he said, "First name terms in my house tonight gentlemen ok". I nodded. "Right let's get a drink shall we", he said heading into the lounge.

I glanced at the RSM he nodded saying, "I tried for selection when I was a young eager lad like you, but I only lasted to week six, I take pride in that I passed test week but it was fucking brutal gents, fucking brutal". Tall man started to nod; you could tell he was lost in thought. He drank his gin down in one swallow and the RSM refilled our glasses.

Tall guy continued, "They will increase weights so you build your base fitness up to a good level, the first four weeks gentlemen are grueling so train hard but you must, must, get to Wales and try the fan dance". I looked at him, 'what the fuck is the fan dance'? He laughed and said, "The fan dance is the nickname the boys from Hereford have given to the hill called Pen y Fan, a beautiful, majestic mountain but a real sadistic bitch that takes no prisoners. Just remember keep hydrated and go for it". At this the door opened and in walked the RSM's wife with a huge tray of sandwiches and nibbles. We changed the conversation and we began to relax; the drink was coming fast and furious, it was good just to sit and chill, the RSM and his wife were the best of hosts.

The following Monday morning, after first parade, the company sergeant majors face appeared at the window of his office and shouted that I was summoned to battalion headquarters. I marched into the headquarters, the RSM shouted from up the corridor, "Front and centre". I thought 'what the fuck', I marched up he gestured his head towards his office. I marched in and halted at his desk. He closed his door then said in a loud voice, "Were you happy with the team that you had last time you were over the water". A bit shocked at this I said, "Aye Sir". He walked out and shouted at the duty clerk to get them here now, he returned and said, "You are up in front of the CO when he appears in camp so wait here, stand at ease". I simply said, "Yes Sir". My usual thought, 'what the fuck'. I preferred you when he was passing me a whisky, what is all the shouting about. He left me standing in his office for about twenty minutes. I then heard a familiar voice outside, it was Knuckles, I heard him whisper, "What do you thinks going on?" I whispered back, "Fuck knows". He moved to one side and peered into the RSM's office I was standing there with a smile on my face as he whispered again, "What the fuck is going on". I shrugged my shoulders; I didn't know either.

A loud voice shouted, "What the fuck are you doing with your head in my office door", it was the RSM. I smiled as Knuckles' head disappeared from view he said, "Sorry Sir, but I thought I got a smell of a something burning Sir, thought I would investigate, but it seems there is only a wet blanket in there Sir". I laughed to myself thinking 'fuck sake Knuckles please give it a rest man', he loved the army but always had the upper ranks right on the wire, he had the gift of the gab. That started the RSM shouting again, "Is everything a joke to you soldier?" Knuckles replied, "Calm down

Sir please, I am a delicate soul you know Sir". I thought the RSM was going to explode, he roared, "Shut up you horrible individual or I'll lock you away do you understand". Knuckles just said, "Yes sir". RSM shouted me out of his office and I saw Alex and Brian standing there. Knuckles made a face as I walked between him and the RSM, I had to look down so as not to laugh, he was up for a laugh all the time but they all knew he was a very good and extremely capable soldier which is why I think he got away with a good lot of things where others would have been locked up straight away.

The CO appeared with another officer. We were all stood to attention as he walked past us, saluted the RSM and said, "Five minutes RSM then we will have a word with these fellows". He walked into the office and closed the door. We were stood at ease and the RSM said, "Right lads, you heard the officer. Five minutes". Out of the corner of my eye I saw Knuckles with his hand up, the RSM said, "What is it? Do you need the toilet? It's not school you don't have to put your hand up man, just say it soldier!". I was praying that he would not come out with anything stupid but, true to form, he replied, "It's a great honour to realise that after all my years in the army, I now am a FELLOW Sir".

Even the RSM had a smirk on his face for about ten

seconds. He went up to Knuckles and said, "That's enough, understand?". Knuckles stood straight and said, "Yes Sir!". Game over.

We were marched into the office where the CO was sitting at his desk. He said, "Right chaps, not going to beat about the bush. You are going over the water again. You are to aid with an 'OP' ok. Questions?". All I could think about was the disruption to my training. He said, "RSM march them out but he will remain for a few minutes", pointing at me. The others were marched out and the RSM re-entered the CO's office closing the door behind him. At his desk, the CO leaned forward and said, "Do you accept my award?" I had no clue what he was talking about but said, "Yes Sir". As I assumed that was the expected reply. He continued, "Good, you are a full Corporal starting today. Well done". The RSM said, "Here, here. Well done indeed". "Keep up the good work. I hear you may want to test your fitness and skills in January for another regiment, is this true?" I said I was, he smiled and gestured his head. I think it was a sign of approval.

I was marched out and we were bundled into another office. A different officer was sitting at the desk. On our entry he stood and said, "Right chaps, we are over the water again tomorrow night. I don't know the details, but you will be briefed when you arrive. Get yourselves sorted out, you all know the drill and the heli will pick you up at 18.45 tomorrow". I asked, "When you said 'we' Sir, the last time it was just us four". He nodded and replied, "I am requested to be present at the comms HQ. Now, listen lads remember if it all kicks off you will know that I have your back". Knuckles just couldn't resist a quip he said "It will be most gratifying to know that we are in an op somewhere eating rations and shitting into a plastic bag and staying silent and that you will have had a shower and sipping a latte". I broke in and said, "Sir, with all due respect". I turned to Knuckles and shouted, "That's enough! Anymore shit like that then you're off the team. You always go too far, have a little respect". I turned and apologised to the officer, he thanked me then glowered at Knuckles saying, "Anymore shite remarks?" Knuckles shook his head and apologised. "Right chaps anything you need before we go, let me know".

Weapons of the British Army

L96 A1 Sniper rifle 7.62 x 51 mm with a muzzle velocity 2,790 ft per second

L1A1 Self Loading rifle 7.62 mm muzzle velocity

2700 ft per second

General purpose machine gun 7.62 mm (GPMG) muzzle velocity 2756 ft per second

Chapter 26

Like before, we stayed out overnight and throughout the next day. We took turns on stag to get us into a good routine, it also helped pass the time. We waited until it was time to board the heli at the agreed location. It was all done the same as before. We landed in Ireland and bundled into an armoured vehicle, transported to the barracks and finally into a briefing room. When we sat down, I noticed that it was the same officer that had briefed us the last time. I was hoping we wouldn't be stuck in a graveyard again but when I looked at the wall behind him I saw large photos and up scaled maps. I realised that the OPs were in the countryside.

The officer nodded to us and started the brief, "We were informed that P.I.R.A were to target an R.U.C. high ranking officer at his home as a warning that no one was safe against P.I.R.A. Intelligence had reckoned they were going to target the officer two days ago so we have been in location now for over a week. Nothing happened but we must keep the security up as the threat was real, some people think that P.I.R.A may have changed their minds or smelled a rat but intelligence think they may still move on this so we will keep the Ops in place until told otherwise".

We were informed that my team was to man the outer Ops. They had closer manned Ops and four soldiers in or around the home of the R.U.C. officer. Our task was hopefully to see them coming, it was the best and easiest route as there was a large boggy area on one side of the house. "We want you to report anything you think could be a potential threat. Radios, night goggles and all other equipment are in the Ops. You will change out with the guys in there starting at 03.15. We have devised a plan so stick to it for the change out. Study the intel in front of you, the plan and routes to the Ops". He finished with, "Thank you gentlemen, I have comms" then left the room. Our officer said, "Ok chaps, let's do a good job I have comms as well". I nodded, "Ok Sir we will study the plans, check our camouflage and we will be ready for our pickup in twenty-five minutes. Just give us time to study". He nodded and left the room.

We went through the plan over and over. As one read it the other was checking equipment and camouflage cream. Once we were happy with the intel, we got a brew of hot sweet tea. I checked the sight on the L96 and had everyone check their weapons and kit again and again until we were all satisfied with every aspect of the journey, the change out at the Ops and of course everything about the mission. I re-checked we had spare batteries for the night scope and a few other items that we had to take with us. I stopped, looked at my watch, we had about eight minutes before getting our transport. I said, "Right guys, lets go through this once again". Knuckles complained, I said, "Again, if you please", so we all went through the whole thing verbally again. I thanked them and told them they were the best guys for this job. Knuckles said, "I think that means you are on the bell at the bar when we get back matey". We all laughed then I said, "Ok lads, let's get switched on and do this".

We were driven out of Belfast on the South bound road into the countryside. One Op was in an over grown drainage ditch in a field overlooking the main road with arcs of fire in the Southern direction. They had a clear view of the surrounding areas. The other was in a lightly wooden area looking up the single track road towards where the house was situated, with views towards the North and surrounding areas. We couldn't see the house, but we were the outer Ops. The other Ops, as we were informed, were a lot closer to the house and of course they had men inside the house too.

There were four vehicles. One of us in each making

it easier for one man to jump out. The vehicles never stopped just slowed down enough for us to get out one at a time with kit. I was in the lead vehicle so I jumped first and staggered a little till I found my footing then got down and waited for the next man to jump from his vehicle and so on until all four of us were off. If we had deployed as a normal patrol the vehicle would have stopped and we would have all piled out but if P.I.R.A or anyone else were watching from a distance, even seeing the lights would have raised suspicion. This way we had four vehicles with about two hundred yards between them, so if anyone was watching and they saw vehicle slowing down then the next one slowing at the same place they would think that there was a pot hole or a tight bend in the road as all vehicles slowed at the same place.

We were dropped about two kilometres from our due location. There was a bend in the road with woods on either side, so we moved into the wooded area and waited for our transport to fade into the distance. We waited about ten minutes then headed towards the first Op. Moving slowly as a four-man patrol team, making no noise. I was trying so hard not to mess up. After an hour of moving slowly and silently, we got into position and went down on one knee to wait at the designated area. We waited for ten minutes as was the plan. By this time our eyes had fully adjusted to the dark and we all had good night vision. I counted ten minutes in my head then glanced at my watch, 03.15 hours. Over the comms came Knuckles call sign, Delta One One. There was movement at the side of us coming in the direction that had been agreed at the briefing. I got a thumbs up from the guy that had just come from the Op, I nodded to Knuckles who faded into the darkness. After a few minutes one more appeared and Brian disappeared in to the darkness. We waited for a further ten minutes then I lead all four of us away and patrolled towards the next Op which was not far away, but moving silently, It took a while. I thought the guys we had picked up from the OP would have led the patrol but the two that came out filed in behind me and Alex. I was trying so hard to do a good job of leading the patrol, this was my first big role in command and I just wanted it to go right.

It was soaking under foot so we moved slowly to lessen the noise. When we arrived at the location we got down and waited ten minutes, then, as before over the ear piece came my call sign, Delta One Two. There was movement from the right hand side. Another guy joined our team and after a few minutes I headed into the Op. Silently the man inside the Op gestured a thumbs up and handed me a notebook. As he placed it into my hand, I tried to take it, but he held onto it, I looked into his face and he mouthed, 'don't lose it'. I nodded and returned the thumbs up. As he moved to go out of the Op, he patted me on the shoulder. It was so reassuring to get that pat on the back from these special forces' guys. Alex came in and settled down. As we waited, I counted ten minutes in my head and waited to hear them move but there was no noise at all. I waited another five minutes, still nothing, thinking to myself that something was wrong, I gestured to Alex to look over the fallen tree to see if he could see them but slowly and silently he turned his head and shook it to say they were not there. These guys were brilliant, we didn't hear a thing.

We got settled into our Op and started stag. I was first. As day break was coming in, I was looking through the scope on the L96 when I saw a lager can. It was a Blue Harp lager tin lying on the road and I thought of the Harp lager advert on the TV, "Harp stays sharp to the bottom of the glass". I could have enjoyed a cool lager right then. Alex stirred and I gestured with my hands that it was his stag he nodded and rubbed his eyes, I put my head down and was asleep in minutes.

Alex woke me and I could see the sun was up. It was my turn on stag again. As the sun rose higher, I could see we were in a little wood and had a good view up the single-track road as well as the open field on either side. This Op was perfect. I opened the notebook; all the ranges were assigned to certain spots in our firing arcs. I looked through the scope at the spots written in the book and agreed with them all. I cast my mind back to Africa and realised the work that these special forces guys put into an Op. Everything was covered it was incredible. My mind was on other things when I heard a noise. I froze and slightly opened my mouth to keep the sound of my breathing low. The noisewas from my right hand side. I slowly looked right and saw a young roe deer eating and moving through the little wood. If I wanted to I could have stretched out and grabbed its hind leg. I lay and watched it for a while, it was as close as I had ever got to a living roe deer, I had shot and killed loads of them before but I never realised how beautiful these animals were. It slowly moved away and I was saddened as I had enjoyed the intimate experience.

We kept stag all that day and into the night. We wrote everything down but saw nothing out of the ordinary, there was the odd car and of course the baker van every morning. A fox, three cows, seventy one sheep a tractor and trailer. I cast my mind back to the farm but shook my head to get my concentration back, you can imagine how bored we were. We heard nothing it was such a peaceful place; the weather was a bit wet in the afternoon, but we were fine and I loved being back in the field again.

Early on our second day, Saturday, we watched a bakers van pull in up the road, the same as it had done the day before. As the van headed up the single track road I saw his brake lights, I thought it must be slowing down for a pot hole or something but then the back door opened and out came four men wearing balaclavas and appeared to be carrying weapons. One had a camouflage jacket on, the others had green jackets and they were all moving very quickly as they headed into the bushes at the side of the road.

Immediately I went on to the radio, no more silent routine, "All stations we have contact. 80 yards on Echo Whisky (the code name for the single track road junction) four armed x-rays wearing masks heading into the field to my right hand side". All went quiet and for a moment that I thought no one was going to come back. I waited for what seemed ages then I heard, "Delta one two", followed by "All copied, report till they are out of your sight". I had the L96 scope on them, they were very good, staying by the tree line low and moving slowly in single file. We watched as the baker van started moving up the single-track road looking as if it was on a normal delivery, I reported it and was told all copied. In my earpiece I heard "Alpha One One (call sign for the unit in the house) just let the baker van do a normal delivery, we will stop the van at Echo Victor. Break, break Delta One One. I heard Knuckles acknowledge then came over the radio from command "Delta One One this is Alpha Zero One. Move to Echo Victors location (that was the call sign for the main road junction) stop and hold the van there". I heard Knuckles saying, "Delta One One moving out now". Alex said, "Let's just take the bastards out now you could get them no problems". I nodded but never lowered the scope, these P.I.R.A guys were good. They stopped, keeping to the tree line at the side of the field, as if watching the house from their location. I reported that they had stopped. I heard a running commentary over the radio of what was happening. The baker van was approaching, I remember the brief from the x-rays location, it was a good four hundred yards to the house and the front door was not in view from there, 'they must be waiting to hit him on the road or move closer once the van is away, I thought'. Over the radio came Charlie One One, the closer Op "We have no sight of them yet". We listened to the whole scenario unfold over the radio. When the van stopped the door opened and out got a man, he went into the back of the van and came out with a plastic tray. He carried the tray to the front door and knocked. The RUC officer opened the door and thanked the man, they chatted for a moment then the door was shut again. The baker returned to the van and reversed out of the drive as if nothing were happening.

Alex looked at the ridge on the road and gave me a running commentary, telling me the four men, wearing masks, made an about turn and ran down to the spot where they were dropped off. I spoke on the radio while following them with the scope. We watched the baker van stop and they all piled in the back . Through my ear piece came, "Break break. Stand down, stand down. Delta One One get out of there. No action to be taken, just get out of there. Let them go ". I couldn't believe it, we had them. Four men bearing arms and a driver. I got on the radio and said, "Alpha Zero One this is Delta One Two, I could stop the vehicle". I received a message back "Negative. Out". I looked at Alex and he shook his head as if to say, 'what the fuck is going on'?

We waited about an hour or so, then over the radio came, "It was probably a practice run. Trying to flush out a tout perhaps. No van delivery on Sunday that's how they will do it, so we will take it that they will hit him on Monday or Tuesday. We will continue as briefed. Out", I looked at Alex who whispered, "Oh well, a weekend with you in here. Fucking great". I smiled and touched his shoulder. He said, "Don't try the hand till it gets really cold, ok". I laughed quietly and thought we must see the funny side of it. Alex went on stag and I was eating some food when Alex whispered, "Knuckles wedding, are you taking anyone?" I nodded, he whispered, "Who?" I shrugged my shoulders, he looked up and said, "Not the Colour Sergeants' daughter?", I nodded and smiled, he said, "You lucky bastard!". I smiled and whispered, "I know". I gestured with my head for him to watch our arcs as he was on stag as he looked back through the scope he said, "You're still a lucky bastard!"

The Sunday morning was wet and miserable, I liked it. After the drizzling rain stopped you were overcome with all the intense smells of the countryside. We received a message that we were to be relieved at 02.40 hours Monday morning.

Alex quietly said, "Thank fuck" but I, on the other hand, would have liked to see what was to happen but the higher officials must be wanting their own men back in place. The morning was very quiet but around 13.00 hours I saw a tractor in a distant field and my mind drifted back to the farm again. I was lost in thought wondering what they might be doing at this moment. I scanned my arcs through the scope when suddenly out of the corner of the scope I saw something move. I thought for a moment my eyes were playing tricks, but I kept the scope on the position. I watched for what seemed like forever. I was about to move back to watch my full arcs when I saw it again. I rubbed my eyes thinking I was just tired. I continued watching the same position which was thick with rough foliage and long grass. I could just make out faint movement in the long grass, I continued watching thinking it might be a deer or some other animal. I felt a slight shudder running through my body, it was almost excitement. Keeping my eye on the scope I slowly stretched my hand out and touched Alex on the arm. My eyes were starting to water, but I didn't want to blink. Alex stirred, whispered "What?". I didn't even want to speak as I realised, I was looking at the side of a face.

Once I made out the face, I could see the

shoulders. The person was moving very, very, slowly in a leopard crawl. I moved my hand away from the rifle slowly and made a thumbs down gesture. Alex whispered, "You're fucking kidding!" I held up one finger then back to the thumb down then back to the rifle trigger. Alex grabbed the radio and whispered, "Alpha Zero One this is Delta One Two, we have contact".

We relayed all the information that we could. This guy was good, moving very, very, slowly. Alex was on his spotter scope, I whispered, "Do you see him?" He answered, "Aye, but only just". "Ok, you watch him. I will back track with the scope to make sure he is alone and for fuck sake, don't lose him". I tracked back slowly with my scope looking for anything out of the ordinary. I picked a figure out straight away, where I first caught sight of movement. Alex was passing the information to Alpha Zero One, the rest of the guys were listening in on comms. After an hour of watching, I was sure there were only two figures. Alex informed me that the first figure had stopped moving and had settled in what looked like the remains of an old. Through the scope I tracked the second figure up to the same position and passed on the location to Alpha Zero One. We continued watching, only blinking when necessary. Our eyes stung but we couldn't lose them. At the distance we were from the figures, it was hard to tell if they were armed or not. The radio was buzzing with code words then it fell silent as we continued watching. I had been exhausted before but the adrenaline had kicked in and I was full of energy now. Over the radio came, "Delta One Two, this is Alpha Zero One. Any sign of a weapon?". I replied, "Negative". I couldn't understand why we were waiting. We had the element of surprise and could have swooped in and grabbed them.

"Charlie One One this is Alpha Zero One. Make a move now. Out to you Delta One Two. Alpha Zero One we will get Charlie One One into a closer position to check for weapons then we may lift them or just observe. You report any movement, Out". We were so busy watching we had forgotten to eat or drink anything. I decided to open my water bottle. A well-rehearsed movement that Alex and I had practiced over and over. With one hand I held the water bottle towards Alex and he twisted the top off but we never lowered our eyes from the scopes. Once the water bottle was open, I dipped my finger in and soaked the glove ends then moved them to my mouth. I didn't realise how thirsty I had been, even the little droplets of water were magical I dipped my finger in and out until my mouth was refreshed enough. Alex did the same, then in reverse we replaced the lid on the water bottle. Alex whispered, "Pity it's not lager eh?". I didn't answer but I managed a smile at the thought of Alex dipping his gloves into lager then into his mouth. By late afternoon My eye was straining so I suggested to Alex he take a break as they weren't moving, I would keep watch. It had been radio silence since they told us that Charlie One One was moving towards them. I whispered to Alex that he should take over in ten minutes and we will keep this up so we could get some rest.

After 10 minutes Alex moved back to his position. I slowly moved away from the rifle, my whole body was aching from staying in the same position for so long. I managed to roll over and stretch, swallowed some water then tried to relax. I wanted to get back in position but I had to force myself to let Alex take over for his ten minute stint. After, what felt like a long ten minutes, I started to move back into position when Alex whispered to me to stop. One of them was looking directly in our direction. There is no way that the human eye could make us out at this distance, especially with all the camouflage and foliage we had around us, but better to have no movement. Alex kept on whispering to stay where I was, I was so frustrated

I just want to get back into position which was just a foot away so I could see what was going on.

Eventually Alex told me it was safe to move back as the x-ray had moved back into their original position. I continued to move slowly and got back into position. I blinked a few times to get my eye to focus again on the x-rays. I told Alex they were lying as still as us so they will have to move now and then for their circulation. As I said this one of them looked directly at our position again. I told Alex not to worry it was just a fluke. Alex replied, "Fucking hope so mate". Alex grabbed the radio and relayed what was happening to Alpha Zero One. We didn't know the position of Charlie One One, but they would have to move extremely carefully to get closer to the targets position.

We kept monitoring the x-rays and after another 2 hours we heard over the radio that Charlie One One was close enough and in good position to view the two x-rays. There was no sign of weapons just two men sitting behind the roots of an old blown over tree. I whispered to Alex, "It's getting grey and will soon be dark. You take a thirty-minute break as we have more eyes on them now". Alex rolled over, grabbed some rations and a few minutes later he was sound asleep. I was starting to feel tired again but kept up the view on these x-rays. They started moving slowly every so often, it must have been to keep their circulation going. I continued to relay this to Alpha Zero One in case Charlie One One hadn't done so already.

As dusk started closing in I was back on stag to watch the two x-rays again. Alex fell quickly into a well-earned sleep. Suddenly over the radio I heard Knuckles voice, "Alpha Zero this is Delta One One. We have a vehicle stopped at Echo Victors location (The junction at the end of the road) Wait, one man out of vehicle drivers side into the boot. He is moving towards the roadside carrying a large bag. He has placed the bag in a ditch to the East of the junction. Man is re-entering the vehicle and the vehicle is moving heading North", Knuckles continued with the number plate, make model and colour of vehicle. There was a reply, "Delta One One, Alpha Zero One did you recognise the driver?" Knuckles replied, "Alpha Zero One, negative. Over". I noticed movement from one of the x-rays I had been observing. I was about to report it over the radio but it burst into life. "Alpha Zero One, this is Charlie One One. We have one x-ray moving out of the area, looks like he's heading towards Echo Victor". Alex was now wide awake and fully aware of what was happening. He whispered, "What's the fucking hold up? Let's move in on these bastards". I replied, "There thinking. Give them time to work it out".

I watched as one of the x-rays moved slowly, heading back the way he had come. I looked as if he was heading towards the junction at the end of the road. They were moving a lot quicker than before but they were still very mindful of exposing themselves too much in these surroundings. I remember thinking if that x-ray realised how much firepower was aiming at him, he would have shit himself. Alex kept the scope on the remaining x-ray as I tracked the other. We couldn't see the junction so I relayed the movement until Knuckles picked him out coming towards it, he then relayed all the movements until the x-ray came to a stop. After fifteen minutes Knuckles came back on the radio, "Alpha Zero One, x-ray moving again. Stopping, waiting, crouching and now turning. X-ray now has a large bag over his left shoulder". I thought this must mean that the x-ray is right-handed, using his dominant hand to help move through the foliage, at least we knew something about him, he's right-handed. Alex whispered, "Let's move on them now! What the fuck are they waiting for?" I told him to calm down, we didn't know what was in the bag. Alex replied, "Well, two guys crawl into a position in the undergrowth, sit for fucking ages then one picks up a strange bag from a dead drop. I bet you it not a fucking fish supper!" I knew he was right, but I declined to answer, "Let them decide ok, now shut up Alex!". He shook his head, rolled over and started eating a biscuit noisily. I touched his shoulder and made an aggressive face whispering, "Shut the fuck up!" He did shut up, but I could tell there was an atmosphere between us. We were both tired and getting on each others nerves. I kept thinking that I just had to make it to 02.40 hours and we will be out of here. I would have liked to have seen it through, but I was exhausted.

The X-ray made his way back through the foliage with the bag to the position he was previously in by the fallen tree. Light was fading fast and we would be in darkness in 15 minutes so Charlie One One was now our eyes and ears. We would still have to be very vigilant until the moon appeared. The moon that night wasn't a full moon but it would give us enough light to be able to continue monitoring the x-rays position. I heard over the radio, "Alpha Zero One, This is Charlie One One. I can see weapons of some description. They have opened the bag and could see that they had checked at least two long weapons. Looks like rifles and at least one pistol verified, over".

As the night dragged we readied ourselves to leave when the time came. I rested up as Alex took stag for his last time. In preparation for the big out I took over stag, it was now 01.55 hours. Alex would be first out then myself. It would be the same procedure we did to get into the OP but in reverse until the bend in the road where we were initially dropped off by the vehicles. We waited and waited. It was now 02.30 hours and we had heard nothing. I wondered if they were there at all. Remembering the briefing, Alex would move out, wait ten minutes and if no one appeared then he would return and we would continue stag then retry two hours later. If they missed the window it could be a long fucking two hours but that was the brief.

I looked at my watch, 02.38 hours. I watched the hands tick by, slowly reaching 02.40 hours. I patted Alex on the shoulder, he moved out and I lay there waiting, staring into the darkness hoping to hear something move. I was about to check my watch again, thinking that it must be coming up to ten minutes as I had been counting it in my head. Alex would be back any minute. I almost shit myself when I felt a hand on my shoulder I looked round and there was a guy I didn't recognise, he must have seen the shocked expression on my face as he just smiled and nodded reassuringly. I had heard nothing, absolutely nothing. He moved over and I handed him the notebook, he gave me a thumbs up then we went through some things using hand signals. When we finished I headed out the OP, trying not to make a sound just as that guy had just done.

I moved slowly until I was in position with the others. As the minutes passed the fourth guy moved into the Op. We waited the ten minutes required then I led the team away. I couldn't see much but I knew there were four of us, so I assumed Knuckles and Brian had done the same from their OPs before they got to us. I kept thinking about the guy that had relieved me and how he had approached without making a sound. It was like he just appeared at my shoulder. After about two hundred metres we stopped. I held out my hand to my side and gestured for the team to go to ground on one knee, I got down on one knee myself. I quietly reached to grab my water bottle and took a swig. As I breathed slowly the voice within me kept saying, 'Stop thinking about It, clear your mind and focus on the job! You are Patrol Commander and you have three men to get out of here!'. I took a deep breath and stood, motioning with my hand to move out. I felt so much better now, I was focused on the job in hand, getting us out of the area.

We patrolled back the way we had come but our pickup point was at another location. It was good to be on the move again. We passed where we were first dropped off as I recognised the bend in the road. We continued on heading up to a field with a broken gate then moved in single file along the hedge. We came to another field entrance with no gate. As I moved I stepped into a puddle making a splash. I froze to keep the noise to a minimum and not cause any more disruption. I moved forward, slower now, until I felt grass under my feet. We still had four small fields to travel through, clearing the fences of each with minimal sound. I went over first while the others covered me and then the next man and so on until we had overcome all the fences. We reached a single-track road. I remembered the brief, we would move along the road edge within the field for eight hundred metres then come to a gate. Once we have overcome the gate we would cross the road and enter another field which had derelict buildings on the right hand side.

After entering into the last field with the buildings, we got into position for an all round defence. I quietly did a full recce of the buildings, maintaining a safe distance until I had circled back to where I had started. I knelt down behind Knuckles and tapped him on the shoulder. When I had his attention I used my hand signals to indicate the way he and I would move whilst covering each other as we moved towards the building.

The building was similar to a barn, but you couldn't make out very much from this distance it was just a black hole with a roof. We began moving to the derelict building. Knuckles on one knee with his rifle trained on the building and I moving forward. I travelled ten paces then got down on one knee covering Knuckles as he began to move forward. We carried this on until I was about five meters away from the opening of the building. I got down on one knee watching for the signal. A few minutes passed, then I saw the pin hole laser light appear on the back wall of the building. I moved closer to the opening and whispered the password, "Sola". From the darkness I heard a voice whisper back, "Fide". This was the agreed response to the password. It was years later that I found out what it meant; the passwords were Latin. When you put it all together it meant – BY FAITH ALONE.

I signaled Knuckles to get Alex and Brian. He turned and headed back into the darkness. On entering the building I noticed a Range Rover with a large horse box behind it. Two men stood inside the building, one leaning against the far wall and the other at the horse box tail gate. Knuckles and the others caught up and we were waved over to the horse box and gestured to get in the horse box. As we entered the guy whispered, "Dump your kit on the rack as you go in". We passed through two heavy curtains then suddenly, we entered what looked like a sitting area with a table and bench seats. I had to squint my eyes as it was so bright. I dumped my gear on a rack and sat down, we all looked at each confused. I looked over to the wall where there was a radio and other equipment, some shelves and four small tv monitors. There was also a tea urn and a huge plastic container on a table. The curtains opened and one of the guys from outside entered, "Fill your boots lads. Get some hot tea and scoff inside you" as he pointed to the plastic container and tea urn. I looked around the trailer and back to the guy. He must have seen the confusion on my face because he said, "It's an adapted trailer. It looks like a horse box from the outside but once the tail gate is up it's a completely sound proof unit. It's also bullet proof so you're safe as houses in here. Get your weapons unloaded, once you've made them safe keep them close with a magazine at the ready".

The guy introduced himself as Stu, he told us the guy outside the horse box was Nick and Ted is up in the woods behind the building. He said, "By the way lads, well done you've done a great job. There will be a de-brief later". As he said it he nodded and made eye contact with each of us individually in what I could only say was recognition for our efforts. He looked back to me saying, "We watched your movement from the bend in the road to the buildings it was faultless. Good patrolling skills mate, well done just watch the puddles from now on". I started to speak but Knuckles butted in, "How the fuck do you know that?" Stu shrugged his shoulders, grinning he said, "There's always someone watching". Knuckles looked over at me laughing, "Fuck sake, you and that puddle. You fanny!". We all laughed, it must have been a pressure release. I tried to stop but found that I couldn't stop, I just laughed and laughed. When we had all calmed down, Stu continued, "It was a very good effort on all your parts. We will move at 09.30 hours, so get some scoff inside you". He removed the lid from the plastic container revealing that it was full of sandwiches, pork pies and chocolate bars. A real feast. He reached in and pulled out a pack of sandwiches and gestured with his head to dive in.

Stu sat with us and chatted about drinking and shagging, your normal conversation within the ranks of the British Army. I always tried to talk in a whisper, but Stu just chatted away normally. Suddenly, his radio burst into life. We went silent as he answered. "Duty calls" he said smiling, he finished his tea and headed back through the curtain.

another chap, we took it to be Nick, entered with a wave of his hand then thrust it into the plastic container pulling out a pork pie and chocolate bar. I figured they must be doing stag the same as we had. Nick poured himself a brew and chatted away, I asked him about the horse box. He said , "It's an adapted trailer. We can have a horse in here too". He pointed to a part up at the front corner, "We knocked that out for the horses head and pull that up" pointing to a strip on the floor, "It makes a partition. Fucking stinks when the fucker shits though, but an excellent surveillance unit. We can have guys one side and a horse on the other if need be". It was very impressive. he slurped on his tea and agreed it was. We chatted away about everyday things as if we were all long-lost friends. I knew the drill; we were not to mention anything until it was an official de-brief, so I joined in with whatever the conversation was but deep down I had so many questions I wanted answered.

Vehicle Patrol at Junction.

A mural painted on the side of ahouse.

Another mural painted on the sideof a house.

Chapter 27

With the warmth inside the trailer and lack of sleep, we began nodding off. The next thing I knew the engine of the Range Rover started and we moved off with a jolt. I noticed a man I didn't recognise, I hadn't heard him enter the horse box. Knuckles said, "You must be Ted, or we have been rumbled and you're IRA". I told him to be quiet and he said, "You're right the first-time mate, now settle back we will be there soon enough". I glanced at my watch and it was 09.30 hours, everything was like clockwork with these guys.

Ted said, "Make your weapons ready, safety on. If the shit hits the fan and we are contacted you will be safe in here but if we have to get out follow my lead". He pointed to a handle and continued, "This is a quick release for the tailgate", he looked at me, "It's ok, there will be no drama. We have a vehicle meeting us after we join the main road, which is three miles from here, along the single track". We all made our weapons ready in preparation. We were all chatting as we bounced along the road when the radio Ted had started squawking. He told us that we had met with the escort and it would be another 35 minutes until we arrived. Twenty minutes passed then Ted said,

"Once we enter the hospital car park I'll give you a nod when we go under the area with the covered roof. You will have around forty seconds to get out of here". He moved the curtain to one side and started winding a small handle "It's a small set of wheels on the outside, when I lower the gate the wheels will keep it off the ground. When I say go, you all run straight out into the waiting Pig and close the doors as quick as you can, they will get you out of the car park. If anyone is watching from a distance, they will see the Range Rover and horse box enter the car park but the vehicle wont stop it will all be done on the move". I told Alex to start passing over our kit, but Ted nodded, "its ok we will have time for that I'll let you know".

After about five minutes Ted gestured to us to stand up and move to the sides of the horse box. He took the table and folded it back against the front wall, then collapsed the seats and fixed it against the side walls. We were cramped before but then we had plenty of room. We had to steady ourselves while the Range Rover and horse box went around a tight corner. Ted said, "One-minute, ok lads!". We were ready to go for it. He counted down from thirty seconds then he touched a button and the whole tail gate lowered. He patted me on the shoulder and shouted go, it was so unsteady under foot I thought for a moment that I was going to fall over as the vehicle rounded another corner.

When I got out off I had about six large steps to take then I jumped into the back of the armoured pig that was waiting. I turned and saw that the tail gate was up and the horse box disappeared around another corner. It was all done in the forty seconds time frame. It went dark as the pig doors were and there was a loud roar from the powerful engine, we were on the move again. We were being thrown from one side of the vehicle to the other, for a while I thought it would never end. When we did stop abruptly the driver shouted in a loud cheery Scottish accent, "Thank you for using armoured taxis that will be £2.80, thank you again chappies!". The doors opened and we were led out towards the unloading bay where we unloaded our weapons and a Sergeant told us to head over to a porta cabin. I looked about as I was walking; I knew I had not been in this camp before. Our officer was waiting for us inside the porta cabin with a big smile on his face, he said, "Good work men excellently done!".

I dumped my gear and sat down. Another officer entered the cabin, it was the same officer that had briefed us at the start. He stood at the front of the room, "Ok lads, well done, good effort. Have you any material on your persons about the operation?". He looked around as we all shook our heads. I replied, "No Sir, it was all handed over to the guys that took over from us in the OPs as instructed in our initial brief". He was about to speak when someone approached from the back of the room. They walked forward and said in a loud, gruff, Scottish voice, "GOOD!". They were dressed in jeans and a black donkey jacket, had long black hair and a stubble beard. He looked as if he hadn't seen a wash for weeks. I thought he looked more like a Player (code name used by soldiers for known IRA terrorists). As he stood at the front of the room, he looked at us with deep penetrating eyes. "Ok nothing is to be mentioned outside these four walls do you all understand? You have been told not to mention anything! If anyone asks you questions say fuck all ok?". He looked directly at me and said, with a frown, "Good enough effort mate". He continued, "If any of you have questions about the operation keep them to yourself, I am not here to answer questions. All you need to know is that you earned your pay doing what your trained to do". He turned, nodded at the two officers, and headed out of the room. Once the door was closed, I said, "What the fuck was all that about Sir?". The other officer said, "You heard what he said". He turned walked out the door and it was slammed shut.

I looked at our officer, he just shrugged his shoulders and said with a forced smile, "Fancy a brew?". I was about to say something when Knuckles said, "It's a fucking beer I want!". I shouted, "I want a fucking beer, SIR!". He shuddered and said, "I meant that", looking at the officer and finished with "Sir". Our officer said, "Ok chaps, tensions are running a bit high just now so just relax. I've got a brew sorted out, you chill out". As he walked past me, he gestured with his head for me to follow him.

I rose from my seat and walked outside, a man dressed in army uniform walked past me with a tea urn and a box full of sandwiches and sweets. I closed my eyes for a moment and breathed in the fresh air. The officer turned and told me to follow him. We walked to another porta cabin at the other end of the camp and gesturing with this head said, "They want a word with you. Once they are finished we will be in the other porta cabin, we will meet you there". I thanked him and he turned and walked away. I thought, 'What the fuck now?'. When I opened the first door to this porta cabin all I could smell was stale cigarettes and cheesy feet, I screwed up my nose as I carried on inside.

When I opened the second door, I looked around the room. There were seven guys in it. When I glanced down again, there sitting on a sofa in a haze of cigarette smoke was Mike from the African operation. Beside him was the man with the black donkey jacket that had just given us a so called debrief. Mike smiled as he threw a packet of cigarettes at me and simply said, "How's it going mate?".

Chapter 28

Sitting in Mike's company again was excellent. I asked him, "Hey, what's with the long hair mate?". He laughed, "Aye, goes with the job. You know the score". We both laughed. He introduced me to all the guys in the room, they all nodded in acknowledgement and carried on what they were doing. I sat back down and Mike said, "Phwoar, you need a shower mate". I knew I did, hopefully I would get one when I get back to our porta cabin. The guy with a padded jacket said, "You will have to wait a while mate they want you and your team out of here. I think you are moving in two hours". I disappointed as I had been looking forward to a refreshing shower, but it was normal routine I suppose.

I was going to ask about the house and the two guys that we had been watched in the woods, but thought better of it. I looked at Mike, it was as if he knew what was on my mind. He lit a cigarette and slightly shook his head and closed his eyes briefly. As I settled back in the chair, he winked and nodded as if to say well done and say fuck all. My mind was racing, I had so many questions but what was I supposed to do? Just blurt them out? No, I held my tongue. I felt a tap on the shoulder and a guy handed me a hot brew, I thanked him and started sipping it. Mike asked how things were back in the battalion, we chatted briefly then the guy in the donkey jacket started cracking jokes, he seemed a fine bloke and we were having a good laugh. With the heat in the porta cabin I started to feel the exhaustion, but I kept smoking, drinking hot sweet tea and chatting. After an hour or so Mike said I would have to get going, so I stood said my goodbyes and headed outside.

It was a relief really to get back outside as I breathed in deep lung-fulls of fresh air. Mike appeared at my side and said he would walk with me. I told him my mind was buzzing with what went on, he stopped me and said, "Just let it go mate, even within our regiment we don't discuss operations with anyone that hasn't been a part of it. It's a need-to-know basis only, just let it go. Once you get back, have a shower and a couple of beers you'll forget all about it". I doubted it. We walked in silence for a moment then I said, "Aye, you're probably right. But you know, anything I do in the army worth talking about I'm told not to mention anything". Mike laughed, slapped me on the shoulder, with a big smile on his face he said, "Welcome to my world mate".

When we arrived at the porta cabin Mike carried

on walking and he said, "Watch yourself mate, see you some time". With a nod and a thumbs up, he disappeared around the corner. I thought I may as well get another brew. When I walked in Knuckles said with a big grin, "Where the fuck have you been darling? I've been up all night worrying and your dinner is in the dog". We all laughed as I told him I was just chatting with an old mate. Our officer glared at me as if to say what the fuck was all that about but I ignored him and stuck my hand into the box pulling out a ham and cheese sandwich wrapped in cling film. Brian handed me a brew, I pulled up a seat and Knuckles lit a cigarette and handed it to me saying, "The cigarettes are tastier that the sandwiches". I puffed away as the officer said, "Jesus guys, must you smoke so much?". We all turned and said, "Aye", then burst out laughing. At this the officer shouted, "Can I have a word Corporal". I looked at him and said, "With all due respect Sir, gives a fucking break eh?". I did feel terrible and it was disrespectful. I looked at him as he stood still for a moment, hesitated, then said, "Ok chaps, still a bit of tension in the air. Can I get you some more tea?" I looked over at Knuckles and shook my head, I stood from the table and gestured with my hand for the officer to sit down at the table he moved forward and sat down. Knuckles handed him a cigarette, Alex handed him a brew and he looked at us all and said, "My names Johnathan by the way". We all nodded and I said "We know, just relax and chill out". He seemed to relax as he smiled and said, "It was very exciting listening to the radio comms". Knuckles said, "Not as exciting as watching Brian trying to shite into a plastic bag". We all laughed as Knuckles shouted, "Fucking hell, it was stinking!". Brian, with his dry sense of humour, said, "What do you mean stinking, all shite stinks". At this we were all roaring with laughter even the officer was doubled up. As I looked around at the guys I thought it's not so bad.

After an hour or so sitting drinking tea and listening to stories from our officer, we readied ourselves for our transport. We were all looking forward to getting some sleep, we were all totally exhausted. Suddenly the door to the porta cabin opened and in walked the other officer with the guy in the black donkey jacket. They stopped in front of me and asked if I was up for another couple of days on a job. My brain said, 'Oh for fuck sake', but I automatically said, "Aye, I am up for it". I looked at Alex, "Aye I am up for it too". They told us they just needed the two of us and for everyone else to grab their kit and get into the vehicle that was waiting outside. The two of them turned and never said a word as they left the porta cabin. Our officer said he would stay behind but the other officer told him there was no need as it's only for a couple of days. Our officer replied, "I would rather stay, if it's all the same". Donkey jacket guy said, "With respect, when we say no, it's not meant for question time its fucking NO. Now your transport is moving in one minute and I suggest you get on it". Our officer nodded his head in my direction, but I could tell he was not amused, as he walked out the door.

Donkey jacket guy and the officer stayed and started chatting amongst themselves. Alex looked at me and mouthed, "For fuck sake". He had a look of disgust on his face, I am sure it matched mine as I sat back down at the table. I was so tired, but I had to look switched on so I drew a deep breath and held it in my lungs sat up right, exhaled and focused myself. We were told to get a brew and have a smoke; I was sick of smoking and drinking tea but thought I better get it while we can.

After a good few minutes of them discussing whatever they were discussing, in low voices with their backs to us, they turned around saying, "The reason for the OP was we have good information of a cache of P.I.R.A weapons. They are buried in a shallow hole under an old collapsed caravan at a derelict crofters cottage". I was handed photo of the cottage showing the remains of the caravan. "We want eyes and ears in the area for a few days. Intelligence has just come through informing us that P.I.R.A plan a visit to the area to retrieve or replace weapons, we are not sure which. It will be in the next day or so.

We don't have the resources to cover all intelligence that comes in about Belfast and the surrounding areas, but it's from a good source so we have to act on what we are given and prioritize". He stared directly into my eyes and said, "I don't normally use green Army but you have been involved with us for a couple of jobs now. Reports say that you carry out the tasks your given with a good attitude and excellent soldiering skills so we needed you to step up for this next job and you did, well done. Oh, by the way your call sign is Tango One One Zero. Base is Tango Zero and your transport is Tango One Two Zero ok. Just remember its surveillance only, we only need to identify players. If you are compromised, use minimal force. Do I make myself clear?". I replied, "Aye, no problem, whatever it takes". The guy nodded his head I think in acknowledgement.

We were shown more photos that had been blown up to a larger scale, showing in great detail where the cache of weapons was. They also showed any surrounding areas that were relevant. We got briefed on route to the area from the drop-off point, highlighting things we would encounter and have to overcome like fences, ditches etc, all good information so we can achieve a silent patrol into the area without disturbing anything, or anyone knowing we were there. He gave us the details of the pickup once the operation was called off or we were relived. We were told that due to resources it would be the regular RCT (Royal Corp of Transport) Tango One Two Zero that would drop us off and pick us up. The cache area had been under surveillance a few times in the past and the best position had been found. A drainage ditch at the edge of a field that was overgrown with lots of cover and perfect views of the weapons cache area. I was then handed a notebook, I opened it briefly and saw it had lots of information, distances and sketches, all very detailed. You couldn't imagine the attention to detail in these notebooks, they were excellent. I was instructed to study the info and photos. We were told, "Ok lads, it's 13.02 hours. You will not be moving until 00.10 hours so plenty of time to rest up and get some fresh scoff". I declined and explained we would stick with the rations as after being on rations or a few days, fresh scoff can go right through you. He nodded and said, "Pease yourself, you can sleep down in here, there are blankets at the back. We will have final briefing at 23.40 hours". I nodded and told him we would be ready, he acknowledged it then walked out of the porta cabin closing the door behind him.

Alex said, "Holy fuck here we go again", as he started undoing his boot laces and pulled his boot and sock off. He quickly put on unscented foot powder and a fresh sock before putting his boot on again and repeating on the opposite foot as I read the brief out loud for him to hear. When he had finished, Alex took over reading out loud as I changed my socks. It was such a relief to have my boots off but I had to get them back on quickly or my feet would start to swell. We went through the whole thing over and over. After about fifty minutes, we had a full grasp on the information and both of us could recite the whole task from start to finish from memory. We asked each other questions on the details in the photos until we were both happy that we knew what we were doing and had memorised the pictures in our head. I stretched out and said we should get some rest and we could go through it all again at 22.50 hours then grab some rations. Alex agreed and headed to the back of the porta cabin to get the blankets. I flicked through the notebook again as Alex threw a massive pile of blankets at me. I took the hint and put the notebook in the map pocket of my combat trousers, took off my jacket and lay down on the pile of blankets. As I stretched out I remember closing my eyes thinking to myself, 'Oh fuck, that's fine'. I must have drifted off to sleep there and then, I woke again at 18.05, had a piss and soon drifted off to sleep again. Oh it felt wonderful to curl up in those blankets.

I awoke just after 21.30 hours. I did some stretches to wake myself up and started going through the info again, looking at the photos and getting my head round it all. I sat on a chair and thought for a moment about the training for the selection course in January, thinking that when I get back I was going to beast myself and get my fitness back to where it was and I must get to Wales on my next leave and get some hill work in on the Pen y fan. I was lost in thought when a voice came from the other bundle of blankets, "Who the fuck are you talking to?". I didn't realise that I was talking out loud. "Sorry mate, I was just muttering". He said, "So, you're still up for that in January? I hear its hard fucking going". I told him I had heard that too, but I needed to get back and do more hill training to get my base fitness back to where it was. Alex told me to calm down and we would be back soon enough. "Then you can get back to training with your pal the Rupert (nickname used by lower ranks for an officer) or you could just go down and have drinks with the Tara". I asked how he knew about that. he told me "Everyone knows, you were seen. Plus, the Tara's wife mentioned it to one of the other wife's while out shopping". "He's ok you know, the Tara?". Alex relied, "Oh aye, you're his blue-eyed boy". "Did you know he went for selection?" Alex pulled the blanket from his head "Fuck off?". I told him it was true, he got up and approached the table and lit two cigarettes. Passing one to me he said, "He's a wanker anyway". I told him he was an ok guy really but he replied, "No! Wanker through and through". I said, "You think everyone's a wanker". He retorted "Aye. That's true, oh well. Fancy a brew?". Alex gestured his head towards the kettle, "Aye, go on then. I will sort us out some rations while you do that. Alex replied, "As long as it's not fucking chicken curry, that wanker Knuckles swapped all my rations so all I had was chicken curry. He even put a smiley face on each tin with a black marker the fucking bastard. I hate chicken curry and he knows it".

We started on our rations and verbally went

through the task again as we ate, smoked and drank tea. At 23.40 hours, right on time as usual, the guys walked through the door. We were briefed again and they asked some questions on the drop off point, the route to the area and about the pick-up to make sure we understood the assignment. They seemed happy with our answers and told us to stay focused.

Chapter 29

Our small amount of kit was ready as we made our way out into an Royal Ulster Constabulary V8 Land Rover. We headed out of the gate and back towards the hospital, just like when we had been dropped off from the horse box. As before, we changed from one vehicle to another only this time it was an old Transit van. I asked the driver, "Holy fuck, how old is this fucking thing?" He replied, "We have to run old bangers or the boyos would pick us out in an instant, this thing is souped up to fuck though". The chap in the passenger seat said, "You know your brief, so let's run through ours".

We were sitting on bench seats on the sides of the van, "Right listen in, we move from here in four minutes. It will take around forty five minutes to get you to your drop off point in the country. There are two 9mm sub machineguns ready with the safety on under our seats. You can reach them if need be. You both have pistols and your main weapons. If anything happens and we need to leave the van you leave from the back doors then follow our lead ok? Have you made your weapons ready?" We both nodded . "Ok, we have comms wired into the van and you're all radioed up. We know exactly where you will be dropped off and the other location for your pick-up point. It should be us again that pick you up but if it runs over three days it will be other blokes ok?. We are at the end of our tour, thank fuck, out of here for sixteen days leave". I told him we were ready to go, "Remember, we are in charge in here ok? Regardless the rank". Under his breath Alex said, "What rhymes with rank? WANK!" gesturing with a masturbating hand motion. I told the driver we understood and that we were ready to go.

As we headed for the drop-off Alex said, "Thank fuck you're in charge, now don't fuck up", he had a big grin on his face. "I'm first at the bar when we get back but you're on the first five rounds". I laughed, "Aye, ok mate. Now focus and let's do this". As we drove out of the city into the countryside, my eyes were starting to adjust to the dark inside the transit van. We were about fifteen minutes away from our drop off point but running around three minutes behind schedule. The driver pulled out a cigarette and was about to light it when I leaned forward and pulled the cigarette from his mouth ."What the fuck?" I said, "No smoking mate", the passenger driver asked, "Fuck up your night vision?" I said, "Aye it will do", I leaned forward and told the driver that I needed my night vision, he did not. He apologised "Sorry mate, but they encourage us to smoke as it blends in while in traffic", Alex pointed out that it was the middle of the night, the driver apologized again, "Sorry I wasn't thinking", I told him not to worry about it but to have a smoke for me once they dropped us off.

As we drove closer, I was buzzing I just wanted to get going. Alex was on one side of the van and me on the other, both our doors slightly open. We handed the ropes that were attached to the inside of the doors to the passenger driver so that when we jumped he would be able to pull them closed. When we approached our deployment corner, I glanced at my watch, 01.32 hours. The passenger driver said, "Thirty feet. Twenty feet. Ten feet. GO!" The van slowed down very slightly as we pulled the doors open and leapt out. I stumbled and slid on the wet road but kept my footing, I watched the van lights fade as it rounded the corner and disappeared. We waited at the side of the road for around ten minutes, staring into the pitch-black night, constantly. Alex moved from the opposite side of the road. Once he was close enough I used hand signals and instructed him to go down on one knee. By this time our night vision was as good as it was going to get. I used hand signals again and we moved off, starting our patrol in the direction of the cottage.

We carefully moved along the road for just over a mile. If a vehicle had approached, we would have seen it coming from a distance. We would have just faded into the foliage cover at the side of the road, waited until it passed then continued our patrol. I knew we had completed the first phase of the route as we approached the bend in the road to the right-hand side. Then we were about to come across our first obstacle, a steep embankment which had a fence at the top. The embankment was a wet grassy slope, we had to watch our footing. I went first, Alex stayed at the bottom waiting for his turn. As I approached the top, I moved over the fence as quietly as I could making sure to scan the area with my rifle. We counted five minutes, then Alex began his climb. When he appeared I held a thumbs up to him and we started moving. I was going over the route in my head. I knew we had six fields to travel through which meant five more fences. Every time we got over a fence, I ticked it off mentally in my head.

Having moved through the fields, we finally arrived at a burn. Alex scanned the area as I crossed it, moving very slowly until I reached the other bank. Once I was out of the burn I scanned the area to cover Alex crossing. We waited a few minutes before Alex began to move, suddenly the bank gave way and he slid towards the water. He managed to catch himself before he splashed into the water, I froze awaiting a splash from the debris but there was virtually no noise. Alex came through the burn and got down on one knee beside me. I could hear him trying to quietly regulate his breathing, he must have held his breath with the sudden shock of slipping as the bank gave way. I reached out and quietly patted him on the shoulder he nodded to let me know he was ready to continue so we moved away towards the wooded area.

We moved in single file, so that we were not clearing two routes through the wood. I was being careful not to stand on twigs, slowly moving my feet and laying them down very gently while also trying to avoid branches at height as we moved. I could hear that Alex's breathing had calmed down and he was back to normal. It seemed like it took hours to cover the small wood, but we had to move very slowly and quietly. I could not feel many branches or twigs under my feet so it was mostly pine needles. and moss. Finally we came to the fence at the end of the wood. As we approached we could just make out the fence, it was in a bad state of disrepair, all the posts were broken or leaning so far over they were almost touching the ground. The wire was just lying on the ground hardly attached to any of the posts, so we just stepped through watching that we did not stand on, or move, any of the wire or rotten posts.

I took my first step from the fence and instantly knew that we were in the marshy area. We patrolled around the side but as we did so the clouds parted and the moon gave a little more light, which was bad for us. If anyone were there watching they would be able make us out with the light from the moon.

When we finally reached the drainage ditch we both got down on one knee, I let my breath out slowly, I didn't even realise I had been holding it. I felt the bottom of the ditch with my hand, it was soft watery mud. The ditch was about four-foot-wide and had a four-foot-high wall on either side, moving slowly we edged our way in an almost crouching crawl. Every so often I slipped in the mud, but we were moving slowly so there was no noise. About twenty yards up the muddy ditch, the walls became a little shallower and we had to get lower and crawl, moving one hand or one foot at a time very slowly to reduce noise. It took a long time but there was no other way to move up a ditch like this and get to our position without making a sound.

It went dark again as the clouds engulfed the moons light and we were plunged back into darkness. I stopped, held up a hand to Alex to stop and we waited in silence. Just listening for anything that might be suspicious and waiting for our eyes to adjust to the darkness again. I heard a hoot not far ahead of us, I almost shit myself until I realised it was an owl. I was about to move when I realised that my boot was stuck in the mud. I stayed still and thought, calm down and regulate your breathing. Once I had settled myself, I began slowly putting pressure on my thigh muscle but still no movement, my boot was stuck solid. I rested on my side and pulled again on the thigh muscle keeping the pressure on, finally I felt the boot starting to come free. I stopped pulling, I didn't want a noise, I moved my boot slowly backwards and forwards in the mud so that the water got under the sole of my boot. That made it easier to pull out and there would be no noise of suction air escaping. I was able to move up the ditch with my boot caked in mud making it about twice the weight. We moved a short distance and realised that the wall of the ditch had collapsed, it had been washed away. We moved into a small eroded D shaped area in the ditch, moving out of the mud and water and managed to lie straight out. I wiped the mud from my boot and we both started to stretch, it was such a relief feeling the blood flowing into our legs again as we had been cramped in this narrow ditch in the crawl positions for so long. With the thought of another hundred and ten yards to go I enjoyed the chance to stretch out. I rolled on to my back slowly and thought I could just stay where I was, but my inner voice said get up and get going. I closed my eyes for a moment then opened and rolled silently over, hand signaled Alex and we headed up the ditch again. We were gaining ground bit by bit but my legs were soaked through and covered in mud. I put my hand forward and felt something. It was big branch, or a small tree, laying up the ditch. Every time I moved I seemed to get caught on its stubby branches, it would have been hard going normally, but trying to do it silently in the dark was testing to say the least. It was hard going, my inner self was screaming every time I got snagged but I managed to control my frustration. I eventually passed the obstacle and moved forward slightly, waited so Alex could make his way past the tree. Like me, he slowly made his way past it in silence. Once he was clear we went forward a little more, I held up my hand to signal Alex to stop so we could rest for a few minutes.

We moved off again and encountered bramble bushes, perfect cover for us but a nightmare when you are trying to get through them quietly. I glanced at my watch, it was 02.50 hours. We had to get a move on as we needed to be in position no later than 03.55 hours. As the ditch opened up the brambles and overgrown grass got a lot thicker. As we moved the ditch was getting narrower and with all these overgrown brambles it was virtually impossible to get through. I stopped and waited for Alex to come in close. I signaled to tell him there was no way we can get through , he held out his hand as if to say, 'Well, what now?'. I thought for a minute then realised that we were about twenty five yards from the OP. I looked up, we still had the cover of darkness, I thought fuck it and used hand signals to tell Alex to follow me. I started to rise up out of the ditch but Alex held on to my shoulder. I looked at him and he held out his hand and mouthed, "What are you doing?" I shook my head and gestured that we were getting out the ditch and leopard crawling. Alex understood and I moved out of the ditch on the opposite side where the cottage was. I moved slowly on my stomach, away from the ditch to where the ground was clear as brambles had grown on the embankment. As I moved I was feeling with my hand for twigs and small branches, any I found I moved gently out of the way. I made sure I scanned and cleared enough space to take into account the size of my shoulders and webbing. As we made our way forward, I figured it would still take a while to get into position but at least we were out of that ditch. Alex lay behind me, every time I moved he waited then moved so that there was no noise, once he finished his move he touched my boot gently to let me know to move again. It was reassuring when I felt the tap on my boot knowing that he was there, in this world of shit with me.

As we crawled past the undergrowth, I raised my head slowly and could just make out the outline of the old cottage. We had crawled a little too far so I moved slowly sideways and headed back towards the ditch again. Finding a way back through the brambles was hard going but moving a little at a time I managed to get back into the ditch. I crouched down, placed my weapon over my head and edged my way to a half standing position, lifted the brambles slightly but did not disturb any of the vegetation on the top so Alex could slide forward too.

It was darker under the brambles and our sight was not great but we made our way forward a little at a time. I remembered reading in the note book that the walls of the ditch had caved in and been washed away creating a large open area. Finding it was easy as we pulled ourselves free of the ditch. We were facing the cottage, this was an almost perfect lay-up position with a massive amount of cover. The brambles had grown over the area and it was almost like a vegetation tent. We had head room, room to move sideways and we had a fantastic view of the cottage and the remnants of the caravan. We could also see the road so far up to the right and a little to the left. I turned on to my back and I could hardly see anything, if I could hardly see out the vegetation then no one can see in. After the nightmare we had to find the OP I can only imagine the hassle the special forces guys had to find it in the first-place. I looked to Alex as he made a thumbs up and I could just make out his big grin of relief. I think we were both exhausted, I returned the thumbs up and he handed me a water bottle. I greedily gulped down the cold water, it tasted wonderful. I handed the bottle back to him and we lay there for a moment, I think we both realised after our muddy crawl that this was really very comfortable. That was the final mental tick in my head, we were here at last. I glanced at my watch, 03.59 hours, I turned to Alex who had the radio out making ready to send the message, "In position" but the radio was not working.

Alex tried to send the message again and again. I asked him to re-check everything again but he made a face and whispered, 'I have fucking checked it!' I signaled calm down and rest up and that I would take the first stag. He ignored me and continued fiddling with the radio. I touched him on the sleeve and gestured for him to leave it and to get some rest, eventually he gave in and rolled on to his side and closed his eyes. I lay there for a while going through the things in the notebook, the distance from the single-track road, the distance to the cottage, locations of certain items of interest and so on until I was well versed in our surroundings. Our report in times were well overdue, we were supposed to report in every four hours. Even when nothing was happening. They would soon realise something was wrong, but if the radio wasn't functional we would just have to follow standard procedure in a no comms situation and hope Alex could get us up and running, he was a wizard with radios. Daybreak was almost upon us, so I waited until it was nearly daylight before waking Alex. He stirred and looked at his watch, he had been out for two and a half hours. I gestured that he was on stag, two hours on and two hours off, he nodded and I lowered my head on to my arm and drifted off in an instant.

I felt a hand on my shoulder, I thought I had been sleeping for about five minutes but as I looked at my watch I had been out for two hours, I hadn't moved and inch since I had lowered my head. Alex gestured that he would try the radio again, I nodded, moving in closely to his ear I whispered, "If it's fucked we will use the lost comms procedure, bug out twenty four hours after the drop as in the brief and bug out of here in just over fourteen hours. That gives us four hours to make our way to the pickup point", Alex whispered that he had remembered it in the brief, but suggested he try the radio again, I nodded and whispered, "Crack on then".

Alex worked on the radio for over an hour. He stripped it down and put it back together, eventually he got it working and we finally managed to send a message. I had asked him to add "Comms was down, ok now" to the end of the message. We waited for what seemed ages, but was only a few minutes, when a reply came through. I patted Alex on the back with a thumbs up mouthing 'well done mate', Alex busied himself decoding the BATCO and showed me. It read, "- In position - Good - You had comms problems - Ok now". It was good to know we had communication with base again. I told Alex to get his head down for his two hours, by now it was starting to look like a nice day which meant we had an excellent view of the cottage and caravan.

I heard the sound of a vehicle approaching, I glanced to my left and saw a green car heading towards us then speed past. I noted its plate number and continued my watch. I woke Alex after two hours and had a sleep myself. We kept up this routine well into the afternoon. I was on stag when I heard a female voice shouting, "Coffee" then, "Coffee come on!". I realised that she must be shouting on her dog. I was slightly concerned, last thing we wanted was a dog sniffing about, but thankfully we saw her walk past our position and the dog just walked along behind her. I thought about a hot steaming coffee, I would have loved a cup but I was stuck with water.

I knew if there was going to be a visit to the cache area it would be done at night. As the light faded we readied ourselves and waited but nothing, not even a car. The odd hoot from an owl in the distance but that was the best of it. We both willed for someone to appear but no sign of anything or anybody, boring to say the least but this was the task. We kept going all night, on two hour rotations.

As day light crept up, I saw a fox beside the wrecked caravan, moving slowly he jumped and pounced on something, in an instant he was gone.

Alex was about to send a message, he touched my sleeve and whispered, "Do you think if I put, 'Seen fuck all, waste of fucking time get us out of here now, you bunch of fucking wankers' they will get our meaning". I smiled, shook my head and whispered, "Stay professional mate". He nodded, "Aye ok, you're right, but I am so fucking fed up". I agreed but it was our job. I glanced up above the cottages remaining roof, it looked as if it going to be another nice enough day. I was just finishing my stag when I heard another vehicle coming towards us from the left but again it sped on past.

After I had awoken from my two hours of sleep, Alex was preparing to send another message but I could hear him fidgeting. I looked over and he whispered, "This thing is fucked again", I whispered back, "Well, fix the fucker then!". He wasn't happy but set about trying to sort it. After about an hour of tinkering he managed to send a 'normal' message then turned and whispered, "Hopefully they will get us to fuck tonight eh". We kept up stag all day but saw and heard nothing. At 18.15 hours a message came through, 'Pick up at 02.25 hours', Alex whispered, "Thank fuck". I was so glad to be getting out of there. I whispered to Alex, "Ok, listen in. We are moving from here once it's dark enough, we can hold up in the woods before we make our way to the pick-up". He asked if it was dark enough but we would have to give it a few more hours.

When we eventually moved out of the ditch, it was overcast and quite dark. I clambered my way silently back through the ditch and out through the brambles. I lay and waited for Alex. Once through we moved off leopard crawling and made our way back to the point where we originally came out of the ditch. I lay and waited for a minute thinking. Alex touched my boot as if to say, 'you move', he touched again and again then I moved to the side and using hand signals gestured Alex to come up alongside me I whispered, "We will not go into the ditch, we will make our way long the top so that we get past that tree. Then we will get back into the ditch". I showed a thumbs up which he returned, and we moved off. It was a long way to leopard crawl, but anything was better than getting past that tree in the ditch. We started to come into some brambles which meant I had to turn back towards the ditch; I just hoped that we had moved far enough along to get past that tree. I sighed in relief, we had come upon the tree but were on the right side of it so we slid back into the ditch and continued on. We stopped at the end of the ditch and took a few moments to rest up before moving into the marshy area. We moved through the marsh with no issues and then started clearing our way through the woods. I stopped at the fence and looked at Alex as he slowly came up alongside. He whispered, "It's ok here eh?". Just as he said that the heavens opened, with a look of disgust he whispered, "I had to open my mouth". Glancing at my watch it was 00.15 hours, we were making good time.

I knew we would have about an hour to get from here to the pick-up point, so we laid up, resting in the pissing rain. When the time came we headed over the fence and made our way back through the fields and over the fences until we made it back to the embankment. Our pick-up was to happen at the bottom. I thought about our brief and went through our pickup details in my head. The RCT guys would drive up and just at the corner pretend to have a flat tyre, put on the four way hazard lights and get out shouting about the flat in gruff Irish voices as they busied them self's pretending to change it. We would wait for the signal words "Mick put the flat in the back", then slip down the embankment and into the open back doors of the transit.

I kept checking my watch as we waited there in the cold and rain. 10 minutes before the scheduled pick-up we made ready and kept a look out for the vehicle. We eventually saw headlights in the distance but didn't move. We lay still until we could confirm it was the vehicle that was sent to pick us up. Right on time the van stopped below us and they were out shouting about the tyre. The orange hazards flashed away lighting up the dark, we heard the clank from tools on steel, cursing and so on as if they prepared to 'change the tyre'. We got ready to move then we heard the code message, "Mick put the flat in the back", at that instant the hazard warning lights were switched off making it dark again. If someone had been watching from a distance their vision would have been impaired for a few seconds giving us enough time to get inside the van. We jumped over the fence, slid down the embankment on our backs then jumped into the back of the transit van, the doors were closed, the front door was slammed shut and off we went into the night.

We were so glad to get out of the rain as it had gotten heavier as we waited. The driver shouted, "Bet you're glad to be out of this shitty weather eh?" We managed to get ourselves up into the side seats while we were speeding around corners, we were sliding down the bench seat trying to hold on tightly. I shouted for the driver to calm down but the passenger driver shouted back, "When we get you back that's us on leave so sit tight".

As we rounded a tight bend Alex slid on to the floor, shouting 'For fuck sake' as he pulled himself back up, the driver just laughed. I grabbed the attached rope that pulled the doors shut, wrapped it round my wrist and held on to it with a tight grip. I spread my legs apart and forced my feet on to the floor of the transit, forcing my back into the side trying to stay in an upright. As we rounded another tight corner, I wished the driver would calm down, I would rather have patrolled back than this. Alex slid to the floor again, I gestured to the rope and he grabbed his door rope, pulled himself back into the sitting position and shouted, "Slow the fuck down!" I shouted over the noise of the roaring engine, "Are you not drawing attention to yourself driving like this!?" He replied, "Do you said see any lights? There's no fucker out in this weather", as he slammed on the brakes at a corner then throttled on again. We were both knackered so forcing ourselves upright was a chore, I kept thinking that when we reach the city he will have to slow down and we can relax.

It all happened so quickly. We rounded a corner at speed I heard the screech of the brakes and I felt a force in my stomach as my body started to move involuntary. I felt pain as the rope bit into the flesh of my wrist. My whole body launched forward at such a force my legs flew upward banging into the roof. A searing pain shot through my back as I felt my whole body stretch, the rage of fire between my shoulders and arms was unbelievable, in one instant I thought I was levitating. I remember seeing the roof of the transit as it buckled, pieces of glass flying past my head, in a hundredth of a second. It was like I would have been able to pick a piece of glass out of the air as everything seemed to be moving so slowly. I felt pressure at the back of my eyes, then everything sped up again. I clattered into the roof , I thought my neck was going to break as my body compressed into an unnatural position. My head slammed backwards and everything started rolling, suddenly I was thrust up and my head was now being slammed forwards.

Chapter 30

I don't remember much, but one thing that sticks in my head was being dragged through what felt like wet grass then being lifted and pushed.

I could feel a pain in my ankles, twisted, tight and aching. My whole body was shivering. I lifted my head slightly and managed to open my eyes but it was so hazy, I tried to focus as I heard voices but it was as if they were in the distance. The pain in my head raged, my ears felt thick and dull, I couldn't hear properly. As I shook my head from side to side, I saw a blurred figure coming towards me. There was pressure on my jaw and I heard a voice but I could not make out what was being said. I stared intently, my eyes began to focus and things began to clear. Someone was shouting but I still couldn't hear what they were saying. My head was forced to the side and my eyes started to focus.

I was looking at a man who was shouting at me, he had white froth at the sides of his mouth. He leaned back and lunged forward, the punch rattled off the side of my face. I lowered my head trying to breathe. When I glanced up my eyes focused, I saw five men standing there. One of them moved closer and said in an Irish accent, "You'll be wishing you were still unconscious, don't ya eh? Or even dead like your bastard mates eh?". I quickly came to my senses and realised I was tied naked to a chair, my hands were tied to a table edge wedging my thumbs under the lip of the table. My wrists were tied so that my fingers were straight out over the table. As I looked around the man shouted again, "You SAS?" I said no, I looked at the rest of the men, moving my head from side to side. I shouted for them to let me go. I felt a punch on the side of my face which caused me to reel backwards putting more pressure on my wrists and ankles. I felt blood pour from my mouth, I went to shout but nothing came out as my whole body started to tremble. I felt my lower jaw shake uncontrollably. Slivers of blood dripped from my mouth, my eyes were welling up, I tried to blink the tears away so I could focus.

I shook my head thinking I was dreaming. A man, with a handlebar moustache, dressed in a long black coat, came close and blew smoke into my face and whispered, "They tell you to focus on a wee dot did they? Pick something", as he gestured with his hand, "You focus but you will tell us what we want soldier. You look a bit young to be one of them SAS bastards". I tried to say something but nothing came out, my eyes were trying to keep focused as I gasped trying to get my breath back. I forced myself to say 'I am not' and shook my head at the same time. He nodded his head and whispered, "Ok, don't you worry boyo, we will find out all about you and what you were up to". With a strange expression on his face he said, "Focus of your wee dot now". He was so close I could smell his rancid breath. I'm sure as he stared into my eyes I saw a glint of sorrow in his, he kept the stare for a moment then he shouted, "Sean!" He moved away but he never lost eye contact with me. I moved my head to one side and saw someone move towards me, I caught the glint of steel as he raised a hammer above his head and smashed it down onto my little finger with such a force the table jolted up and down. I felt my whole body go rigid and my neck became stiff, my head was rolling to one side before the sheer thrust of pain came raging up through my arm. My stomach muscles braced, my head flung back and the scream came from way down inside my body and roared out of my over-stretched mouth. I opened my eyes, tears blinding me, I tried to focus on the man in front of me but my body was shaking so violently I couldn't. Then I saw it, the hammer coming down again on the next finger, I thought my head was going to burst. I tried to hold the scream from leaving my mouth, thinking for a millionth of a second, if I hold the scream there will be no pain but involuntary my mouth wrenched opened and the pain raged through my convulsing body.

I came to, staring at the stone floor. The pain in my arm raged. I lifted my head slightly and saw someone come into my blurry vision, they shouted, "What's your name soldier? What the fuck were you doing? Where were you?" I shook my head as I tried to say something, but nothing came out of my shuddering mouth. I looked into his eyes searching for some sign of kindness, nothing but a cold dark stare looked back at me. He shouted at me again, "What's your name soldier?". He clenched his teeth, moved back and swung the hammer again. I felt the agony of the hammer striking my third finger, the table jolted upwards and my backbone straightened with such a force my head flung back and my mouth wrenched open. A scream raged through my throat, I started to shake uncontrollably again. I thought I was about to faint, my eyes were bulging out of their sockets, my neck muscles were so tight I thought they would snap. This time he didn't even give me time to stop screaming as I saw the blur of the hammer pass my line of vision before it smashed into my fourth finger. I started trembling uncontrollably and could feel bile wrench up through my throat, out of my mouth. I felt the burning sensation in my throat as I tried to scream but nothing came out. I lunged forward; then everything went black.

I came to in a haze, I knew I was conscious as I felt the pain in my hand and arm, my chin was rested on my upper chest. I didn't want to move, it hurt so much. I tried to control my breathing, I could see the floor and there was blood on my thighs. I dared not look at my hand but almost involuntarily I glanced left and saw through eye-lashed slits the remains of my fingers, white bones sticking out of blood mashed flesh stuck to the table. I could hear voices, I dared not move as I tried to breath shallower staying very still trying to focus my brain. I heard a voice saying, "That cunts just moved", another voice said, "He's not going anywhere". I heard something scraping on the floor then a weird sensation as my body moved. In a shuddering jolt, as a wave of pain rose from my testicles, my eyes flung open and a scream propelled out from my mouth. I saw a figure move forward again and thrust some long item under the table. I thrust upwards as the electricity jolted my uncontrollable body. The bindings bit into the flesh of my ankles and wrists, my eyes were raging in pain. He thrust again but missed me, and hit the chair. I screamed and jolted automatically but there was no pain sensation. I heard a voice shouting, "Like that do ya eh?" He thrust the electric probe, this time hitting his target, my body jolted rigid. I slumped into the chair as my head rocked from side to side, the man with the handlebar moustache came up to me, looked me in the eye and said in a whisper "Right, you ready to talk now? What's your name?" I couldn't remember, he asked, "What's your number?", I shook my head I tried to say something, but it was just a garble. I looked into his eyes for mercy as he said again, "What's your name soldier?" I looked through swollen eyes as tears spilled out, I tried to say something, but I couldn't remember anything.

In the films they slap the prisoner about a bit then ask their number, rank and name and they give the answers no problem, without hesitation. It's all ok in the movies and very entertaining but having just had my fingers smashed with a hammer and my testicles electrocuted I couldn't remember anything at all, I think my brain was starting to shut down.

I shook my head and managed to say, "I don't know", he nodded and whispered, "What do you mean you don't know?" I honestly couldn't remember anything; I just tried to concentrate on keeping the pain away. He said again, "What unit are you? SAS?" gesturing with his head. I shook my head and he said, "That's better, if you're not SAS then you are based here. What regiment are you and where are the barracks?" I said I didn't know, which was true, I couldn't remember. He looked at the ground then back to me, stared in to my eyes as he shook his head he said, "No ID tags soldier, all you bastards wear dog tags. Where are yours?", I shook my head again and told him I didn't know, "You're fucking me about soldier". I shook my head thinking' where were my ID tags'? He moved away and I started to garble something. I forced myself upright, hoping he would not move back, he stepped away and nodded to another man who came forward with a set of pliers.

He tapped the pliers on my nose and grinned. I shook my head and managed to shout 'No', but at that moment he thrust my head backwards. I heard the pliers grind on my front teeth then force was applied but as he pulled. The teeth came free with no real pain, he looked in shock at the three teeth, it was my tooth bridge that he had pulled. He turned and said, "Look at this for fuck sake", still holding my tooth bridge in the plyers. I slumped back into the chair in a daze and started to drift away, I felt an odd sensation in my head, not sure what but a weird sensation. I was left to sit there for a while, I tried not to move to keep the pain at a bearable level. I realised someone had just came up to the side of my head and whispered, "What's your name and what the fuck were you up to?" I shook my head as he said, "I can make them stop you know, I really can. What was your mission?" My brain started to work again, I thought about our task. I tried to say something, but it was just a blur of incoherent garbage that came out. I felt a reassuring hand on my shoulder as he squeezed then patted my shoulder he whispered in my ear, "You're 22 regiment SAS. You've no id tags. You were covered in stinking mud and you look as if you been hiding somewhere for a good while". I shook my head and managed to say, "No", he said, "We think you bastards are all over the place, now listen in closely. What was your mission? Where have you been? May as well tell us because your two mates are dead" I must have pricked up slightly, had I heard right, only two men were dead? What two? Was Alex ok? What happened to Alex? My mind raced. He must have seen my slight reaction, he said, "Well, well, would you look at that lads there was more than just you in the van eh. How many of you bastards were there eh? They left you for us to find, now that's not mates are they eh? Young Patrick here said that both guys in the front were well mangled. He only managed to find one pistol where are your weapons?" He slapped my upper arm, "You bastards won't move without your weapons". I couldn't see the man that was talking to me, but I could see the five others standing by a gas bottle on a small bench against a white stone wall. I listened to the guy at my ear as he said, "I can stop this". I tried to say something but my throat was so dry, I forced myself to say, "There were two of us", at that I saw a man approach wearing a glove holding an iron poker. He thrust my head backwards, I felt the heat come from the cherry red tip of the poker as he held it in front of my eye, I tried to move my head away but it was in a vice like grip. He said, "You will talk you fucking British bastard". I heard a voice say, "Just hold on there Sean". He let go of my head and I watched as he forced the hot end of the poker into my right forearm, my body arched in a rigid movement as the heat melted my skin. I could smell the burning flesh, my body fought against the restraints but I could only move slightly. I howled, he moved away and stood in front of me. I gasped for breath trying to think the pain away. He smiled and shouted to the others, "Let me blind one of his eyes, that bastard will talk to us before long". My whole body started to shake with terror.

I jolted in the chair when I heard a loud bang and a noise like something crashing, I went ridged as a rush of cold air chilled me. I heard gun fire, I waited to feel the pain of being shot. I looked up in horror when I saw a man fall towards me, his head banged off my shoulder, his body hit the table before falling to the floor. My hand raged in pain as the table was battered to one side, a man moved just in front of me, he fired his weapon again and again at the person that had just fell to the floor, the noise was so intense and the smell of carbon forced up my nostrils. The gun fire continued around me and then as quickly as it started it all went silent. My ears were ringing with the noise I heard voices, but it was all muffled.

Chapter 31

Panicking, I looked around, it had all happened so quickly. I was in a daze I glanced from side to side trying to make sense of it all, a face came into my view. I focused noticing he had long brownish hair, I reeled backwards as if trying to get away from him. He knelt down beside me and said my name, "You're ok mate, British army" nodding his head, "British army, do you understand?" Saying my name again, he put a hand on my shoulder and tapped gently it was so reassuring, he nodded his head saying "It's over mate, you're ok". "British army", I said in a whisper, "British army", he nodded, "Aye that's it, British army". I nodded saying again, "British army". I felt a lump in my throat and tears formed in my eyes. I heard someone say, "Fucking hell!", but the person in front of me glanced at the man and shook his head slightly, the man nodded and bent down and started to undo my ankle ropes. The other guy kept patting my shoulder and saying, "You're ok now, you're ok mate it's all over". I could see the smoke from the gun fire hanging in the air. Someone else appeared in front of me and shone a light into my eyes, first the right then left, and nodded. I felt my right hand become free as the rush of blood went into the fingers, he said, "Ok mate, can you squeeze my finger with your right hand?" My hand was swollen from being tied so long but I squeezed, he nodded and said, "Ok mate, with your eyes can you follow my finger?" He moved it slowly from side to side, nodded again, turned slightly and went into a pack pulling something out of a small packet. I saw him plunge something into my thigh, I looked at him he smiled and said, "Its morphine mate, you'll be fine now", he patted my right knee and began pulling something else out of his pack. I heard someone on a radio saying something but all I could make out was, "Move in now, out".

The morphine worked quickly and the pain dissipated, but I was still in such a daze. They kept asking me questions and I just nodded or grunted. I felt something being placed over my shoulders it felt rough but warm, I heard car engines and the screech of tyres. Looking down at my fingers the blood had congealed but my hand was still tied to the table, someone bent down in front of me and said, "You're ok mate, we will leave your left hand tied ok, we are going to take the legs off the table do you understand? It's so that we can get you out of here without disturbing your hand, so we must take the table top with you, do you understand?

The legs are secured by bolts and wing nuts so it should come away, if not we may have to saw the legs off ok. Do you understand?" I felt my eyes welling up impairing my vision, so I had to blink the tears away. I tried to say something but the lump in my throat stopped me, I nodded and garbled something. He said, "Ok mate, it's ok". He stood up and nodded at two guys, I saw the two men stand either side of the table and slowly lift it. The guy who had just talked to me bent down, I heard a squeak as he undid the wing nuts on the legs, then a tapping sound as he worked away the bolt from the table leg. I could feel the table move about as he removed the table leg, I saw his head bobbing up and down and heard clatter of wood on concrete as the legs came free. When all the legs were removed the guy approached me and said, "Ok, we will hold the table steady, then lift you up and get the stretcher under you. Then we will place the table on top of you ok, we will secure it to you without disturbing your injury". I nodded as my eyes filled with tears and I started to shake, I felt a nip on my right side, I jolted my head upward and saw a man putting a needle into my right hand and placing a piece of tape over it to secure it, he fitted a long plastic pipe to a bag. He whispered, "It's an IV drip, we have to get fluid into you". He stood at my side holding the bag above my head. I felt many hands on me as I was lifted out of the chair and slowly moved until I was in a horizontal position. I could see the roof of the building; a stretcher was laid up against my back and then I was laid gently onto it and covered with a blanket. I felt a weight on my thighs and movement as they secured the tabletop to the stretcher. I could see there were four guys on the stretcher now, carrying a corner each. as we moved I could just make out another couple of guys, one of them nodded and winked at me then he moved forward and patted me on the right shoulder saying, "You are safe now, it's over",he winked again.

I felt the wind bite into me as I was taken out into the fresh air. I could see the two doors were hanging off the building I had been in. It was dark outside, the fresh air felt cold but wonderful. I was laid gently into an ambulance, two guys came inside with me and told me were about to move off. They placed an oxygen mask over my face, lifted my head gently and securing the elastic round my head and the doors were closed. As we moved I heard one guy say, "23.37 hours, thirty-five minutes to run as long as they secure the route, they have assured us they would and we would have a clean run in. Thank fuck". He glanced at me, winked, said, "Soon be there mate". The internal light was on in the ambulance; I just lay there and watched as they changed the bag on the drip. They kept checking my blood pressure, shining a light into my eyes and they spoke to me constantly. I closed my eyes, but they said, "No stay awake, we need you to stay awake. It won't be long now, but you must stay awake. Are you cold or hot? Do you feel any pain?" They just kept talking to me. I shook my head and the guy bearing over me said, "Ok, you tell me when you feel pain", again I just nodded. I stared at the roof of the ambulance and saw a union jack sticker, I focused on that sticker for what seemed like forever, it just felt so relaxing staring at this sticker. They asked me where I was from and what I did as a hobby, my sisters name, a heap of fucking stupid questions. I felt like saying just leave me to sleep but every time I closed my eyes they shook me gently and asked more question, what's your favourite colour? What car do you drive? Do you prefer Blondie or Madonna?

As they continued to ask me questions, I just kept nodding or shaking my head. When the Ambulance stopped, the doors opened, and I felt a blast of fresh air. I saw more faces as I was moved out of the ambulance and into a long corridor with bright lights. I was moving so fast the lights became a blur. I felt pressure on my side as we rounded a corner, then through more doors and finally into a room with lights so bright I could hardly see. I blinked as someone came into view wearing a mask over his mouth, he said, "I've seen worse you'll be fine". Was I supposed to feel reassured by this? More faces came into view then moved away then reappeared, I tried to focus then I felt a cool sensation in my right hand.

Chapter 32

I remember being moved and cold wind rushing over me, the slam of a door and I heard someone say, "Just settle down". I heard an engine roar with power and unsteady movement. I remember a warm water sensation over my body rubbing roughly, I tried moving my legs as a voice whispered, "Settle down, settle down. You're ok, just settle down".

I was warm but my mouth was so dry, I heard a door open and close, footsteps coming closer then pressure on my right upper arm. I tried to move but was told again to settle down, I heard a metal clink as I drifted off. When I came too again my vision was blurry, but I am sure I saw someone walk away from me. I looked around trying to focus, a light was on behind my head. I was so warm and there was pressure of something taught over my body, I could hardly move my legs. I tried to move to the right but as I did I felt pressure on my left shoulder I looked round and focused on my left arm it was elevated, as my vision became clearer I started to panic. I was looking at my hand and its bandages. I tried to move my hand towards me, but it was strapped up so tight. I took deep breaths trying to calm myself when suddenly I remembered what had happened to me. Beads of sweat poured over my whole body and I started to shake. I glanced again at my bandaged hand. I managed to turn my hand slightly towards me, I saw finger tips at the end of the bulky bandage. I shook my head, was it a dream? I looked as the door opened and closed, a female face came into my view. She held a finger to her lips and whispered, "Its ok, settle down". I could feel the pressure on my arm again. I tried to speak but my mouth was so dry then I heard the metal clink again and the door was shut. I tried to sit up, but I had no purchase in pulling myself up, something held me tightly. I shouted for help, there was a noise as the door open quickly. I heard loud footsteps approach me, it was the woman from before. I managed to say through a dry throat, "Help me". She leaned in and said, "It's ok, settle down now soldier". I watched her as she checked the equipment at the side, she looked down at me and smiled. She patted my chest and asked if I was thirsty. I nodded and she disappeared for a few minutes before returning to held a wet cloth over my lips, I tried to move my lips to get moisture but she moved it away and told me to take just a little at a time. She placed the wet cloth back to my lips, it felt amazing to get something to drink.

My right arm and thigh were very painful. I managed to say to the nurse through a rasping throat, "It's too tight, my legs". She pulled at the side of my bed and suddenly I could move my legs again. I tried to sit up, but she said to lie where I was. I asked "Where am I?" She placed a hand on my shoulder and replied, "Just rest, I haven't to talk to you", she smiled again and started to quiet me again saying, "Get some rest, I'll see the consultant and tell him your awake. Just lie still ok". After she left I looked around to see if I could see anything in the dim light, it looked like a hospital ward with five empty beds, all the curtains were closed. At the far end there was a desk with a table light on. I heard a door open then a face appeared in front of me, I could smell the coffee off his breath as he shone a light into my eyes. He moved to the bottom of the bed to grab the clip board that was hanging there. He kept nodding to himself as he flicked through the pages on the clipboard, eventually he said, "Ok, that's fine". He turned to the nurse and said, "Let them know he's awake". He turned back to me and told me to rest before moving to the bottom of the bed to return the clipboard and leaving. I let out a long breath and tried to push myself up a bit more, I moved around and pushed using my right hand on the bed, after a while of this I was sitting up slightly. I could see a bit better but now I was rather uncomfortable. I looked around, there was not much to see but I could smell the disinfectant. The door opened and in walked the nurse again. She gasped, "What are you doing?". I was all at one side and I must have looked uncomfortable, so she placed her arm round my shoulders and hauled me over and up at the same time as she moved my pillow and laid me back down. I was more comfortable and I was upright so I could see a bit more. My right forearm was bandaged. In my mouth I felt the gap with my tongue where my teeth used to be, I could only feel the sharp pegs that had held my bridge in place.

I closed my eyes and it all came flooding back, the hammer connecting with my fingers, the heat of the poker on my arm, the pain, the terror I felt. My body started to shake, sweat poured from my brow as the nurse comforted me saying, "Its ok, its ok". I must have started to struggle but again she said, "Shhhhh, shhhhh its ok, settle down. You're ok, they will be here soon". I was thinking 'Who are THEY?' She offered me more water, her reassuring voice settled me as she placed a hand on the back of my head, lifted gently and put a glass to my lips. I felt the water pass over my dry lips, I must have drunk greedily because she stopped me, saying, "A little at a time". I asked again where I was, but again she replied she was not to talk to me just attend to me. I watched her as she took my blood pressure again, she looked around thirty. She had short black hair, but she looked very tired. As I settled back down she moved away yawning, she stood at the end of my be and wrote something on the clipboard then returned it to the bed end and left. I tried to say something but suddenly felt very sleepy and I closed my eyes.

I woke in a daze as I heard someone whisper in the distance. I moved my head to one side and the nurse appeared and asked, "You ok soldier?" I grunted as she said, "Want some more water?". She held my head as I drank down the cool liquid, I looked up at her and she smiled, "That's enough, ok", I nodded. She asked if I wanted to sit up slightly, I nodded and grunted, "More water", she nodded as she hauled me up slightly. I looked around and saw three men, two sitting on chairs and one person standing in the background. I tried to focus then I recognised one of them. I said, in a raspy voice, "You've had your hair cut". Mike smiled, saying "Aye, that's right mate. How do you feel?" I told him my arm was burning, he told me to rest and they would be just next door. I asked again "Where am I?" Mike walked over, placed a hand on my shoulder, and said, "You're in London mate". I glanced, wide eyes, at him and said, "Eh?".

Someone else came into view, an older man, he said in a well-mannered officers voice, "You were transported here three days ago, now you rest up for the next couple of days. Ok Corporal?". I acknowledged his instruction, he said, "Good man. You get some rest" then headed out the door.

Mike again said they were going to be next door. He turned towards the nurse and said, "Senior Sister, or Captain. Otherwise known as the lovely Shelley here, has been looking after you round the clock, so if you need something one of us will be by the desk", He turned to the Nurse smiling and said, "Ok Shell, thanks for everything. We will take it from here, you get some rest. We'll see you tomorrow at around 11.00 hours, thanks again".

She said it was her pleasure as she leaned in and patted my shoulder, saying with a smile, "You'll be fine". I watched her go then focused back on Mike he told me again to get some rest, I was about to say something but was overcome with tiredness.

When I woke, I could see light coming through a small slit in the curtain. I grunted and someone appeared at my side. They asked if I wanted some water, I tried to speak but my throat was sore so I just nodded. I tried to sit up a bit but the person had to help me into an upright position. I was handed a glass with a small amount of water in it. I held it in my right hand but as I moved a pain burned through my arm, I tried to get the glass to my mouth, but couldn't. He smiled, "Here, let me help you", holding the glass I drank it all down. He told me it was 06.10 hours and that I was to get a bed bath at 07.00 hours, he winked, "You may be lucky, there are some bonnie nurses here". He moved a chair over, sat down, and told me what was happening in the news that day. I looked at him and asked what had happened to me, Alex, the rest of the men? I wanted to know. "Don't think about that now, you just get your strength back mate and we can talk then".

We chatted until the door opened and in came a guy in a white uniform pushing a small trolley. The guy at my side rose from his chair and said, "Bath time mate". I must have looked disappointed as he smiled and said, "Sorry son, all the bonnie nurses are probably at breakfast". The guy with the trolly approached my bed and said, "Good morning, and what happened to you then?" The guy I had chatted with turned and said angrily, "You were briefed weren't you?!" the guy in white looked a bit sheepish, as he continued, "Don't talk, just wash and tend the dressings". White coat man nodded and set to work.

After a wash and a good clean he changed my dressings, there were lots of little ones on my arms, thighs, neck and shoulder. He peeled away the dressings, cleaned the wounds with a brownish liquid, patted them dry and then redressed them. He never said anything else as he worked, he just glanced at the guy sitting beside me every now and then. When he was done, he nodded and walked away. I croaked a "Thank you", but he just turned, nodded again and walked out the door. "Feel better now eh?" the guy sitting with me asked, "You want to get some clothes on?" I grunted an 'aye' as he opened a small bag and produced a green army tracksuit, vest and socks, he said, "Ok mate, I'll dress you. Now the vest will be ok, but I have modified the track suit jacket on the left hand side to accommodate your bandages". He moved me upright, I felt all dizzy and very lightheaded, but he dressed me slowly taking care and stopping if I winced in pain. I noticed that the left arm of the track suit was removed at the seam, he unhooked my hand from the stand that had been keeping it upright then pulled the track suit over my bandaged arm and zipped it up. He lifted my arm and hooking the bandage to the stand again, said, "Once the catheter is out we will get you bottoms on ok".

I sat there, dressed from the waist up, but at least I was upright now. I looked around and stared at the desk with the light on, he asked, "You ok? You're a bit white". I felt lightheaded and sick, I looked at him as he said, "You're going to be ok mate". I remember struggling for breath, breathing in short gasps, he held on to my arm and shoulder. I screamed and shouted, "NO!". He settled me back down and asked if I was ok. I felt tears build up in my eyes, I couldn't see. I was breathing rapidly. He said, "Its ok mate, its ok, settle down". I screamed again "NO!" It was almost involuntary, my brain saying, 'Why are you doing this?' My body shook in terror and I screamed, "LET ME GO!".

He stood over me with his hands on my shoulders pushing me back into the mattress, he kept saying, "You're ok mate, settle yourself. Your safe here ok. You're safe here". Safe? Would I ever feel safe again?

I felt the pressure coming off my shoulders, all I wanted now was to sleep. I heard him say, "Its ok, rest now mate, rest now", I heard him sigh and in a whisper say, "Too early, far too early". I felt as if I was as light as a feather and I drifted off.

I woke to a pressure on my arm and a clink sound. I opened my eyes and this female smiled and asked how I was feeling. She pulled me up slightly, gave me a little water and said, "That's better now isn't it?" I saw her glance to the right and nod, then a face appeared. It was Mike. He smiled and said, "Remember me mate?" I nodded, lifted my right hand and pointed at him grunting, "Just keep up, ok", He laughed, "That's right mate, when did I say that to you?" I replied in a raspy voice, "Africa then Gibraltar". He smiled, "That's it mate, that's it", he turned to the female and said, "Ok if we try and sit him up a bit?", her face came into my view as she asked me if I wanted to sit up.

They both pulled me up into a sitting position and she said if I felt sick or dizzy to give her a shout. I did feel sick and dizzy, but I said nothing. Mike sat on a chair and asked how I was feeling. I tried to say something but the lump in my throat stopped me. I leant forward trying to swallow it down, I felt tears pricking my eyes and I tried to blink them away. I felt so embarrassed. Mike kept smiling telling me everything is going to be ok. After I had calmed down, he said, "You still as good with a rifle are you?" I nodded gesturing toward my hand and said, "I think so", he said, "Aye, you have a talent mate". I managed to get rid of the lump in my throat and blinked away the tears saying, "Mike-". He leaned in close and said, "Its ok mate, just forget it just now and get your strength back". It was almost as if he knew what I was about to say. He grinned and said, "You're in London now, this is your ward. We are just outside. Want something to read mate?" I shook my head, he looked at the ground and I could see him nodding to himself then he turned and said, "You're ok now mate, you're safe here. Just rest up and we will debrief you as soon as we think your strong enough, ok?" The female, who I now remembered was called Shelley, butted in saying, "I think that's enough, he looks tired again". I shook my head and said, "No I'm not tired, but I am thirsty". Mike stood and said, "I'll get you some juice and a magazine or two, you rest up. There are some of the guys next door. Shelley here will look after you".

I must have been tired because I don't even remember falling asleep but when I woke up again my arm ached. I looked up and there was a pull up handle above my head. I grasped it with my right hand and hauled, twisting my backside until I was upright. I looked around and to my delight I wasn't dizzy or nauseous. Shelley appeared from behind her desk and said, "Well, well, feeling better are we?" I nodded. My bed was all wet, she looked under the blankets and confirmed my catheter was leaking. "It's ok, let's get you cleaned up; do you think you could manage a bottle for your wee?". I nodded feeling a little embarrassed, it must have shown on my face, because she smiled and said, "its ok, no need to be embarrassed. I am a nurse you know".

Mike returned just as Shelley finished tucking in the sheets and I was all clean and dry, I even managed to get a pair of boxers on, me wriggling and Shelley pulling but they were on. Mike brought bottles of diluting juice and a couple of mags. He winked and said, "The middle ones quite interesting mate". I looked at it as he showed a bit of the front cover, it was an escort magazine. I tried to smile but in a flash I saw the hammer batter on to my finger and I started to shake again. He sat down on the edge of my bed patted my shoulder and said, "It's ok mate, you've been through the mill I know, but its ok". Shelley held my hand and smiled, "Listen to your pal here, it's ok". I was so tired my eyes were heavy I tried to keep them open, but I drifted away again.

I woke thirsty and hungry; I had not thought about food for a while but suddenly I was starving.

Shelley was about to go off shift but she sorted out coldwater and a bottle for my piss. It's hard sitting there trying to piss into a bottle but after a few moments there it went, I handed it to her and asked if I could get up, she shook her head, "Maybe tomorrow, but you rest up. What do you want to eat?". I told her anything would do, she replied, "No, you tell me what you would like". I shrugged my shoulders, I couldn't think of anything in particular, I just wanted food. She held up a finger as if she had and idea and told me to wait a moment then left. When the door opened again in came a guy with a huge grin, he placed the escort mag back in the pile and said, "Ok mate, I wanted a read of that". I smiled and told him to help himself. "Right then, what do you want to eat? Pizza, burgers or KFC maybe?" eventually I settled on a pizza, I didn't care I just wanted food. This was a good sign surely.

When he left I settled back to wait on my food, that's when I started to recall what had happened. I shook my head and the images went away, I told myself to get a grip, sort my shite out. I pulled back the sheets and saw, for the first time, that my stomach, arms and thighs were covered in small dressings. I remembered the guy changing the dressings earlier. I remember my fingers, but had it all been a bad dream? A stabbing pain in my hand brought me back to reality, I looked at my elevated hand, no it was real. I sat there deep in thought for what seemed ages, then the door opened and I heard the squeak of wheels. Mike appeared saying, "How's it going mate? You feeling better eh?". I nodded as I watched him pushing a unit with a TV and a video. he stopped at the bottom of my bed, he had run out an extension cable, and switched it on. "The tv channels are shit but we have heaps of videos, what do you fancy?". I shrugged and said 'whatever you've got', he said, "The Deer Hunter, Convoy and the American Werewolf in London", I was about to answer when I heard a voice from the door say, "And I got blue movies in the back of my car". I looked up and saw someone I thought I recognised but I wasn't sure, he smiled and asked if I was feeling better, I nodded. He said "Pizza will be here shortly". I sat back as they put in the film, 'Convoy'. They both pulled up chairs and we started, ten minutes later the pizza arrived. We ate and chatted our way through the movie and into the small hours of the morning.

QRF "Pig" on Patrol

QRF 2 "Quick Reaction Force 2" On Patrol

QRF 1 "Quick Reaction Force 1"at Falls Road
Junction.

Chapter 33

The consultant said, "We will have to do a lumber puncture, I'm not happy with some of the things we are monitoring", I felt fine but still very tired. I was wheeled away on a trolley into a room full of shiny stainless steel and bright lights, told to get into a position with my knee up to my chest, I felt a sting at the bottom of my spine then it was all over. I was trolleyed back and left to rest.

The following day the consultant came through the door with two of the guys, they hovered around while the doctor looked at my notes then said, "We did the lumber-puncture and there is a trace of blood in your spinal fluid, not much, but there is a trace. I would like you to have a CAT scan". He explained it was a scan of the brain, a needle will be inserted into the Femoral Artery in my groin and inject dye which would travel over the brain while they viewed it on a monitor. I was shocked but he assured me it would be fine, he turned to the two guys nodded and left. "Ok mate, because of this we will have to inform your family", one said, "Ok, but I don't want anyone here" I told him. "If they insist, we can't stop them" he replied. "I'll phone myself", I said. One of them disappeared and returned with a trolley phone, he said, "Sorry mate, but we will have to be here. It is under the official secrets act so not a word". I stared at him for a while, I did understand but the reality of it all had not sunk in until then. He continued, "Just say you were in a vehicle accident, which isn't a lie. Try and stay as close to the truth as you can when telling a cover story". We practice that in the regiment, if you stay close to the truth it is a bit more believable and easier for you to remember, I nodded as I lifted the receiver.

My Mum answered on the third ring and she was not happy when I told her I had been in an accident. "I am fine, but my fingers are in a bit of a mess", which wasn't a lie, I was now reading off a piece of paper that one of the guys was scribbling notes on, I continued, "The doctor said they want to do a CAT scan". Immediately she said, "I am on my way". I insisted, "No Mum, honestly I am fine". She was not taking no for an answer. I said, "Mum, listen. I am fine, I am in London and getting the best of treatment", I read the piece of paper and said "Mum you can phone the consultant if you like but I am fine honestly", all I got was, "I am coming down, your brother will be coming too. Your sister will have to stay with your Grandmother, what hospital are you in?" I tried again, "No Mum, honestly there's no need..."

suddenly, the telephone was taken out of my hands. One of the guys spoke into the phone, "Sorry about that", he introduced himself as Sergeant Jones. I looked at him, he winked and continued, "We have the authority to transport you to London so let us make the arrangements for you", I did not hear what Mum said but he replied, "We will have you picked up from the door tomorrow morning at 05.00 hours, is that ok for you? Good. Ok, as I said 05.00 hours to Aberdeen, flight at 07.10 hours arriving in London at 08.40 hours and we will be waiting for you when you arrive. We will take you straight to the hospital. His scan is scheduled for 12.45 hours tomorrow so plenty of time to see him before. I take it there will be two of you coming down? Oh good. Can I have both full names please?" He nodded scribbling on a piece of paper, "You can pick up your tickets at the British Airways desk, thank you so much I will hand you back to your son. Thank you again, look forward to meeting you tomorrow".

He handed me back the phone I said, in as cheery a voice as I could manage, "That's good of them eh?". She never said much, then there was a long silence before she finally said, "Well, do you need anything?" I told her I had everything I needed, she continued by saying, "Oh by the way your Dad was in the army and he was injured. He never got this special treatment, I'm not sure what's going on. When was your accident?" I said, "Yesterday, it's a new army now Mum", she told me to take care and they would see me tomorrow. There was a whisper beside my ear, "Tell her that accommodation will be offered in the Union Jack club, for as long as they need". I repeated what he said, she replied, in a sarcastic tone, "Well that's very nice of them, ok my loon see you tomorrow love you", then she hung up. The guy who had whispered in my ear asked, "What did you tell her?". I told him I said it was yesterday I had the accident. He sighed, walked around the ward for a bit then said, "Your brother, is he trustworthy?" I nodded, "Yes very much so". He thought for a while then continued, "Ok, we may have to tell them, I'll see what the boss says. You get some rest, we have all this in hand".

The next day I got up and was wheeled into the shower room. As I sat on the shower chair, Shelley told me to sit and wash myself. She fitted a plastic bag to my left hand. I looked down at all the little dressings and she told me it would be ok; she would redress them when I had dried myself. I was dressed in a new army tracksuit, all clean and showered. I almost felt presentable. I was chatting away to one of the guys when I glanced at the clock, 08.45, I thought that's them landed now. I really was looking forward to seeing them both. I asked how long their journey is to here from the airport, he smiled and said, "It's about an hour from Heathrow, but depends on traffic" I slowly watched the clock tick past as the guy was telling me about the new house he just brought and all the things he wanted to do to it, I nodded along. It was very interesting, but I longed for the clock to go faster. I was getting sleepy again, I think with the heat in the ward, when I heard the door open. I looked over and there was my Mum and my big brother. They smiled and Mum hugged me, I saw tears well up in her eyes but I reassured her I was fine. The guy who had been chatting to me, stood up and said, "I will leave you to catch up, I'll be at the desk if you need anything". I nodded, thanked him and he left.

My brother came round to the other side of the bed and asked if I was ok, I just nodded as I tried to swallow the huge lump that had formed in my throat. My eyes welled up but I managed to say, "I missed you both". Mum hugged me again and my brother asked what had happened, when a well-spoken voice, from behind him, said, "I can fill you in on that if you'd like, unfortunately he was knocked out for a bit, but I was there". My Mum spun round and there in full dress uniform was a Colonel. He held out his hand and shook both of theirs. He continued, "We were in a convoy and a reckless civilian car went out of control causing our driver to swerve. He hit the verge, that's what caused the lorry to topple over and down the embankment", he smiled, "Everyone is ok, except his hand was stuck under a heavy piece of equipment. Very unfortunate, but he looks fine doesn't he?" My Mum said, "That's all very well, but why was I not informed straight away?" "Well I can only apologise about that, it was all such a mess and we had the best interests of your son uppermost in our minds", he smiled. My brother asked when I would get home, the Colonel told them, "Not for a while I am afraid, he will get the best of treatment here. You can talk to the consultant in an hour or so, he will be doing his rounds. Your accommodation is all booked and, please, stay as long as you wish. The duty driver is on standby for you coming and going from the hospital and anything else you require".

He smiled, shook their hands again and said, "I have a meeting to attend but it was very nice to meet you, anything you need just ask". They both thanked him, he turned to me and said, "Good man", then walked away.

Once he was out of ear shot my Mum leaned in and whispered, "I do not believe a word of it by the way, but they do seem to be looking after you". I started to tell her it was all true but my brother butted in, "Do you know that there are two men outside this door, two at the door at the end of the corridor and another two men and him at that desk", he said pointing in their direction. I tried to tell them they were mates, but they didn't believe me. My Mum just looked at me and said, "Aye right, let's get this scan out of the way first. I have a few questions for the Colonel myself". I asked her not to say anything, "Don't Mum, honestly, don't ok. It's just great to see you both".

I was taken away on a trolley for the scan, my Mum and brother said they would stay in the ward. The next thing I knew I was in a room and this chap appeared. He explained what was about to happen "Keep very still when we are doing this, if you move your eyes you can see the three monitors up there on the left. Ok, let's get started". Padding was placed around my head with Velcro straps and straps over my body to keep me still. I felt a nip on my thigh as he begun, talking me through the process, "First the dye over the left side", it was a weird sensation, I felt my eye flicker, it was a terrible feeling. He said, "Over the right side now". I felt sick, I had flashes in my vision. I was told to stay still but my arm started to tremble, I saw a picture in my head, coming and going. A lorry in front of me then it went back to normal. He said, "This is the last one". There was a strange noise as the dye was injected in and I could taste salt on my tongue. There were lots of flashing lights and images which seemed to go on for ages. A face appeared in front of me saying, "You're done, get some rest now and I will see you later". I tried to nod but my head was still secured tightly. The taste of salt and metal in my mouth was terrible. Next thing I knew I was back in the ward and someone was telling me to rest.

When I woke up, I moved my eyes and tried to sit up. Mum appeared at the side of my bed asking how I felt. I had felt better but said I was fine. The day came and went, my Mum and brother left saying they would be back tomorrow as I drifted off to sleep again. The following day we were informed that I was in need of a few operations on my fingers once they had healed and that I had suffered a small bleed in the brain but it was not a problem, probably caused by the head trauma. When the consultant was telling me this, I saw him glance over at the two guys standing beside him, one of them nodded, I looked over at my Mum, she had seen it too.

Later that afternoon the Colonel appeared again and spoke to my Mum and brother. They had decided to leave for home the next day so he wished them all the best and told them, "If you need to come down again just phone this number and flights and accommodation will be provided", he handed them a card. They sat, had coffee, and chatted, I just sat on the bed as everyone talked over me, and nodded every so often in my direction, as if I were not even there. Eventually he stood up, wished them both a safe journey home then left. My brother went for a smoke, as he did every hour or so, the guys took him out on to a fire escape, he said they were all a good laugh. It was sad when the time came for them to leave, we all hugged. They wished me well. As they were leaving one of the guys gave my Mum the number for the trolley phone, and they were off.

Chapter 34

Over the next few days I had the same routine, woke, breakfast, shower, watched the news then a video. Once, sometimes twice a day, the consultantwould visit. Two days after my Mum had left, the consultant came and explained about the CAT scan, "There is no problems in your head. If there had been, theatre were standing by. You have been through a lot and something had to give, you're only human". Someone, who was standing by my bed, cleared their throat as if to say that was enough. A nod from the consultant, 'message understood'. He continued, "Your wounds are healing fine, your hand will be seen in a day or two.", he asked if I needed anything, I shook my head as he replaced the clip board on the end if my bed. He left followed by the person who 'cleared their throat'. I could hear their voices outside the door. When the guy came back in he sat down at his desk, I asked if there was anything wrong but he just brushed it off telling me everything was fine. I knew I wasn't being told the whole story; I didn't even feel like I was being told much of it at all.

All my small dressings were changed on a daily basis, my hand was still bandaged and had to be elevated as much as possible. The consultant had told me it would have to be kept immobilised, they would leave it bandaged but monitor it for signs of infection. One day I asked Shelley what all the small dressing were covering, she whispered, "Its burns but they are healing". I asked where I got the burns from, she just shushed me but I repeated, "Where from?" She just shook her head and said, "Rest up, ok?" That was the end of it.

Most afternoons I chatted with some of the guys and again at night, such was my routine. I was starting to get my strength back and was walking around the ward, but when I went for a shower, they said I had to go in a wheelchair. It was only two doors down in the corridor, but they insisted. This routine carried on for the next couple of days, shower, brew, TV and looking at magazines. I was a little bored but slept a lot, the guys tried to keep my spirts up with funny stories and the odd joke.

Chapter 35

By now all the small dressings on the burns were removed and left open to heal, my hand and wrist were still bandaged and had to be wrapped in cling film when I showered. I was managing to walk about no problem, getting stronger all the time. One day, on the way back from my shower, I stopped to have the usual chat with the guys. When I entered my room there were chairs set out in the middle of the ward facing my bed space. I was handed a brew and the tv had been wheeled out of the way. I asked the guy at the desk what was happening, he just told me to relax they would be here in twenty minutes. I asked, "Who's they?" He replied, "It's the debrief mate". I felt my stomach turn and I stared to shake slightly. I walked over to the window and opened the curtains, I looked out thinking back to what had happened, until now I had managed to get it to the back of my mind and not think of it, but now it all came flooding back. A reassuring hand was laid on my shoulder and a voice said, "Its ok, just rest up till they arrive. It will help you get your mind straight, help you understand better", I nodded and sat back on my bed. I could feel the anxiety creeping in.

Twenty minutes later the door opened and in walked a large group of men, one of them I recognised as the Colonel that had been here before when my Mum and brother visited. They were all dressed in civvies which was strange. Some of them nodded in my direction as they settled down in the chairs, I noticed Alex at the back, he was the last to enter the ward. He sat with Mike who nodded and smiled to me. I nodded in Alex' direction his eyes met mine but he lowered them instantly and stared at the floor, I noticed that the top of his head had been shaved and there was scar tissue covering the top of his skull. I looked around the group but I didn't recognise any other faces, the colonel nodded and the doors to the ward were closed.

One of the men walked over, asked if I was ok and handed me an ice cool bottle of water saying, "It will help your dry throat mate". I was about to say I was fine but thought better of it and just took it. They were all staring at me with expressionless faces, it was very daunting, eventually the silence was broken, and to my surprise, it was Alex that spoke first.

His voice was shaky as he started, "As you are aware we were involved in an accident. The driver lost control on the wet road causing the van to swerve and hit a tree almost head on then rolled down and embankment. I came too in the back of the van. I managed to find my torch in my top pocket and shone it around. The van was laying on its side and I saw you crumpled into the back of the passenger's seat, by the position you were in I thought you were a goner. I managed to move you slightly, I checked your vitals and you were breathing but very shallow and your pulse was faint. I checked for broken bones, none, but you had a head injury, it looked like a flesh wound so I decided I had to get you out of the van. With an effort I managed to get one of the back doors open, pulled you out and on to the grass bank and get you into the recovery position. I went to the front of the van, I saw the driver and passenger, both goners, a right mess they were in". Someone cleared their throat as if to say 'just the facts'. Alex continued, "I tried the radio in the van but nothing. I tried our radio, it was fucked anyway but I had to try. With the van on its side the remaining head light was shining up towards the road. I tried everything to get the radios to work but nothing, so I decided to go and get help. I knew I had to clear the van of weapons and stash them. I managed to get the weapons out of the back of the van but I had to go to the front again, fucking terrible, I pulled one pistol from the passenger but the driver was wedged to one side and I couldn't get to him. The two sub machine guns that were under their seats were now in the back of the van. I unloaded all the weapons, hid them up the bank to the right of the van and covered them with foliage. I hid the rounds and mags in another area, keeping my pistol with me. I tried to get a response from you but still nothing. I went up to the top of the embankment and waited but there was no sign of any cars coming in the distance and the weather was getting worse. I headed away in the direction we had come from. I knew from the maps that we had studied there was a farm along the road, but I couldn't remember how far back it was so I started running, thinking if a car comes I would commandeer it and get help. It felt like I had run for ages before finally reaching the farmhouse, it was set back from the road and I slid on the mud at the entrance and struggled to get through the mess. I banged on the door, no answer so I just booted it in. I was looking for light switches because the place was in darkness when I heard a noise upstairs, I shouted for help and I could see a light come on as it lit up the doorway. I checked my watch; it had been twenty-three minutes since I left you. A voice shouted, "Who is it?" I called back that I needed help and if they had a phone I could use. An old man appeared at the top of the stairs asking what was going on. I explained that there had been an accident and I needed help, the old man gestured with his finger to a door telling me the phone was in there.

I booted the door open and was standing in the kitchen, I switched the light on and picked up the phone. The old man appeared in the doorway wearing his Pajamas. I held my pistol up towards him. He told me there was no need for that and I was hurt, he offered to help but I just ignored him and dialed the emergency number. I got through on the fourth ring, explained what had happened and was told to get back to the scene of the incident as quickly as possible, quick reaction vehicles were being dispatched. I then told them I had asked for help from a civilian and would take his car and make my way back.

The old man said he had some medical experience and could treat me head injury but I shouted back, "Fuck that, where are the keys for your car, I will have to commandeer it". He said he would drive me and handed me a towel for my head. We jumped into the car and we headed back to the crash. I sat in the back with my weapon on him all the time. He told me again that it wasn't necessary but I just told him to keep driving. I told him roughly where to head, and I asked if he was a doctor, he said he had medical training but, no, he was not a doctor he was a vet. Retired now, but in the circumstances, he would be able to help so we headed back up the road. We drove through dark night until we turned a corner and saw the head light still shining in the distance. He told me this was a bad bit of road and had caused a lot of accidents. As we rounded the last corner I saw another vehicle had stopped at the side of the road. I thought there is no way the QRF could get there that quickly and as we approached the vehicle took off but I managed to get the number plate. We stopped, I got out and slid down the embankment to where I left you. I searched all around but you had gone. The old man slowly made his way down to me, unsteady on the wet embankment; he approached the front of the van, looked in saying, "Dear God". I told him there was someone missing. He asked if I was sure, of course I was sure I was pointing at the ground where I had left you. He said that the people in the car have come across the accident and may have taken you with them to a hospital, either that or you have woken and wandered off yourself in a daze. After about ten minutes, vehicles appeared, there were voices shouting, lights everywhere, the quick reaction force had arrived. It had taken them about twenty-one minutes be on scene".

He paused for a moment then continued, "I explained to the officer what had happened, that you were missing, and told him the location of the hidden weapons and munition. He said they would start a search of the area as you couldn't have gotten far on your own and to check if you had been taken in to any of the hospitals. They also relayed the plate of the vehicle I had seen over the radio so everyone was on the lookout for it. I was taken into the land rover ambulance when it arrived and was treated. Five minutes later the officer returned to get me to verify the plate again, he asked if I was sure. Of course I was bloody sure. He grabbed his radio and started talking into it, I wasn't sure what he said but before I could ask what was going on the ambulance doors were closed and we left".

Alex stopped talking and lowered his head.

I jumped when a voice from the other side of my bed started talking, he introduced himself and explained that he ran all the operations for the regiment in Belfast under the control of the Colonel, gesturing with his hand toward the colonel, he continued, "A call came through to us from brigade informing us of the incident and that the car that was seen leaving the scene was that of a known player (terrorist) and registered to his cousin, possibly a soldier may have been lifted and we needed help in finding him. Realising who you were and you were working for us, that's when we got the ball rolling. Every tout (informant) that we knew was contacted, it took a while but in the end one came through, thanks to him we got a break. There were three possible locations you could've been. We knew they couldn't have moved too far, they would have never chanced it with the usual roadblocks. Information came through from 14 Intelligence which verified our previous intel from the tout, it was either a derelict farmhouse, an old sawmill used now for storage of heavy plant moving equipment or a disused warehouse. I split the guys into three teams of five using six vehicles. The first team to arrive on scene was at the old farm house, they drove past and there was no sign of anything but just to confirm they dropped a couple of guys off to recce the area. Whilst that was happening the other team approached the area near the sawmill, but as they drove past one of the guys in the back caught a glimpse of a small glow from a cigarette. He could just make out a dark shadow in the wooded area, back off the road, possibility a dicker (look out) but we needed to confirm. They dropped two guys down the road out of ear shot of the dicker then the vehicles continued and waited half a mile down the road.

Two of our guys made their way back along the lower bank, once in position they radioed that the person we spotted was definitely acting as a lookout. It was agreed that this was quite possibly the location you were being held; it was all reported back to ops. A few minutes later it was confirmed by the guys on the ground that there were three vehicles round the back of the sawmill, one being the vehicle reported leaving the scene of the accident. 14 intelligence managed to get all relevant information on the structure of the building, concrete block, asbestos roofing, eight skylights, a normal door north and south, a glass door east into a reception or office area and two large main wooden doors facing the entrance road on the west side, door hinges inward opening, the lot. The other team were at the disused warehouse. They saw no sign of anything so turned around and headed back towards the sawmill. We didn't have time to fuck about so I radioed our guys on the ground and had them make an arrest of the dicker, after few moment of persuasion it was confirmed that you were held in the main building. By this point we had everyone heading to your location".

There was a brief pause, "Once all vehicles arrived, roadblocks were set up four miles either side of the access road to the sawmill by RUC and green army. As the information came through we put a D.P.A. (Deliberate plan of action) in place, the dicker was secured and lifted by other team members. Two guys made their way down towards the sawmill staying under cover, I suggested just eyes on the building for the moment. More information came through about the sawmill, who owned it, how long it had been disused as a sawmill and what was now inside. We heard over the radio that lights were on in the main building, we thought we better get some eyes in closer and to confirm that the main doors were still old wooden doors. There were no sentries present so it wasn't too difficult to get nice and close. We also dropped two guys off further up the road so they could recce the south side. It was now a waiting game, someone said we couldn't storm in without proper intel, I agreed but we would have to improvise. Once the south team were in position, they confirmed there was approximately 100 metres from the tree line to the sawmill. We checked weapons and removed the back doors of a vehicle. Over all our comms we heard what none of us wanted to hear, north team reported a loud scream from inside the building. We moved forward to some closer observation points in preparation".

"North team radioed that they had eyes on X-rays, 5 confirmed but there may have been more. All this was relayed back to base, moments later it was confirmed we had control and authorisation to assault the building and it came from the top. It was rescue at all cost".

D.P.A.

Eight-man assault team, not including driver.

Two men on the North of the building to make their way to the side of the large wooden doors.

South team to gain access through the side door.

Three, including driver in the vehicle up the main road, ready to free wheel silently down 19-degree angle towards the building using the vehicle as a battering ram. The explosive diversion to go off at ten yards from the doors.

East team to set an explosive charge, by way of a diversion, wait on ground north and east for stragglers.

South team to make way through side door taking out x-rays. North-west team enters as vehicle crashes through door.

(I have given all soldiers a letter rather than a name just to make it easier to understand)

SOLDIERS

A, B North team made their way to the side of the main wooden doors.

C, D South Team at side door of the building, picked lock ready to gain access.

E, F East Team set explosive charge for diversion.

G, H Inside back seat of vehicle with the doors removed.

R Driver of the battering ram vehicle.

THE ASSAULT

R Driving vehicle with seat back as far as possible from the dashboard.

G, H Inside back seat wedged sideways into seats to brace against the impact.

E, F Waiting for go with explosive diversion.

C, D Ready to gain entry

Relaying all information back to base, it was confirmed, standby, standby.

GO

R Vehicle freewheeling round corner on to the sawmill road gathering speed round the last bend. Wheels straighten up heading for the wooden doors.

R Calling out the distance on radio fifty yards, forty yards, thirty yards, twenty yards.

A, B Standby doors

Over the radio came "TEN YARDS".

E, F Set off the diversion charge, just before the vehicle crashes through wooden doors.

C, D Wrenching the door open and move inside instantly taking out two of the armed x-rays.

A, B Moving through the smashed doors taking out another two armed x-rays.

G Take out the x-ray from the vehicle.

A Moved forward taking out last x-ray, at the side of the captive. Initial assault was done in fourteen seconds.

Captive checked and treated on scene, table legs removed, captive secured into stretcher and moved. Building secured, searched, and handed over too RUC, thirty-three minutes. We vacated the area.

Chapter 36

I looked over at a guy sitting crossed legged and arms folded, as if he were in his living room watching the tv. I asked if he were soldier A. Smiling and nodding, he said, "Remember my face mate?" I told him I did and thanked him, he shrugged saying, "No problem mate, that's what we train for", the Colonel stood and looked at his men, "Well, that's a job well done". Nodding his head in appreciation he turned on his heel and stared directly at me, "What do you say soldier?" I didn't know what to say so I replied, "They are dead sir, and I am alive thanks to you and your men". He nodded and said, "Good man. Your injuries will heal and you been through a massive ordeal but you're a British soldier so chin up, step over the wall and move on ok". I nodded, "Yes Sir", the Colonel continued, "I don't need to remind you that you're under the official secrets act?" He stared at me for a moment then nodded his head, walked through the seated men and out the door.

We all sat there in silence. Eventually, someone from the back said, "Well I've got gardening to do when I get back as long as it's still dry, when are we leaving anyway?". "Right now, let's make a move", someone else said and they all stood up to leave. A voice said "I want to get some new jeans", another voice said "Me as well". Just like that, these men were going about their lives like nothing had happened, what self-control and professionalism they had within their job. I felt quite emotional and asked if I could shake their hands, they all stopped and one said, "But you'll be in Hereford next week mate". I glanced at the guy in charge, he nodded saying, "If you're up for it and the doctor says its fine". He rummaged in his pocket and brought out a plastic bag, it contained my identification tags. He smiled, "They were found in the boot of the car that lifted you, one of the guys came across them while searching the vehicle". I thanked him and he said, "I will see you later". I rose from my bed, shook everyone's hand, and thanked them all individually. Most of them said 'ok mate thanks' some just nodded. When they left, I sat back on my bed but was overcome with a rush of dizzyness.

I noticed one of them spoke to Alex, in a whisper, he nodded as they all walked out. Only Alex and I were left in the ward. He came over, sat on the edge of my bed and said, "I should never have left you mate, I am so sorry". I told him it was all over now, but he turned to me, looked through pained eyes and said, "No mate, I should never have left you". I went to touch his shoulder to comfort him but he winced away and stared at the floor. I said, "Listen, we'll have a pint once I am out of here, relax mate it's over", he shook his head and sighed, "No mate, I'm away tonight". "Back to the battalion?" I asked. He shook his head and replied, "No, I'm headed to Australia". I stared at him "Did I just hear right, Australia?" He nodded, "I was asked if I wanted a transfer to the Australian army. I have nothing of family here, so I said yes". I started to say, "You can't. We are a team and once I'm back on my feet we will….", he stopped, "Not anymore, now you get yourself better". He stood from my bed and said, "I am sorry". He turned and walked away, I shouted after him, "For fuck sake, Alex!" He stood at the door and looked back, I said, "Fucking hell mate, don't leave. Years from now we'll have a pint and a talk about this". Tears welled up in my eyes as he shook his head and said, "I can't, I'm sorry". He turned and walked away. I was devastated, I couldn't understand why he would want to leave.

Later that the day Mike came back in and I asked him, "Where did all these little burns come from?" He told me to forget it, move on. I told him I needed to know. He took a deep breath and said,

"Ok, you asked. They are cigarette burns mate. They must have been testing your level of consciousness by putting cigarettes out on your skin". I looked in horror at my arms and legs, as he said, "Well, you did ask. Forget it mate, it's past now. Step over the wall and get going with life. Right, what we are watching tonight then?". He said it as if nothing had happened. I didn't care, I told him anything. He handed me a bottle of cold water but I wished it were a beer.

Weapons of the British Army

<u>Sterling L2A3 (Mark 4) Submachine Gun 9 mm (SMG)</u>

<u>Browning Pistol 9 mm muzzle velocity 1100 ft per second</u>

Chapter 37

The rest of the day was a bit of a blur. I was checked over by the consultant, once he had finished he signaled towards the two guys at the desk and a wheelchair appeared. I was wheeled down the corridor, through a series of doors then out into a waiting car. As we pulled away, I asked where we were going, one of them explained I was to be taken to get my teeth sorted. I was tired but it was nice to finally get out of the ward and see the hustle and bustle of London.

After forty-five minutes in the dentist's chair working on my teeth, I was fitted with a new bridge. As I was leaving, the dentist remarked, "Lucky we still had the original impressions of your teeth. Where will I send the bill?" With a grin on his face. I thanked him and headed outside into the waiting car. It was great to have my teeth back, at least I could smile and talk properly rather than sounding like a hissing snake.

As great as it was to have my teeth fixed, I couldn't get the thought of Alex leaving for Australia out of my mind. I tried to distract myself with some movies but it didn't help much. In the afternoon I chatted with the guys as I walked up and down the corridor, I was starting to feel so much stronger.

That night I slept right through until the morning. I got up, had a coffee and I was asked to shower at 08.00 hours. I nodded and minced around the ward watching the news. When 8o'clock rolled around I headed to the shower room, I stood in the warm water for ages, it felt so good. Returning to my ward, I could smell polish. I entered to see three cleaners finishing up, all the other beds were made up, the curtains opened and my bed made perfectly. Lying on my bed was a brand-new track suit and trainers. It was unusual, something must have been going on. With a little help, I got dressed, usually I was asked if I wanted a brew but today was different. I sat on the edge of my bed looking out of the window, the sky was nice; it was blue with grey patches and it looked as if it would be a fine day. If only I could get the fuck out of the ward. About twenty minutes later I heard a commotion outside the ward, a female voice saying, "In here is he?" A male voice replied "Yes Mam", then the female voice instructing their male companion to wait outside. The male voice protested but was told that they would wait outside.

I wasn't sure what to expect. In walked this female dressed in a blue skirt and jacket. I looked at her as she approached my bed space, high ginger hair, handbag draped over here arm, then suddenly I recognized her. I tried to stand but she told me not to get up. She stopped beside my bed, and asked, "Are they looking after you?" I nodded managing to say, "Yes Mam", she replied, "Good, I have eleven minutes in my schedule and I wanted to see you in person and thank you for being so brave". I was still gob smacked as I looked at Prime Minister Margaret Thatcher, I was so overwhelmed and just managed to stammer out, "Thank you, Mam".

The eleven minutes of our chat were private between us and I will keep it that way, but I will share this with you.

When she was about to leave I thanked here for visiting but she replied, "No, it is I that should thank you. For being a British soldier, a protector of our country and the people against the terrors of the world. I thank you and the British people thank you". As she walked towards the door, I felt amazing at her inspiring eleven-minute talk with me. She opened the door slightly paused then closed it again, she turned and faced me and said, "Do you think that the debrief helped you?" I told her it did and she said, "Good, that was my idea. Some people thought it was a bad thing for you but I said NO we must do this for you. I asked my

SAS to debrief you properly, on the whole horrid affair and our capabilities when having to use force". I thanked her again and she said, "I hope it helps you now and in the future, and I do look forward to hearing of your progress".

With that she opened the door and disappeared. I was smiling from ear to ear, I kept thinking of her words over and over, they were so inspiring for a young soldier that all I wanted was to get back out there and protect my country and be a soldier again. I was lost in thought when one of the guys appeared and casually and asked if I wanted a brew. I nodded. "Coming up, oh by the way, not many people get a visit from her. She has bigger ball than I have". I had to agree, what a woman. I kept thinking about her words of encouragement, it put me on a high all day.

The day after my 'visitor', the guys outside my door said their goodbyes. I thanked them all and they told me they were all heading back to Hereford. One of the guys sat by me and said, "You have been through a terrible ordeal, hopefully your wounds will heal and you get yourself right back into soldiering again. By all accounts your training record is exceptional, so keep it going mate. It's now up to you on how you handle the hardest part". Pointing to his head, "Once it passes through your iris there no turning back, it's in there etched into the back of your skull never to be removed. It will haunt you, but think of it, and deal with it, and get it back deep down into your subconscious. Find a way of being able to think of something that will put it out of your thoughts. Deal with it, as if you were dealing with something you could hold in your hands, if you don't want it put it away, it will always be there but you should always have a way to set it to one side". As he stood up, he shook my hand. I thanked him for the advice but he laughed, "We will see you in a week or so in Wales", he smiled again, patted my shoulder and headed away, he was the last to leave.

An hour later the door opened and there was a guy in a wheelchair being pushed in by a porter. He noticed me looking over puzzled, he said with a grin and a Liverpool accent, "How's it going mate?" He pointed to his leg, which was in plaster and said, "Clipped by a taxi, legs fucked. Broken in three places but hey ho, beats playing soldiers eh?" The porter pushing him left him by his bed but he managed to wheel himself over to mine, put out his hand and said, "My names Ripples, Grenadier Guards". He asked what had happened to me, I said I was in an accident and my hand was badly injured. He nodded but would not leave it, "Fuck that, what's with all the burns?" I told him I didn't know as I was unconscious, he seemed satisfied with my answer. Pointing to his plastered leg and smiling, "They think I'm going to be on light duties for a year, fucking excellent, sitting around chilling". I was lost in thought for a moment when he interrupted, "Are you okay?" I brushed it off and told him I was tired, at which he said, "Fuck off, you jock bastards never get tired. I remember drinking with some of you jocks, fuck you can't half drink". I let him talk, he talked and talked I listened with the occasional smile and a nod but really, I could not take in what he said. I was just thinking about getting my handhealed, getting stronger and getting back to training.

The next day the consultant removed my bandages, I reeled back at the smell. My fingers were black and it was hard to make out flesh from dried blood, he said, "We will gently wash your hand, your fingers seem to be ok but time will tell. Ok son, be aware that those fingers may have to be removed if they don't take". I nodded my understanding, but inside I screamed 'Are you fuck taking my fingers off!'.

There were metal spikes sticking out of my knuckles, I asked what they were, he explained,

"They had to rebuild the bones piece by piece, the spikes go through the centre of the bone and held them in place while we stitch it all together. 186 stitches in all, internal and external. The internal stiches will dissolve, we will remove the outer stiches in a week. The metal spikes will be removed in around 6 weeks. Once that's healed we will operate again". I asked how long it would be until I could start my training again, he shrugged, "If the fingers take, probably a year maybe more", I couldn't believe it, a year. "Yes a year, it was touch and go if they were to be saved anyway", he smiled, "It will be ok, you have the best of care here so chin up. You could have been discharged this morning with a fingerless hand but there is hope now, so accept it".

Once he left I looked down at my hand, it was weird seeing metal sticking out of my knuckles but there was no pain. My whole arm ached but the most painful was my right forearm, but no pain in my hand.

I was asked if I want to go home for ten days, did I ever. I wanted to go to the farm, but I thought I would just be in the way. I was limited to what I could do, moping around Mum's house was ok but watching TV was something I just was not into, I had sat around enough lately.

Chapter 38

I made the most of my time at home and started to walk ten to fifteen miles a day, I had my hand wrapped up and tucked into my jacket. I was getting bored, but I had to push myself. I kept doing sit ups and squats, anything that did not involve my left hand, which looked horrendous now.

My brother visited one Friday, we sat and laughed till the wee hours, it was great to be back in his company, he really was my hero. Saturday night there was an engagement party at a local pub come dance hall. I said no, but my brother insisted, "Just you sit at the back, you'll be fine. I get the drinks in, you chill out". Eventually I agreed to go, my mother didn't approve but she relented, saying if I felt any pain to come home, she reluctantly said, "I'll wait up, phone me and I will come and pick you up if there are any problems".

The party was in full swing when we arrived, I slinked round the back of most people and sat with my hand inside my jacket, it felt good to be out hearing laughter and singing, some good music was being played. My brother appeared with a couple of pints, the happy couple came up, I wished them all the best, it was nice to see them again. I sat back down and watched the party; my brother was very protective of me and my hand, if anyone came tooclose he kept them at bay. I told him it was alright, but he ignored me.

I noticed a lassie going about with a camcorder, she was in the middle of everything filming what was going on. I watched as she moved about and laughed and chatted with everyone. After an hour or so when my brother was up dancing with some girl and I was about to light another cigarette the lassie with the camcorder sat down at the table with her back to me, watching people dance or fall over with too much drink. I offered her a cigarette, she accepted, took a light and went back to watching the party. She was laughing and waving at people that she must have known, she was the life and soul of the party. I sat there feeling a right fool. As she turned to flick her cigarette she looked at me, our eye's met for a split second then glanced away, I smiled and she asked, "Are you not hot with that jacket on?" I told her I had an accident and my hand was in a bit of a mess. I couldn't believe it when she said, "Let's see it then". Without a thought I took my hand out from under my jacket, with its the spikes out the knuckles, stitches all over and black Fingers, it was not a pretty sight. All she said was, "Is it sore?" Not the reaction I expected. I said, "No, not just now", she laughed and said, "It will be fine, I'm sure it looks bad now but give it a month it will look a lot better". I smiled, I couldn't believe I was sitting chatting with her, she was so beautiful, and her hair was perfect. I introduced myself and she told me her name was Margaret, I said, "Nice to meet you", she was about to answer when she was pulled away towards the dance floor. She turned as she was led on to the floor and said, "Yes, nice to meet you too". I nodded thinking what a beauty.

I lowered my eyes back to the table, I began to smile as I noticed the camcorder still sitting on the table. I thought to myself she has to come back for that so I'll get to speak to her again. I must have been grinning from ear to ear as my brother came up with another pint and asked gesturing to the camcorder, "Who's is that?" I turned my head and nodded towards Margaret on the dance floor, he asked how my hand was and I told him it was agony. "Let's get you home", I shrugged him off, and said, "No way, wait until she picks up her camcorder".

It was about half an hour before Margaret returned to collect the camcorder. She smiled and said, "Thanks for watching this for me. You're sweating, are you alright?" I felt the bead of sweat run down my face, I forced a smile and told her I was fine. She screwed up her nose and thanked me again. I said, "It was nice to meet you", she smiled, "I hope your hand gets better soon. Bye then", and she was gone, lost in the massive crowd. I lowered my head on to the table, I was in so much pain when I felt a hand on my shoulder. My brother asked if I was ok, no I was not. "Right let's get you out of here now", he said, as he pushed most people out of the way as I walked out, it was like running the gauntlet. When I got outside I gulped in the fresh air, my hand was pulsing in agony with every beat of my heart. By the time we got home the pain was driving me mad, I felt dizzy. My mother berated me, "I told you not to drink for goodness sake. Right, up the stair and bed now", I didn't argue. When I returned to the hospital in London, the ward was empty. I still had a tv so I sat there watching it feeling sorry for myself. My hand was in agony, it seemed to be so painful all the time it was relentless. I didn't want pain killers, but they left them on my bed side cabinet just the same, but I was determined not to take pain relief. A fortnight later I was picked up by two guys from Hereford. They drove me from the hospital to Wales with a food stop and smoke breaks. After five hours of congenial chat and jokes we finally arrived at the Special Air Service base. As we drove through the gates I felt such a buzz at being allowed to enter, the newly named Sterling Lines.

Chapter 39

A year and three months and three painful operations later, the surgeon told me that my hand was now as good as it will ever be. With the loss of over twenty-five percentage of movement, strength and grip. I did mope about for a few hours after I was told that, but I said to myself I better put the last remaining seventy five percent to good use. During that time, I had taken some leave back home and, with a lot of Dutch courage, I asked Margaret out on a date. That was over a year ago at this point and every time she saw me, the first thing she would say is, "How is your hand?"

She was wonderful, I thought she was the most beautiful lassie I had ever seen. She had been married before and had young kids but that was fine, I felt like part of a family and I really got on well with them all. I was up and down the road as often as I could be, every time I wanted a rail warrant the Clerk just handed it over, no questions. Sometimes even a flight from London to Aberdeen if he was in a good mood. I didn't care which as long as I saw Margaret and the kids as much as I could, we all had a lot of fun and I loved every minute of it.

I had to report to an officer if I was in London, with what I was doing weekly or by telephone if I was back home or at other training camps. I was left to train and get stronger by myself. In London the officer would fill in some detail on a form about my health then we would have a coffee and shoot the shit for an hour or so. Every so often he would invite me to one of his father's clubs. I loved it sitting on lovely leather sofas and being waited on hand and foot, how the other half live. They were all good to me and I was greeted warmly whenever I walked through the door.

I managed to get on a parachute jump course at Brise Norton, thanks to a friend that pulled some strings. It was such a buzz. I had trained hard and my fitness level was high, but my hand was still weak. I really enjoyed the course, I felt it was a great achievement for me when I passed the course and was awarded my wings. I had really struggled; my hand was still hurting like fuck from the last operation, it had not properly healed yet. I learned later that if you operated on a part of your body in the same place it takes longer to recover after each operation, but when I was offered the chance to get on to the parachute course nothing was going to stop me, I pushed through the pain and managed it, I was so proud of myself. I started training even harder when I was in London, but I also trained with 2 Para. At first the guys all wanted to know who I was and what I was doing there, but it soon became the norm for me to appear for a few days, train hard with them then disappear and I was accepted after a while.

Between home, 2 Para and London I was remarkably busy. Always on the go. I also trained at Sterling lines in Hereford most months, for a week or so with the guys. I made a lot of good friends; some are still best mates to this day.

Excellent soldiers, totally focused in getting the job done right. They passed on knowledge to me in fitness, health, weapons, unarmed combat, survival, and military tactics. I would spend days looking, listening, and learning. Their moto is, 'WHO DARES WINS', but really it should be, 'Train hard, Fight easy'. Every time I appeared at the base, I always thought it was an honour to have the opportunity to train and learn from these guys. Always, in the back of my mind was training and going for the SAS selection in the future, maybe being one of the few to be able to wear a sand coloured beret with a downward pointing Excalibur cap badge.

One cold morning myself and a few others from

the regiment jumped from the back of the four-tonner truck. My breath was visible in the cold air as I pulled on my bergen, there in front of me in all her glory was the majestic Pen y Fan mountain. I took a moment, full of thought, I had been waiting to do this for a long time. I smiled, so much had happened since I sat and listened to the guy in the RSM sitting room telling us to get to Wales and do some hill work, now I was here for the first time. I was lost in thought when one of the regiments guys said, "Hey, you're first fan dance mate, take a good look. It will be etched into the back of your skull forever. The ultimate test 'man verses nature', you ok?" I nodded as he turned and headed off saying, "Ok lads, let's do this". We followed behind him, even with the hefty load in my bergen it felt like it was a weight off my shoulders, I was free. I was so excited and nothing was going to slow, hinder or stop me from doing this, even if it killed me.

Ten months had gone by and I continued to train hard with the guys wherever I was, London or Hereford. My hand was getting slightly stronger but the rest of me was at a new height of fitness and stamina after all the fan dances I had completed. I think I knew every nook, cranny and stone having completed over thirty of them. Each one was different one way or another, if anyone was going to the hill I went too, even with the guys doing their selection course. I would turn up with the regulars from the regiment and stick with them, we would see guys on selection struggling on their first fan dance. One of the guys said, "You have to be ultra-fit for selection, look at some of these fucking guys they come here unprepared in fitness and mind". I never said anything I just looked, listened, and learned, but secretly I knew I had to train harder and stronger if I was to go for selection.

I realised that I wanted to stay at Hereford more and more, no one ever said anything. I would just call ahead and join in with whatever training they were doing in the training wing. There was the odd weekend I would be invited to stay and go out on the town with some of the guys, or down to someone's house for a party, it was an excellent time. I always ended up pissed, but I was up and going first thing Sunday morning regardless of the banging in my head from the night before. Nothing worse than being out for a run, getting into your second sweat and all you can smell is stale whisky. I pushed through it, head down and got on with it, sometimes I ran even more just to push myself that bit further.

Once a month I looked forward to jumping on a train and heading up the country for a long weekend, to see Margaret and the kids. She would pick me up from the train station with the kids and we had a ball. We would go out for meals, toy shops, buying sweets and crisps, it always made me smile hearing them giggle and laugh. Margaret kept saying to not spoil them but I would wink and say, "What do you think boys, pictures (cinema) tomorrow followed with pizza and ice cream?" It was always met with a cheer. Margaret kept saying they were always tired out when I came home, I winked and said I knew. She would blush and say 'Method in your madness soldier', I nodded and would say, "Something like that".

Sunday mornings we would just go out walking in the woods if it was nice, I would show the boys what you could eat and how to track a roe deer or a badger print or how to make a fire from a spark stick. They would gather tinder for the initial start, then small twigs, then large and larger. I would show them how to make a fire safe for the outdoors and I would laugh and see Margaret smile as they would argue who would try and light the small fire, it was so much fun. Back home again Margaret said, "They miss you and so do I", I nodded and would say I have to try for selection she would smile but there was a sadness in her eyes at the thought of me going away down the country again. One day she asked me when was I going for selection, I told her it was just under 3 months. I told her that I had to go for it, she told me she understood but I said we should enjoy the time we have together and not think about it.

Just over two weeks later back in Hereford, it was 05.00 hours Thursday morning . I was about to go for a run when I was joined by three others, who I recognised from the regular regiment. One asked if I minded if they joined me, I told them it was fine but it was not usual for someone to turn up and run with me. They asked my route, I suggested the nine mile route that I ran now and then. One of the guys said, "Let's just see how far we can go", I nodded and said, "Aye, no bother", but I did start wondering what was going on when I saw a four ton truck up ahead. One of the guys gestured for me to get on the truck, I must have looked at him a bit strange as another guy said, "It's ok, we will get to the hills sooner". As we drove along I asked what was going on, one said, "Nothing mate, we just want to check your fitness", my stomach went ridged. I tried to make eye contact with the guys, looking for the usual reassuring wink or nod but they all looked at the floor or out the back. My mind was racing, thinking all sorts of stuff, maybe I have out stayed my welcome at Hereford. The truck went on for what seemed like forever until it finally stopped and we all piled out and headed up a hill, the pace was fast, but I just tucked in behind the lead guy.

I tried to regulate my breathing but my mind was still racing with the thought of what was going on. We ran for over an hour, stopped for a few seconds then off we went again, I hardly had time to catch my breath. We stopped again about thirty minutes later and started doing press ups then off again, this routine carried on for a total of three hours. I was exhausted but I never let them see that I was starting to struggle. The rain was hammering down, but we never stopped, on we went. The guy behind me was right on my tail, up over ridges, burns, then down hills, it was relentless, but I carried on. When we stopped we got into the press up position, by this time my hand was really in agony with the pressure from the press-ups. I felt as if I were about to vomit, I swallowed it back and carried on with the press ups, suddenly we were up and on the go again. I was knackered but it was such a relief to get the weight off my hand. About an hour later we rounded a corner and there was the four-ton truck,

I thought thank fuck. As I went to slow down, I realised that the guy in the front never stopped and he ran right past the truck, I was about to give up when Mikes voice came screaming into my head "Just keep up!" I straightened myself and tucked back behind the lead guy and off we went, I was exhausted but I pushed my legs, one in front of the other, just to keep going.

We ran for another hour after we passed the truck, same routine thirty-minute intervals, down to press ups then off we went again. At last we rounded a corner and I could see the four-tonner in the distance. I had realized a few hours ago, I was being tested in fitness, stamina and attitude. We ran up toward the four-tonner, as we approached it the black smoke came from the exhaust pipe and off it went, I never missed a footing and kept my pace.

We had ran for another thirty minutes or so now and the pace was opening up a bit more. I was right on the heels of the guy in front, I was so tired but I was never going to give in. Finally we stopped, I was shocked that we had come to an abrupt halt. At that, the four-tonner appeared, and we jumped on. We were all covered in mud and soaked through, but I looked away and smiled slightly to myself thinking, 'You did ok there matey'. When we got back, I had a long shower and went for some food. Someone stopped beside me and said, "See you again tomorrow then eh?". I asked, "What's happening tomorrow?" "05.00 hours, we are doing the fan dance", I didn't react I merely nodded, finished my food and left.

I went straight to bed, I was so knackered. Little did I know what was about to happen. I think I was sleeping for about an hour and a half when the door opened and I was told to wear camouflage combats, kit and get outside. There was no shouting just told to get outside, "No bergen, just webbing, now move it. You have five minutes to get outside". It was a mad rush, but I managed to get outside within the small-time frame, wearing my combats. I signed for a SLR rifle then was briefed. I was to be dropped off and I had to make RVs, handed a small compass and a piece of parachute material with a sketch of hills, roads and a river and other prominent points. Next thing I knew I was in the back of a four-tonner alone, I was driven for about an hour then dropped off, given a map reference, and had to point to my RV point on a map using a blade of grass. I asked the time frame to get to the RV point but all I got was, "You better get moving, time started 10 seconds ago". I headed off into the inky black night. I made the first check point, was given another map reference and off I went to the next RV, as I left I was informed that I was two minutes behind, and I better get a fucking grip.

It was over three hours later before I arrived at the next RV point. I was told to complete different small tasks and asked questions on basic military tactics. Once all the tasks were completed I was given another map reference. I pushed myself off towards the next RV with total determination. I was so knackered I had to concentrate on getting my legs moving.

Day break came and went, I carried on the whole day. I went from RV point to RV point and I was beyond exhaustion but knew I had to keep going. I ran down hills and staggered up as fast as I could, at each RV they always said you are behind the time and to get going. After I had done whatever test they had for me and answered all questions, some on military others on random categories, I was off again.

Finally, at 22.10 hours I arrived back to my room; it had been twenty-four hours of hard going through the elements, I was exhausted. I had stopped wondering what it was all about hours and hours ago I just had in my head 'keep fucking going'.

I showered and fell into to bed; I remember thinking about what if they come get me again but I drifted off to sleep. The next day no one mentioned the last twenty-four hours, so I thought I wouldn't mention it either, I was still pretty tired, but I had to stay focused. One of the guys was off to Portugal the following day and he asked if I fancied a pint, I said I did but deep down I knew I could have been doing with getting my head down but thought may as well join in as it was Saturday night.

Over the next few days, I was tested on weapons, unarmed combat and other skills I had learned, I always stayed focused and did well. My hand was in agony after a full day of unarmed combat, but I had to push through, I ate my meals with one hand just to rest the injured one. I was due to return to London on the Friday, as normal on Thursday afternoon I did some gym work. This Thursday, while I was training, three guys came into the gym, the same guys that tested me on the hill. They nodded and winked, that was reassuring, then one guy said, "Do some pull ups mate", so I jumped up grabbed the pull up bar and started the exercise. On the twentieth pull up he said, "Ok mate" but before he could say anymore, I knew what he was going to say and I had dreaded it. "Now hang from your left hand", I knew straight away I couldn't, I tried, but with limited grip, I slipped off the bar. I jumped up again, grabbed the bar with both hands then released my right hand. I tried to hold on, but my left hand had neither the strength nor the grip of my right. I kept going until I was told to stop. I was worried because I hadn't be able to hang from my injured hand.

I was instructed to get a shower and they would see me later. I felt defeated, full of remorse at not being able to do a small task like hang from one hand.

I showered, got dressed and was about to have a coffee when the guys came into the room. One of them said "Look, we know you're going for selection in January and we can't stop you from doing it. Being honest your fitness is great and you made excellent timings on your last twenty four hours on the hill. We also we have really learned a lot from you about the time you were held in Ireland, but we have to give you a heads up mate. You won't make it through selection with that hand", gesturing with his head toward my left hand. "We can't give you any leeway on selection", after a short pause he continued, "Listen, your attitude and dedication to training, after what you have been through, is second to none", I glanced at the others and they were all nodding in agreement. I stared out of the window, I was devastated. I asked "Is that my time training with you guys over, am I going back to my battalion now?" Surprisingly, he said "No mate, there are still some options for you if you want it ".

Chapter 40

Over the next few months I trained in close protection, otherwise known as a bodyguard, it was excellent still training with the guys. All the different scenarios with lots of new skills to learn, not just the physical side of the training but you had to learn so much more. It was a real eye opener what wasinvolved but I really went for this bodyguard training. As normal adopting words from my Dad, 'look, listen and learn', you can bet your last pound I did exactly that.

Now having realised, and accepted I was not going for selection, I put it right out of my head. Now it wasn't something I was going for, it was something I was doing. It gives you a totally different outlook, I had to focus and focus hard on the training, these regular regiment guys train extremely hard and get the job done and don't accept second best.

Margaret said, on one brief visit up the road, "You're a different person now, you seem brighter and happier". She was right I did feel better knowing I had something to look forward to, a purpose. She went silent for a moment then said "You always have something, you have us. We love you so much. When your done and you have the military out of your system, you could always come home and get a normal job and we could be an everyday family. I have a good job we would manage moneywise", she smiled at me as she teared up. I moved forward and held her close and whispered, "I love you too". I stared up at the ceiling and I knew at that moment that I wanted to marry her, realising she was my purpose, my only real purpose in life now, it was almost like I could breathe more clearly. I moved back from our embrace and said, "Hey, let's get...", but she stopped me and said, "No not now, but when you're done with the army definitely". It was almost like she knew I was about to ask her to marry me. I looked into her eyes, she smiled that big beautiful smile and said, "See I know you better that you know yourself", I leaned in and kissed her as I felt the buzz through my whole body.

Over the next six months I started really enjoyed training and working in close protection, I felt part of a team, but I knew deep down my army days were coming to an end. Passing selection was my life's trophy at one time, but now I realised that Margaret was my life and always had been ever since our first kiss.

One of the guys was leaving the regiment, after

eight years' service. I had worked close with him during my close protection training and we became good friends. One night at the bar, I said, "Thanks again for all the help mate, it is very much appreciated", he said "its ok, you'll do ok. You have dedication and commitment, in this life that means a lot". I asked why he was leaving, and he replied, "I have done my bit and beat the clock, so time to move on and settle down. My wife's pregnant now and she does not want me going all over the world for months at a time with the regiment, but mostly we have been trying for a baby for years. She is thirty now and she let me do my thing with the regiment, so she thinks it's her time now".

I had to agree with her, I asked him what he was planning to do. He told me he was planning to be a bodyguard in the private sector, "Lucky you, big money eh". He said "Aye, I will do it for a couple of years to give us a nest egg, then I will see what happens. Here, you should contact the firm" I told him I had no chance as it was only regiment guys they hired. He drank his pint, once finished he laid his glass on the bar and said, "You may not have been badged mate, but your regiment trained. Think about it". I was deep in thought, when, someone bumped my arm with his, smiled and said, "It's your round", I nodded and was about to order when he whispered in my ear "He's right you know".

A few weeks later, and a bit of research into private bodyguard work, I had been talking to a few guys I knew about getting a job. I asked what was involved and they all said the same, "We trained you, you'll do ok". It was then I decided, ok time for a visit.

I had a mid-week break for 2 days, so I booked a flight up north, hired a car ad drove home. I arrived at the door at 20.45 hours. When Margaret answered the door, she looked worried at first, then flung her arms round my neck saying, "You're home, is everything ok?" I told her I had to speak to her and that it was very important. We went through to the sitting room, I sat down while she fixed us a drink. When she settled down I drank a big gulp of whisky and started, "I want to come out of the army and get a job". She beamed a smile, "I will be based in London, but I should get more time off". She asked what I would be doing, I had told her that I would trying to get work through this firm, in close protection or a bodyguard in the private sector, "It will be good money", but she replied "I don't care about the money, all I care about is you. Is it safe and who will you be guarding?" I told her I was not sure yet I have still to contact the firm, but I stand a chance of getting work.

She said, "If we get more time together, then it's a thumbs up from me". We hugged each other so tightly I whispered, "I love you", she replied, "I love you so much", as we tightened our hug.

Chapter 41

Two weeks later, I travelled to London. I entered a massive building, found the floor I required and up I went. I sat there in my best suit and tie with razor sharp creases in my trousers. I was offered a drink by a secretary, I smiled and declined, I was to nervous. I had never had a job interview before. My palms were sweating, I wiped them dry. I was told to enter the large door on the right., I breathed deeply, knocked and entered. A guy dressed in a designer suit, jumped from his seat, made his way towards me, he shook my hand "Grab a pew mate, fancy a brew?" I had expected a well-spoken businessman, not this welcome at all; it did settle me down a bit.

He mentioned a few things and the guys back at Hereford, I only nodded, thought for a moment, then I asked a few questions. He smiled and answered them correctly, I relaxed, he was ex regiment. I said "I will have that brew now mate, if that's ok", he replied "Yes sure, no problem. By the way, I have heard a lot about you mate", I only nodded, the door opened and the secretary asked what I would like to drink. The guy leaned back in his chair, said, "So, you want work? I can give you work, when are you out?" "Soon hopefully, just thought I would see if I was suitable", he nodded, "Yes of course, I get a lot of the guys down here testing the water, as you would say, wanting to know all about it". I said "Look mate, I was never badged I have only...." but he held up his hands and stopped me. He leaned forward saying "You come highly recommended from friends of mine ok, that's enough for me. Just get out of the mob and when you are ready, get down here. If you weren't suitable, you would have never been given the address". I was so chuffed, as the door opened and in came the secretary with our brews.

I left the office with a spring in my step and headed off across the city to see the officer I had to report to weekly. At the barracks I went straight to his office. He was pleased to see me, we shook hand and he offered me a seat. "Not seen you in months, you are looking well, very smart too", he said. "Ok so what you been up to, I have been filling in your report myself, so I know you've been up in Wales most of the time. You are supposed to contact me on a weekly basis you know. The last time was five weeks ago, not good enough". I was about to apologise but he waved his hand and said, "Its ok no bother, you're here now". I took a deep breath and I sat forward, "I would like to leave the army". He leaned back in his chair and rubbed his head, asking, "Ok, why or shouldn't I ask?" I told him it was time to move on, he shrugged saying, "Oh come now, what's going on? I need a bit more than that". I shrugged my shoulders and told him it was my time. He rose from his desk moved to a filing cabinet and pulled out a bottle of 'good stuff', poured a couple of drams and handed one to me. We clinked glasses and both said cheers. I sipped it slowly, it was a good dram. He stood, looking out of the window, then turned and said, "I was never privy to what happened to you, but I have an idea. I know where my weekly reports have been sent. If it is your time to go then I salute you, young man. I will sort the paperwork out but it will take a while. I will see what I can do. I will have to put this into this week's report". I nodded and said, "I have to leave sometime". "Yes, you're right, ok that's over now. What are you doing tonight? Let's have a few down 'Fathers' club eh? Some of the old timers have been asking about you", he smiled. I nodded, "Aye that would be fine, maybe my last time I get an invite eh", he shook his head, "Not at all. Right, I must phone my wife and let her know I will be late tonight, she was none too happy the last time I went drinking with you". I remembered it well, I smiled, he was a true gentleman, once he had a few drinks he was also a great laugh.

It took eight weeks from that date to get out of the army. I trained up at Hereford for another two weeks until it was made official I was to get out. I was told to report to London Wellington Barracks. When I left Wales there was no piss up or anything, just the odd wink or a nod and the occasional 'See you mate' as I handed my kit back. That was fine with me, I knew the score, so I packed up and headed out of the gates for the last time. I did glance back full of memories, but I shook myself and thought, 'Hey let's make some new memories'. I jumped into the waiting transport thinking; I was so lucky to have had that opportunity.

Back in London I was allocated a room, unpacked, and went straight to the gym. I had to keep training, I did the same routine almost every day except when I was back home, where Margaret and I enjoyed our time together planning our future. While in London I trained hard right up to the very last day of my military service.

The officer I had to report to basically left me to train and do my own thing most of the time, he knew if he needed to get a hold of me, I would be out running, in the gym or in my room. We had the odd drink here and there and I was invited to the club a few times, which was a fantastic laugh, but it meant that if I drank, I had to train even harder the next day. I met his wife, who was very classy and extremely elegant, but once a few gins were inside her she let go all the upper-class stuff and was very down to earth. It was great being invited out in the city to some of the top night spots and exclusive clubs, for a boy that was brought up in a pair of wellies and hand me down clothes it was a real eye opener. How the other half of society lived, no thought of money or they seem to act like it. I still kept a low profile, the grey man as I had been taught, but it was hard when you were in the centre of things so I tried to enjoy myself as little as possible, all the time I wanted to see Margaret and the boys, I did miss them. At every opportunity I was up the road and able to relax and enjoy their company, I loved it. I did wonder about working from London, I would still be away from Margaret, but I would be a civilian earning good money.

Chapter 42

The day I left the army I had to march up in front of the Commanding Officer of Wellington barracks and was released from the military. Normally you would go back to your training depot, but I think strings were pulled a bit. As I stood there, he moved an envelope towards me and motioned for me to pick it up, I broke step and retrieved the letter. I noticed it was hand written, I went back to the 'stand at attention' position and said, "Thank you Sir", he merely said, "All the very best to you, I am just sorry that I didn't know you a lot better, I have heard you are a very capable soldier, but this is your choice". I thanked him and told him it was time to move on.

As I walked away from his office, I glanced at the hand written letter. A voice shouted to me, "Don't go without a visit to my office", it was my Reporting Officer, as he rushed past in a hurry to go somewhere. I answered, "Yes, ok Sir". When I got back to my room I looked at the back of the letter and smiled, on the rear of the envelope was typed, 10 Downing Street.

I said my goodbyes to the friends I had met and went to the Officers office. He wished me well and shook my hand, but as I was about to release the grip he said, "I know you're a civilian now, but do me one last favour. Be at the Buckingham bar, just outside the barracks here, at 14.00 hours ok". I asked why and explained I was due to fly north at 16.00 hours. He said, "Your flight has been changed, sorry. I contacted Margaret this morning and told her you will be flying tomorrow instead", I replied, "Without telling me?" "Oh settle down, Margaret was quite happy so there's no problem", he released the grip on my hand. I said, "Ok, but not another piss up. I was out my head yesterday with drink", he nodded, and said, "My fucking head is still banging too, but no, please don't ask questions just be there. You have a room booked at the union jack club for tonight, your kit will be delivered there". I was very hesitant, but I trusted him, so I said I would. "See you sometime soldier, please keep in touch, do you promise?" I nodded, of course I would.

I left the office thinking, 'I am not happy with this at all. It's 11.25 hours I will scope this place out now, I don't like surprises. Time to do what the guys at Hereford trained me to do, a bit of surveillance'.

I packed the remainder of my gear and handed it into the guard room. Before I left, I asked to use the phone, Jerry, the Guard Commander said, "Sure mate, last free call on her majesty eh". I smiled and said, "Aye you're right there". It was only then I realised I would no longer be part of a huge, amazing, organisation that looked out for one another regardless what regiment or part of her Majesties service you were in. You could always count on support and the comradery. In a hundredth of a second I thought about what had happened in my life, from the first time I enjoyed a smoke with Mike, the guard commander at Glen Course barracks, to here, another guards room in the last moment of my military career. A chill went down my spine as I dialed Margaret's number. I said, "You heard I won't be up the road till tomorrow then?" She asked if everything was ok, I told her it was just the blokes wanting a send-off. She laughed, "Well don't get too pissed, your flight is just after 11 o'clock. I'm not working tomorrow so I will pick you up". I said, "Excellent, I promise I will be a good boy tonight". She laughed and told me she loves me, and I told her how much I loved her too before I hung up the phone.

I shook Jerries' hand and wished him all the best. He replied, "No problem Jock, you take care. It's been a pleasure mate, I will never drink whisky again". I laughed and told him, "Whisky is the water of life, it's been a pleasure mate, you take care". He winked and said, "If you ever need somewhere to stay and I am on guard duty, there's a fucking good hotel round the corner you civvie bastard", We both laughed then I turned and walked out of the army.

Out of wellington barracks guards room, onto Birdcage Walk. I turned right, walked up then right again onto the lane that lead into Queen Ann gate, up to the roundabout and right again, on to Petty France road and walked towards the Buckingham bar. I glanced at my watch, 12.15 hours, 1 hour and 45 minutes till I am supposed to be there. I went inside ordered a half pint whilst I looked around for any known faces, but I didn't recognise the few that were there. I forced the half pint down, the barmaid offered me another as she bundled old newspapers up but I asked for one of the papers, she told me they were yesterdays but I could easily have one. As she handed me the paper she asked again if I wanted another drink. I declined, telling her I only wanted a quick thirst quencher. I smiled, walked out of the bar and turned left, crossed the road with the paper under my arm. I sat at the café next to a souvenir shop, ordered a large coffee, and glanced at my watch, 12.55 hours.

I was facing the Buckingham bar, I had a good view of the front door and I knew I could make out faces at that distance. What I was doing was a bit over the top, I knew that, but I did not like surprises, even if it is just a piss up. I glanced at the paper that I held in a way that if anyone walked past me from behind they could not see my face, but I could still keep an eye on the bar door. At 13.52 hours I saw two blokes walking towards me on the same side as the bar. I watched them come closer and as they slowed and headed into the bar, I recognised one of them. I involuntary said "Holy fuck", I apologised to the couple in the seat beside me for swearing, paid my coffee and headed towards the bar.

I stopped at the bar door, took a deep breath and sorted my leather jacket. I opened the door and as I entered the barmaid said, "Back again love?" I nodded to her as I stood behind the two figures at the bar, they turned slowly and I involuntary started to shake, it was my old Colonel and my old RSM. For a moment no one said anything we just stood and looked at each other, then the Coronel said, "How are you?" I was so emotional, I felt the tears build up in my eyes. I forced them back, but must have still been shaking. The RSM gave me a hug and said, "What the fuck did they do to you?", his embrace was so reassuring, the Colonel patted me on the shoulder and said, "It's ok now, let's get a seat", he turned to the barmaid and said, "A bottle of Glenlivet, 18 years old and three glasses with ice if you please". Before we made our way to a table the RSM turned and said, "It's good to see you again", I nodded, it was good, "I would have contacted you but!" The Colonel cleared his throat, for us to stop talking and said, "Let's talk over at the table gentlemen".

We sat there in silence as the drinks were poured. The Colonel raised his glass and said, "Your health, young man". I drank down the whisky, I cannot explain the feeling I had at that moment, it was like I was safe or comfortable it was so reassuring. The RSM started and said, "We were told you were off limits and to be left alone, no contact. That's why we had to wait until you were a civilian, how have you been?" I stared at the table for a moment and I felt the Colonel put his hand on my shoulder saying, "It's ok, you enjoy your dram. Cheers", as he raised his glass. I told them so much had happened since I last saw them and the Colonel said, "We can imagine, we are not aware of the details, and it's not important now, but I was informed you had a bad time over the water", the RSM said, "Those bastards". I shook my head and told them, it is in the past now, I have managed to get it into my sub-conscious mind and very rarely recall it. I was lying through my teeth.

Our 'Army' conversation lasted for almost two hours. The Colonel placed his hand on my shoulder, as he did the RSM winked. The Colonel said, "I know you've made your father proud". I only nodded, as we clinked glasses I said, "Cheers Dad".

Epilogue

I stayed with the security firm for well over a year and a half, working with a variety of people from the music industry, film stars, visiting dignitaries and many others. I sometimes got bored, quickly realising that some people on this earth have got a talent, providing them with unlimited funds and little grasp of reality, living in a make-believe bubble.

It was a great honour to work alongside these ex-regiment guys and be a part of the team. I classed everyday as a school day, look, listen and learn, but we were all civvies now and we had great respect for one another. So long as we could do the job, we could work as a team or on some occasions work alone on the smaller tasks, these guys were the best in the business. I felt I was incredibly lucky to have landed a cracking job like this and the money was excellent, but I did miss Margaret and the boys. I had promised them we would spend more time together once I got my feet under the table with this firm, but it seemed like all I did was work. I saw them when I could, flying up the country for a day here and a weekend there.

Realising that I missed them all so much I decided to give it all up with the firm and head home to be a real family. I asked Margaret to marry me and she said yes, so we planned it all together and we married a year later. It was the proudest day of my life. After getting a normal everyday job it was such a difference from what I was used to, but I took to it like a duck to water and loved every minute of being a family man. I was also spending as much time at the farm as possible.

Margaret and I are just meant to be together.

I know that in marrying someone like Margaret my Dad would be enormously proud.

As a boy, I was brought up in a country environment working on the farm. I always wanted to make my Dad proud, he never showed much pride in me or my achievements, but I always strived for that privilege.

He died when I was only fifteen years old.

I had to make him proud of me.

But doing what?

I JOINED THE BRITISH ARMY.

My life took off.

From Africa to Northern Ireland and everything inbetween

THIS IS HOW I

MADE MY DAD PROUD.

A work of fiction Based on a true story.

Printed in Great Britain
by Amazon

32050066R00255